All Bat, No Glove

I hope you enjoy going through this... I look forward to spending more time with you ——

Mr McKelvey

All Bat, No Glove

A History of
the Designated Hitter

G. Richard McKelvey

McFarland & Company, Inc., Publishers
Jefferson, North Carolina, and London

LIBRARY OF CONGRESS CATALOGUING-IN-PUBLICATION DATA

McKelvey, G. Richard, 1935–
    All bat, no glove : a history of the designated hitter /
G. Richard McKelvey.
        p.   cm.
    Includes bibliographical references and index.

    ISBN 0-7864-1944-X (softcover : 50# alkaline paper) ∞

1. Designated hitters (Baseball)   I. Title.
GV869.2.M34   2004
796.357'26 — dc22   2004017519

British Library cataloguing data are available

On the cover: Edgar Martinez *(Ben Van Houten, Seattle Mariners)*

Manufactured in the United States of America

McFarland & Company, Inc., Publishers
  Box 611, Jefferson, North Carolina 28640
    www.mcfarlandpub.com

Contents

Introduction

The basic elements of baseball remain essentially the same as they were when the first professional game was played in the 1870s. Rule changes are often approached as if baseball had been delivered from on high in a nearly perfect form in the 19th century.

The four bases are set in a square configuration with each of the four being 90 feet from the pair on its left and right.

There are three outs for the visiting team in the top half of each inning, and there are three outs for the home team in the bottom half of the inning. Nine full innings comprise the normal length of a game except when rain shortens it or when a tie game lengthens it.

Nine players on a side play nine positions that are prescribed within the playing boundaries of the field. On July 14, 1946, in the second game of a doubleheader, Cleveland Indians manager Lou Boudreau stunned and amused the baseball world with his specially designed defensive maneuver against the Boston Red Sox' Ted Williams, one of the game's best all-time hitters. When Williams came to the plate and was ready to hit, he saw a strange infield shift aligned against him. Shortstops had always played on the left side of the infield, and now Boudreau, the Indians' shortstop, had positioned himself near the second baseman on the right side of the second base bag. The "Williams Shift" went against the normalcy of the game.

The pitcher throws the baseball to a hitter who is 60 feet 6 inches from him. That distance was established in 1893, and it has remained the same ever since. The height of the pitching mound has been changed occasionally as attempts were made to help either the pitcher or the batter. The interpretation of the size of the strike zone has been altered slightly from time to time to aid either the thrower or the swinger.

Lights were installed in major league stadiums to illuminate play. Cincinnati's Crosley Field, home of the Reds, was the first major league ball yard to be equipped for night baseball. Artificial illumination first replaced the sun for a ball game there on May 24, 1935.

Changes in baseball, when they come, often come slowly. It wasn't until 53 years later that every major league ballpark was equipped for play after dark. The Chicago Cubs, who play in historic Wrigley Field, were the last holdout. On August 9, 1988, Wrigley Field's new lights were turned on, and the Cubs played the New York Mets in nocturnal baseball.

Artificial surfaces have replaced natural grass in some parks. Baseball fans were first introduced to the game played indoors on "fake" grass in the Houston Astrodome in 1965. Other teams began to install and use artificial surfaces in their ball yards, even though their games were played outdoors. Recently, a number of those teams have returned their playing surfaces to real grass, which provides part of the beauty of baseball.

Baseball has a history of offering consistency for those who have watched it being played, and who have developed a fondness for the nuances that take place within its regularity.

Before 1973, baseball's last major rule change had been made in 1901. That year the National League legislated that a foul ball on a two-strike count would not result in a strikeout. The American League accepted the same rule in 1903.

In 1973, baseball's most drastic change was legislated. It was so drastic that one league accepted it and the other league did not. The American League's owners voted to add one player to the traditional nine-man lineup. Their league began to play a "10-man game," in which a designated hitter (DH) had a regular spot in the batting order, and he or a replacement for him batted for his club's pitcher(s) throughout the game. Baseball in the National League continued to be a "nine-man game," with only that number of players for each team active in the game at any one time.

The American League owners, who approved this change to the basic rules of baseball, were hoping that designated hitters would provide a spark for the sagging offenses in their league. The hitters in their league had posted a number of poor offensive seasons as they watched the National League's batters top them in many of the offensive categories. The American League's owners were also hoping that an explosion in hits, homers, and runs would entice more people to come to their ballparks and enable them to catch and then pass the National League in the annual attendance race.

Since 1973, the designated hitter had been a topic for discussion and debate. There have been a few times when it looked as if the designated hitter might be eliminated in American League games. Designated hitters have become expensive commodities for many clubs, but they have also helped to produce increased offense for the league's teams.

Only once did the National League come close to adding the extra hitter to its lineups. Other than that one brief moment, the league has remained steadfast in its resolve not to have designated hitters in its lineups during the regular season.

Since 1973, major league baseball has been played with two different sets of rules which have resulted in two different games. There are the purposefully designed, power-laden, "10-man" lineups in the Junior Circuit that are hoping for offensive explosions that produce victories and whirling turnstiles in their ballparks. There are also the more traditional, strategically-oriented, "nine-man" National League lineups. The Senior Circuit's leaders want baseball to be played as it was originally designed.

There does not appear to be an end in sight for this tale of two leagues.

ONE

The American League Falters at the Plate

On April 6, 1973, in Fenway Park, Boston, the New York Yankees' Ron Blomberg stepped to the plate to face the Red Sox' Luis Tiant. It was Opening Day and Blomberg was about to become major league baseball's first designated hitter (DH). Blomberg drew a walk in his first at-bat, beating seven other designated hitters to the plate in the four games played on the American League schedule that day. Orlando Cepeda was Boston manager Eddie Kasko's choice to fill the new role for the Red Sox. Tony Oliva and Billy North were the designated hitters in the Minnesota Twins–Oakland Athletics match-up. The Baltimore Orioles and the Milwaukee Brewers had Terry Crowley and Ollie Brown in their lineups, and the California Angels and the Kansas City Royals tapped Tom McCraw and Ed Kirkpatrick to fill the role for them. On Opening Day, these eight hitters were spread throughout the teams' lineups. North led off for the Athletics and Crowley hit in the eighth spot for the Orioles. The others were in the fourth, fifth, or sixth spots on the clubs' lineup cards. Together, the eight designated hitters were 8-for-32 for a .250 average in the first day of designated-hitter baseball.

Four more American Leaguers made their first appearances as designated hitters the following day in their clubs' openers. Mike Andrews and Rico Carty were in the role for the Chicago White Sox and the Texas Rangers. John Ellis was the Cleveland Indians' DH in their game against the Detroit Tigers, who had Gates Brown as the club's "10th man." The four designated hitters had a .133 average from a combined 2-for-15 effort. Together the 12 designated hitters in the openers were 10-for-47 for a .213 average. The offensive onslaught by the new players in the lineups had not yet been seen!

On January 11, 1973, the American League had approved the use of designated hitters to bat for pitchers in their games. The National League had rejected the innovative idea, and their pitchers continued to occupy the #9 spot in their batting orders. The insertion of a DH in the lineup was an attempt by the American League to increase the offensive part of their games, to create added excitement, and to draw more fans to its ball-parks.

The vote had been taken during a meeting at the Sheraton–O'Hare Motor Hotel in Rosemont, Ill. When the owners and general managers of the American and National League teams left the meeting "each looked as if something dire had been done, something evolutionary, something bizarre. Commissioner Bowie Kuhn told what: the American League was going to run a three-year test on the DPH — designated pinch hitter. The National League had said no thanks, not for us."[1]

It was not a surprise that the leagues would have arrived at different decisions. The National League (the Senior Circuit) was usually slower than the American League (Junior Circuit) to accept change. In 1961, the American League had expanded to 10 teams with the addition of a new Washington club to replace the one that had relocated to Minnesota, and a new club in Los Angeles. The National League was not ready to make the leap, but they did so one year later when they added the New York Mets and the Houston Colt .45s. In 1961, the Junior Circuit went to a 162-game schedule while the Senior Circuit remained at the traditional 154 games. It took the Senior Circuit a year to catch up with the other league. There was discussion about whether or not they would also jump on the "designated hitter bandwagon" within a short period of time.

The American League's owners were responding to recent patterns in the game that had propelled the National League to the lead in a number of offensive categories. League batting average and the total number of hits and runs in a given season usually favored the Senior Circuit's hitters. The designated pinch hitter was an attempt to help the Junior Circuit take the lead in these and other areas from the older and staid Senior Circuit.

Baseball's offensive side had held sway during the early 1960s. The hitter was the center of the game, and the pitcher usually took a position in the background. A well-pitched 1–0 game was appreciated by some, but a 10–7 slugfest made for a much livelier ballpark. Offensive baseball, with a multitude of hits, runs, and home runs, brought crowds to their feet. The ballpark was alive with excitement and expectation when players were scooting around the bases.

Ted Williams, who had returned from military duty during the Korean Conflict, had led the American League in hitting in 1957 with a lofty .388 average, and he took the crown again the following season with a .328 mark. In June 1960, he hit his 500th career home run, and he joined one of baseball's most elite groups of players. He would go on to total 521 four-baggers before he retired at the end of the season. In his final at-bat, "The Splendid Splinter" powered one of the Orioles' Jack Fisher's pitches for a climactic home run in Fenway Park.

A dramatic home run highlighted the 1960 Fall Classic. The series between the Pittsburgh Pirates and the Yankees was strange in terms of the twists and turns it took along the way. Going into the seventh and final game of the series, Pittsburgh had won the first, fourth, and fifth games by the scores of 6–4, 3–2, and 5–2. New York, affectionately known by fans as "the Bronx Bombers," had picked up their victories in games two, three, and six in an overwhelming offensive manner. They had bombed the Bucs, 16–3, 10–0, and 12–0.

In game seven, on October 13, the Pirates came to bat in the bottom of the ninth inning with the score tied, 9–9. It had been another offensive outburst. New York had scored twice in the top of the inning to create the deadlock. Pittsburgh second baseman Bill Mazeroski was the lead-off hitter in the Pirates' at-bat. Ralph Terry was on the mound for the Yanks, and he delivered an inside pitch to "Maz," who drove it over the left-field wall for a series-ending, walk-off home run that sealed the 10–9 victory and delivered the 1960 World Championship to Pittsburgh.

During the seven games, New York, in a mighty offensive show, hit .338, banged out 91 hits, and scored 55 runs—all World Series records at the time. The accomplishment of New York left-hander Whitey Ford, who threw the Yankees' 10–0 and 12–0 shutouts, pales in the recall of many compared to the runs his team had scored.

Home runs were a focal point the following season as well. The baseball world awakened to a dual assault by the Yankees' Roger Maris and Mickey Mantle on one of the game's greatest achievements. Babe Ruth's 1927 record of 60 homers in a season was in jeopardy of being broken. In the past, only a few players had come close to breaking the hallowed mark.

The most serious challenges had been mounted in the 1930s. The Philadelphia Athletics' Jimmie Foxx (1932) and the Tigers' Hank Greenberg (1938) had fallen only two homers short of matching the Babe, and, in 1930, the Chicago Cubs' Hack Wilson had slammed 56. In 1947, the New York Giants' Johnny Mize and the Pirates' Ralph Kiner each hit 51. Kiner had another outstanding season in 1949 when he blasted 54 four-baggers. Mantle registered 52 in 1956, and the Giants' Willie Mays powered 51 during the 1955 season.

In 1961, Maris and Mantle waged a two-man challenge of the fellow Yankee's mark. For some time it appeared as if either or both players might reach or surpass Ruth's long-standing record. However, late in the season,

Mantle suffered a series of injuries, and the race ended for him at 54. Maris continued on, battling self-inflicted pressure as well as a lack of support and a measure of anger from many who didn't want him to reach 60 and break the icon's record. The new 162-game schedule provided Maris with additional opportunities to catch and pass Ruth.

On September 26, Maris hit his 60th home run off the Orioles' Fisher to tie Ruth. The Baltimore pitcher had become a item of trivia as the player who had served up Williams' final home run and Maris' record-tying shot. Since Maris had hit his 60th homer in the 159th game, there was the possibility that an asterisk would be attached to his accomplishment. There had been talk that baseball commissioner Ford Frick had suggested that an asterisk be placed next to a tie or a new record if it took the player more than 154 games to accomplish the feat.

On October 1, the final day of the season, Maris blasted a pitch from the Red Sox' Tracy Stallard into the stands at Yankee Stadium and the new mark of 61 was his. Since the Yanks had played a tie game on April 22, the memorable homer came in the team's 163rd game. Maris had played in 161 of them.

An asterisk was attached to the record in many listings of home-run hitters until commissioner Fay Vincent removed it in the 1990s. Frick denied that he was responsible for the notation. He said that the idea had originated with Dick Young, one of the outstanding baseball writers of the time. Frick described his thinking and the eventual resolution of the issue:

> Late in the 1961 season when it became apparent that Maris had a great chance either to tie or better the Ruth mark, newspapermen raised the question as to how any new record would be handled. The commissioner was asked to make a ruling. The ruling was a simple one. In case the record was broken in 154 games the Maris mark would be recognized, and the Ruth record would be dropped. If the Ruth mark still stood at the end of 154 games but was subsequently broken in the eight additional games of the 1960 [1961] season, then both records would be recognized as official and given equal billing in the record book....
>
> Detailed information on each record was carried side by side. They still are. Page 311 of the 1972 Red Book carries a complete record of the 61 home runs hit by Roger Maris. Page 312 carries the same full report of the 60 home runs hit by Babe Ruth. No asterisks! No apologies! Just two official records of two great baseball accomplishments that fans will never forget. I still think it was the right decision.[2]

Mantle and Maris weren't the only players banging home runs in 1961. Eight major leaguers had more than 40. The Twins' Harmon Killebrew and the Orioles' Jim Gentile, who each hit 46 homers, followed Maris and

Mantle in the American League's list of the home run leaders. The Tigers' Rocky Colavito belted 45. The San Francisco Giants had a pair of players with 40 or more round-trippers. Cepeda powered 46 and Mays had 40. A year later, a major league record of 3,001 round- trippers was set.

Frick was alarmed by the hitters' increasing output, and he sought to remedy the situation. At one point he said, "I would even like the spitball to come back. Take a look at the batting, home runs, and slugging record for recent seasons, and you become convinced that the pitchers need help urgently.[3]

Following the 1962 season, Frick gave the pitchers some aid when he persuaded the Major League Baseball Rules Committee (MLBRC) to enlarge the strike zone that had been made smaller in 1950. The smaller strike zone, which had been delineated as being from the batter's armpits to the top of his knees, had hurt pitchers and had been a huge help to hitters. It had taken away a pitcher's high and low strikes, and it had allowed the hitters to concentrate on a smaller hitting area. With the change that took effect for the 1963 season and beyond, strikes began to be called if the ball was over the plate and between the top of the batter's shoulders and the bottom of his knees. "The result would be a second golden age for pitching — the number of homers fell by 10 percent, the number of runs by 12 percent, and overall batting averages dropped by 10 points, all in one season (1963)."[4]

During the 1950s, in an "era of the offensive game," major league teams had combined for an average of 17.7 hits and 8.8 runs per game. (These and the following statistics are the combined totals of both teams in a single game.) The high points in the two categories were registered by teams in the American League. In 1951, they averaged 18 hits per game, with the White Sox leading the way with 1,453 hits during the season. A year earlier, the American League clubs had scored an average of 10 runs per game, with the Red Sox at the top of the list, scoring 1,027 runs.

The lowest figures for hits per game in the decade were reported by the National League in 1952 when their average was 17.1. That season, the Senior Circuit's clubs averaged 8.3 runs per game, which was also the lowest during the 1950s. The 1952 Pirates, with 1,201 hits and 515 runs scored, sat at the bottom of the loop in these areas as well as in the number of wins and losses.

The comparative figures for the six seasons after the readjustment of the strike zone following the 1962 campaign indicate changes in the offensive nature of the game. Even though expansion came during the 1960s, weakening many pitching staffs as clubs had to go deeper into their pool of minor leaguers, hitting and run-scoring statistics went down.

The combined statistics for both leagues show decreasing numbers in both batting average (BA) and runs per game (RPG) from 1963–1968.

Year	BA	RPG
1963	.246	7.89
1964	.250	8.07
1965	.246	7.98
1966	.248	7.99
1967	.243	7.54
1968	.237	6.84

After 1962, there was a decline in the major leagues of over a hit per game from the previous decade when the average dropped to 16.6, lower than any single season during the 1950s. The runs-per-game average dipped to 7.89, which was also lower than it had been in any year during the previous decade. In 1966, the National League registered the high for hits with 17.6, which was lower than the average for all major league games during the previous decade. The highest average for runs scored after 1962 was 8.2 in the American League in 1969, which was also below the major league average during the 1950s.

Not to be overlooked in the changing times of decreasing offense were the outstanding pitchers that batters had to face during the 1960s. The Hall of Fame could field a formidable staff of pitchers who were active and collecting wins during the decade. The National League featured Don Drysdale (25–9 in 1962), and Sandy Koufax (25 wins in 1963, 26 wins in 1965, and 27 wins in 1966) with the Los Angeles Dodgers, an aging but still effective Warren Spahn (23–7 in 1963) with the Milwaukee Braves, Phil Niekro with Milwaukee and the Atlanta Braves (23–13 in 1969), Tom Seaver (25–7 in 1969) with the New York Mets, Jim Bunning (19–8 in 1964 and 19–9 in 1965) with the Philadelphia Phillies and the Pirates, Bob Gibson (20 wins in 1965, 21 wins in 1966, 22 wins in 1968, and 20 wins in 1969) with the St. Louis Cardinals, and Juan Marichal (25 wins in 1963, 21 wins in 1964, 22 wins in 1965, 25 wins in 1966, 26 wins in 1968, and 21 wins in 1969) and Gaylord Perry (21–6 in 1966) with the San Francisco Giants. American League hitters had to face the likes of the Yankees' Whitey Ford (25–4 in 1961 and 24–7 in 1963).

On July 2, 1963, a monumental match-up took place between two of the National League's top hurlers. In a 16-inning marathon between San Francisco and Milwaukee, Marichal and Spahn, who was 42 years old at the time, nearly laid the two clubs' offenses to rest as both pitchers went the distance. They scattered 17 hits between them, and Mays' walk-off homer off Spahn in the bottom of the 16th inning provided the game's only run. Marichal gave up four walks and struck out 10 Braves during his outing. Spahn doled out a single base on balls to go with a pair of strike-outs. The San Francisco right-hander threw 227 pitches and the Milwaukee lefty delivered 200. There weren't any "pitch counts" controlling the managers' decisions that day!

There were a number of outstanding pitching performances in 1968. Drysdale posted six shutouts in succession, and he set a record of 58⅔ consecutive scoreless innings. Gibson tossed 13 shutouts, went 22–9, and had a 1.12 ERA, the stingiest in the majors since the Red Sox' Dutch Leonard's 0.96 ERA in 1914. The Cardinals' dominating right-hander also fanned 17 Tigers in the first game of that season's World Series. Detroit's Denny McLain, who is not even in the Hall of Fame, went 31–6 to become the first pitcher in 34 years to win more than 30 games.

Beside the change in the strike zone and the dominating pitchers, there were other causal factors in the offensive decline.

By the end of the 1950s, relief pitchers were being used more often and earlier in games than they had been when a starter was expected "to go the distance." Managers were beginning to make more use of their teams' bullpens, and batters were increasingly having to face more than one or two pitchers in a game. That was an added challenge for batters, who now had to adjust to the different styles and repertoires offered by each pitcher.

During the 1950s, before the increased reliance on relief pitchers, the two major leagues posted the following complete-game statistics:

Year	National League	American League
1950	498	500
1951	459	479
1952	444	505
1953	430	434
1954	377	463
1955	385	363
1956	360	398
1957	356	354
1958	356	387
1959	376	366

The highest annual per-team average for complete games during these years was 62.3 in the National League in 1950 and 42.6 in the American League in 1952. The lowest annual average in the National League was 44.5

in 1957 and 1958. The lowest per-team average of complete games in the American League was 44.3 in 1957.

The average number of complete games per club began to fall off during the following decade even though the statistics in some cases indicate that there were more route-going performances being turned in by pitchers. That was due to the increased number of clubs in each league, which resulted in more games being played. The comparative per-team averages for the 1960s show a downward trend in comparison with the figures for the 1950s. The highest annual per-team average for complete games during the 1960s was 45.9 in the National League in 1963 and 42.6 in the American League in 1968. The lowest annual per-team average in the National League was 40.2 in 1967, and it was 32.3 in the American League in 1965.

The Pirates' Elroy Face was at the top of the list when it came to recognizing the accomplishments of those who came into games out of the bullpens. In 1959, at the turn of the decade, Face made 57 game appearances, and all of them were in relief. He racked up a remarkable 18–1 record. That same season, the Cardinals' Lindy McDaniel, pitching mostly in relief, posted a 14–12 mark.

Face had perfected the "forkball" to confuse the hitters, and others were beginning to add an effective new pitch to their arsenals— the "slider." Frick hadn't gotten the spitball legalized, but the forkball and the slider were there for hitters to try to handle.

In 1968, the combined major league batting average dropped to .237, the lowest in the 20th century. The 6.84 runs per game for both teams was the second lowest in the century, with the 1908 clubs holding a seven-hundredths of a run lead in futility. The American League's clubs hit at a paltry .230 clip. The once-mighty Yankees, who finished in fifth place in the 10-team league, had an overall .214 batting average! The Red Sox' Carl Yastrzemski captured the batting crown with a .301 average, and the runner-up for the title, Oakland's Danny Cater, hit only .290. Rick Monday, the 10th best hitter in the American League in 1968, batted .274.

Hitters were also being challenged by a different style of ballpark. Gone were many of the short and inviting home-run targets. Stadium architects, especially for National League clubs, were creating "The Era of Symmetry." Older parks, with both their idiosyncrasies and their charm, were being replaced by modern facilities that were similar in design and had been constructed for both baseball and football games.

Ebbets Field and the Polo Grounds fell victim to the wrecking ball in 1960 and 1964 respectively. However, their replacement wasn't necessary since their former occupants had departed for the west coast. Their new homes represented the new-wave ballparks. On April 12, 1960, Candlestick

Park hosted its first San Francisco Giants' regular season game. Baseball's new symmetry was represented in the "Stick's" dimensions. The fences down the left and right-field foul lines were a uniform 335 feet from home plate and it was 400 feet to the center-field wall. That was quite a difference from what the Polo Grounds, with its short foul lines (279 feet in left field and 257 feet in right field) and its cavernous center field (483 feet to the deepest part of center field), had offered batters.

Chavez Ravine, the Los Angeles Dodgers' new home, officially joined major league baseball on April 10, 1962. The park, which was playfully referred to as the "Taj O'Malley" (for owner Walter O'Malley), had left- and right-field foul lines of 330 feet, power alleys at 385 feet, and the center-field fence 400 feet from home plate. It replaced the Los Angeles Coliseum, which had been the relocated Dodgers' home since they arrived. The Coliseum had been constructed for the 1932 Olympic Games and was hardly suitable for baseball. The left-field wall was only 251 feet from home plate, and a 40-foot-high screen which extended 140 feet toward center field was built on top of it to add a bit more of a challenge for hitters. The Dodgers' left-handed-hitting Wally Moon developed an inside-out swing, and he lofted "Moon Shots" over the short left-field fence. For a short time, some were fearful that Moon, whose best season in home run production had been in 1957 when he hit 24 for St. Louis, might challenge the Babe's record in the misshapen Coliseum.

In 1964, Shea Stadium in Flushing became the home of the New York Mets, who had played their first two seasons in the Polo Grounds before it was razed. The distance in Shea to the left- and right-field walls was another example of the symmetry in the recently constructed major league ballparks. The distance down the lines was 341 feet and the center-field fence was 410 feet from home plate.

The same symmetry was represented in Busch Stadium in St. Louis, which opened in 1966 to replace Sportsman's Park, which had been the home of both the Browns and the Cardinals. A fair fly ball hit more than 330 feet down the foul lines would land in Busch Stadium's stands. A drive traveling 386 feet or more to the power alleys and 414 feet to center would reach home-run territory. Conversely, Sportsman's Park had featured a 351-foot left-field foul line and a very inviting 310-foot right-field foul line, but the center-field wall was a distant 422 feet from home plate.

New stadiums also came to the clubs in Anaheim and Houston in the 1960s. The early 1970s welcomed the opening of other symmetrically-designed ballparks in Cincinnati, Philadelphia, and Pittsburgh.

Whether it was because of the quality of the pitching, the size of the strike zone, the style of the stadiums, or any number of other contributing factors, the 1968 season had produced an eye-opening low point in offensive baseball. Following the season of offensive impotence, a number of changes were introduced throughout baseball to get the bats going again.

On December 3, 1968, the MLBRC took three actions that were aimed at helping hitters resurrect the offensive side of the game. The committee, which had the authority to make changes without consultation with owners and general managers, voted to lower the pitcher's mound from 15 to 10 inches, to shrink the strike zone to the 1950 guidelines, and to enforce the existing rule about illegal pitches.

The batters were being given the advantage again. The higher mound that had given pitchers greater leverage was lowered and, once again, they were throwing at a smaller target area. Both of these changes were aimed at benefiting the hitting game.

There was also a set of experimental rules that would be available during 1969 spring training. The American League, traditionally more on the cutting edge of change than the National League, approved the experimental rules subject to approval of the participating teams. The National League did not approve their use.

There were four plans available for use when American League teams were playing each other in pre-season contests. For the first time, a designated hitter was introduced to baseball. Two of the plans involved this innovation. The first plan allowed for a designated pinch-hitter who could be used twice in a game for anyone in the lineup without forcing that player out of the game. The pinch-hitter could not enter the game as a fielder. The second plan involved a permanent hitter who had to be declared before the game to hit for the pitcher. This was similar to what would later become part of the American League game. A third approach involved the use of a pinch-runner who could be used twice with the player he ran for remaining in the game. The final experiment was intended to be a time-saving measure. It involved the awarding of an intentional base on balls to a player after a notification of intent had been made to the home-plate umpire. The batter would take first base without a pitch being thrown. The lineup card for games in which the first three options were used would contain 12 names—the nine starters along with the designated-pinch hitter who could be used twice in the game, the permanent hitter for the pitcher, and the designated pinch-runner.

The spring training experimental rules were not used during the regular season. However, four minor leagues did experiment with a variety of approaches during their regular seasons in attempts to increase the scoring punch.

The Triple-A International League provided for the use of a permanent pinch-hitter to be designated before the game to hit for the pitcher. During the game, the manager could change to another designated hitter for the one who began the game.

The Class AA Eastern League's plan involved the use of a pinch-hitter for the pitcher, but that hitter could be inserted into the lineup to hit for the pitcher at any point in the game, and the hitter or a substitute for him had to continue as a designated hitter in the lineup for the remainder of the game. The Eastern League's experiment was in place through the 1970 season, after which the MLBRC voted to discontinue it.

The Class AA Texas League used a more complicated approach to help improve its teams' offenses. A manager could employ a specific pinch-hitter as often as he wanted, but only for one man in any given inning. If the team batted around, the pinch-hitter could hit for the same batter again in his normal turn. Every time the pinch-hitter was used, the player he batted for was required to leave the game.

Another approach was used in the Class A N.Y.-Penn League. That league employed a hitter designated before the game to hit twice for any player in the lineup without forcing that player out of the game. Also, for two seasons at the Class A level, intentional walks were awarded when notification of intent was given to the home-plate umpire.

Substitution in baseball had been allowed only for incapacitation through 1891, when it became permissible to pinch-hit or pinch-run for any player with that player being required to leave the game. On June 16, 1892, John Montgomery Ward became the game's first pinch-hitter when he went to the plate to hit for the Brooklyn Dodgers' pitcher and singled. The experimental rules for 1969 were the first time that a player could be hit or run for without having to be replaced in the game.

Commissioner Bowie Kuhn commented about the experiments:

> The DH debate we stirred up in 1969 was altogether healthy ... I think the public was beginning to believe that we were finally awake. Executives like Lee MacPhail of the Yankees believed in the DH and were beginning to make some progress in the American League. Certainly, if change in any area was coming, the more venturesome American League would be the place for me to seek allies. They had precipitated expansion in 1961 and 1969, forcing the reluctant National Leaguers to follow suit both times.[5]

Statistics from the International League's 1969 regular season showed the desired increase in offensive performances. The following figures represent the 1968 and 1969 seasons. The first are the pitchers' figures for the season when they batted for themselves, and the second are the designated hitters' figures for the year they batted for pitchers:

Batting average, .160 up to .261; runs scored, 225 up to 511; hits, 514 up to 958; home runs, 24 up to 108; walks, 162 up to 425; strike-outs, 1,173 down to 628.[6]

In 1969, the International League's pitchers experienced two changes when designated hitters were in the opposing lineups. It was more difficult to keep the opposition off the scoreboards, but they were remaining in the games a bit longer. They tossed 67 shutouts in 1969 when designated hitters were in the lineups compared to 103 the previous season. During the year of the DH experiment, the number of complete games rose from 311 to 362.

During the 1969 major league regular season — sparked by the changes that had been made before the campaign by the MLBRC: lowered mounds, shrunken strike zones, and enforcement of the rules regarding illegal pitches— the hits began to mount. The two leagues reported 6,871 more hits and 1,124 more home runs than in the previous season. The American Leaguers, who had averaged .230 in 1968, hit 246, and the National League raised its average from .243 to .250. Pete Rose won the Senior Circuit's batting crown with a .348 average and Rod Carew captured the honor in the American League with a .332 average.

In 1969, there were signs of offensive improvement, but pitchers were not ready to roll over and play dead. In 1961, when Maris broke Ruth's record and powerful offenses were a central part of the game, the majors' 18 teams produced only four 20-game winners. In 1969, even with the rule changes that were aimed at getting offensive baseball going again, the major leagues' 24 clubs produced 15 20-game winners, with nine of them pitching for National League clubs.

There had been positive signs in the major leagues in 1969 when there were increases in batting averages, hits, runs scored, and home runs, but the American League's offensive output didn't continue to grow beyond 1970. The league's batting averages rose above the 1969 mark to .250 in 1970, but fell to .247 in 1971, and then slipped to .240 in 1972. The National League's averages for those seasons were .259 in 1970, .252 in 1971, and .249 in 1972. In 1970, the American League's hitters increased their output in hits (16,404), home runs (1,746), and runs scored (8,109), but they fell below those numbers during the following two seasons.

In 1971 and 1972, the American League only topped the National League once in these three categories. In 1971, the Junior Circuit's home run production exceeded that of the Senior Circuit. There was a growing divide between the two leagues in the number of runs scored. In 1971, the Nationals had topped the Americans by 129 runs, and they stretched that lead to 824 in 1972.

American League pitchers were still improving their stats at the expense of the hitters. In both 1971 and 1972, the Junior Circuit's hurlers' ERAs were lower than they had been in 1969 when the league average was 3.62. In the first of the two seasons the American Leaguers posted a 3.46 ERA, and they lowered it to 3.06 in 1972.

More was still needed to jump-start the Junior Circuit's offenses. League president Joe Cronin was on a crusade to find an approach other than lowered mounds and smaller strike zones to improve the slumping offensive play.

TWO

The American League
Suffers at the Gate

The American League owners were drawn to the idea of a designated hitter (DH) when the clubs' offenses during the late 1960s and early 1970s didn't rebound in the manner they had hoped they would. It was about hits, but it was also about putting people in the ballpark seats.

Besides the sagging offensive numbers, the American League owners had also watched glumly as the National League's clubs had beaten their teams in the turnstile race in recent years. Joe Cronin, the American League president, and others believed that it was exciting, offensive baseball that brought fans to the stands, and, at the time, the Junior Circuit's teams were not providing such a product.

Although not much had separated the two leagues in terms of attendance figures during the 1940s, the American League had finished ahead of the National League in seven of the 10 years. During the 1950s, the Senior Circuit had held sway, leading the majors in attendance during six of the 10 seasons of the decade. In 1958, the Nationals topped the Americans by over 2.8 million fans.

In 1961, the American League welcomed 1.4 million more fans than the other circuit, but that was the only year the AL led in drawing power during the decade. The increase was primarily a result of that season's American League expansion from eight to 10 teams and an increase in its schedule from 154 to 162 games. The Maris and Mantle home-run race also played a part in drawing additional fans to the Junior Circuit's ballparks.

The National League had its own expansion to 10 teams in 1962, adding the Houston Colt .45s and the New York Mets. The Senior Circuit went on to lead in annual attendance the during the remainder of the 1960s. In 1965 and 1966, it outdrew the American League by a little more than 4.7 million fans each season.

Both leagues set regular-season attendance records in 1969 after they expanded to 12 teams. Montreal and San Diego were added to the National League, and Seattle and a new Kansas City club, to replace the one that had left for Oakland for the 1968 season, joined the American League. The National League led the way with 15 million admissions, and the American League drew 12.1 million customers. In 1969, each circuit was split into two six-team divisions— Eastern and Western — and the new alignment paved the way for the expansion of postseason play as a pair of League Championship Series (LCS) were

American League president Joe Cronin (1959–1973), the major proponent of the designated hitter (National Baseball Hall of Fame Library, Cooperstown, NY).

added. Two teams in each league were now headed for the postseason, and their fans had added reasons to go to the ballpark.

The Senior Circuit continued its attendance draw during the first three years of the 1970s, topping the American League each season and putting 5.4 million more fans in the seats in 1971. The Junior Circuit fell under the 12.1-million mark they had reached in 1969 in each of the three seasons. From 1969 through 1972, the National League outdrew the American League by a dominating 36 percent.

The American League's 1972 attendance figures were disappointing in a number of respects. The league's total attendance was 11,438,538 with only three of its 12 teams surpassing the million-fan mark. Detroit drew 1.89 million, Boston welcomed 1.44 million to its park, and Chicago had 1.17 million fans go through its turnstiles. The World Champion Oakland Athletics drew a disappointing 921,323 customers, becoming the first World Series winner to sink below the million mark in more than a quarter of a century. The New York Yankees played in front of 966,328 people, finishing under the million-fan mark for the first time since 1945. Eight of the 12 American League clubs reported that they had finished in the red in 1972.

That same season, the National League posted a total attendance of

15,529,730, and nine of its 12 teams attracted over a million fans. In that group, the Mets counted 2,134,185 people coming to modern Shea Stadium. Only Atlanta, San Diego, and San Francisco had fewer than a million fans watch them play that season.

The National League had been on a stadium-building binge. Modern stadiums are not always better for the game, but new ball yards can help draw fans. Since 1963, the National League had outdrawn the American League by more than 30 million paying customers. Part of their success was attributed to their foresight in constructing a number of new stadiums, each with ample parking areas on the site.

The American League played in historic and legendary ballparks such as Chicago's Comiskey Park, which held its first game in 1910; Boston's Fenway, which opened its gates in 1912; New York's Yankee Stadium, which was dedicated in 1923; Detroit's Tiger Stadium, which had been in operation under different names since early in the 20th century; and Cleveland's massive Municipal Stadium, with seating for 70,000 and an opening date of 1932. The National League could only match the special nature of those five parks with storied Wrigley Field, vintage 1916, on the north side of Chicago.

The Senior Circuit had made its move to "modern." During the 1960s and early 1970s, because of relocation, expansion, and modernization, the National League built 10 new ballparks that were enticing fans to come to the games. They appeared to be operating with the slogan: "If you build it, they will come."

Candlestick Park in San Francisco opened in 1960, and it was the first heated, open-air stadium in the world. That design ingredient was a fan-friendly attempt to combat the often chilly and windy San Francisco nights. The Dodgers moved from the Los Angeles Coliseum in 1962 and made their new home in the six-level, 56,000-seat Dodger Stadium.

In 1964, the circular, five-tier Shea Stadium in Flushing became the home of the Mets, who had played their first two seasons in the Polo Grounds. Two years later, Busch Stadium, a two-tier masterpiece in St. Louis replaced Sportsman's Park.

The Astrodome, the "Eighth Wonder of the World," had risen in Houston to house that city's National League team. The game's first indoor stadium opened for the Astros (formerly, the Colt 45s) on April 9, 1965. The original plan was to grow real grass under the dome, but that didn't work out. That led to the quick development of an artificial surface to provide a different kind of green on which to play. The many new elements that were part of the Astrodome turned it into a tourist attraction for many visitors to the Texas city who had limited or no interest in baseball.

The Braves arrived in Atlanta from Milwaukee for the 1966 campaign, and they took up residence in Atlanta–Fulton County Stadium, which had been built a year earlier and was used that season by the Atlanta Crackers, a Braves farm club. The San Diego Padres came into the Senior Circuit via expansion in 1969, and they played their games in San Diego Stadium, which had opened in 1968 as the home ballpark of the Padres of the Triple-A Pacific Coast League.

Cincinnati and Pittsburgh both inaugurated their multi-purpose stadiums on river banks in 1970. They joined the other circular, symmetrical ballparks, and they were similar to the Astrodome as stadiums with synthetic turf playing fields, although their games were played outdoors.

Philadelphia was next in line to open a new stadium. It was of the "cookie-cutter" variety like the ones in Cincinnati and Pittsburgh. On April 4, 1971, Veterans Stadium, soon to be known simply as "the Vet," held its first game. By moving from Connie Mack Stadium (formerly Shibe Park) in congested North Philadelphia to 14 acres of open land in South Philadelphia, the Phillies' organization provided the fans with better roads to get to the park and a vast parking lot when they got there. These were both welcome ingredients in most of the new parks that had come onto the National League scene. "The Vet" also incorporated modern features that were appearing in other venues. The stadium didn't have stairways. Two miles of ramps, eight escalators, and four elevators provided access to the stadium's 65,454 seats.

Better access roads and convenient parking at "the Vet" were a welcome change from Connie Mack Stadium. It was usually difficult to find a parking spot on the streets of North Philadelphia. After a space was found and the car was maneuvered into the available space, the driver would be approached by a neighborhood resident who would offer "to watch" the car during the game. That meant that if the driver paid the going asking rate (which would vary according to the whim of the person doing the "watching") he was pretty well assured that his hub caps would still be on the wheels of the car when he returned after the game.

Only Montreal, which joined the league through expansion in 1969, was in sub-par housing. The Expos would occupy the small, single-decked Jarry Park until they took up residence in Olympic Stadium in 1977.

The American League had not been on a building spree. Anaheim Stadium had opened in 1966 for the California Angels, who had played in minor league Wrigley Field and then had shared Chavez Ravine with the Dodgers after becoming a major league franchise in 1961. The Minnesota Twins, who joined the American League the same season as the Angels, took up residence in an expanded Metropolitan Stadium in Bloomington, which had opened in 1956 as a playing field for a minor league club.

Oakland-Alameda Coliseum was completed in 1966, and it welcomed the Oakland Athletics from Kansas City two years later. Turnpike Stadium in Arlington, Texas, vintage 1965, became Arlington Stadium in 1972 when the Senators moved out of Washington, D.C., and became the Rangers.

Royals Stadium in Kansas City was the first new construction in the American League in the 1970s. It opened in 1973 to provide an improved ballpark for the Royals, who had been an expansion team in 1969. They had been playing in the city's elderly Municipal Stadium, which had been rebuilt in 1955 in preparation for the move of the Athletics from Philadelphia to Kansas City. At that time, a piece of the National League became a part of Municipal Stadium when the scoreboard from old Braves Field in Boston found a new home in the Kansas City ballpark.

The future of the American League's campaign to regain the ground it had lost in the attendance wars wasn't going to be waged by providing new, modern stadiums. Their owners had another plan in mind.

On December 1, 1972, at the major league winter meetings in Honolulu, the American League owners voted unanimously to request the use of a designated pinch-hitter who could hit for the pitcher without forcing him out of the game. Their intention was to have this rule change in place for the 1973 season. The request was later defeated by the Major League Baseball Rules Committee (MLBRC) that was composed of members from both leagues by a 5–3, vote with one abstention. Earlier, the proposal had been defeated 7–2, so the American League had gained a bit of ground. The MLBRC suggested that the experiment be tried again in the 1973 spring training, and in the minor leagues. Earlier that week, at baseball's annual business meeting, the highest minor leagues had been asked to use the experiment in 1973. There was mention at the time that the Texas League might vary the experiment and go with an eight-player lineup, skipping the pitcher altogether.

Cleveland Indians' general manager Gabe Paul spoke about why he supported the use of a DH, saying, "The game has got to be more offensive…. The stadiums and the pitchers are getting bigger. You can coach a pitcher a lot easier than you can coach a batter. Maybe we even ought to juice up the ball.[1]

Lee MacPhail, who had been a proponent of the DH for some time, was serving as the Yankees' general manager in 1972. He would follow Cronin as American League president (1974–1984). He heartily supported the use of designated hitters:

I can tell you the advantages we felt it would accomplish. First, it would increase the offense of each team. Second, it would enable some clubs to retain a player, important in the club's past, who possibly was no longer able to do the job defensively. Finally, clubs would not have to remove pitchers for pinch-hitters. All of these, we felt, justified the rule change.[2]

This was not the first time that the idea of a designated hitter had been advanced in baseball. Philadelphia Athletics' manager Connie Mack had made the suggestion as early as 1906. Two decades later, at a league meeting on December 1, 1928, National League president John Heydler moved that his clubs vote to allow the use of a DH. The major reason for his proposal was that he thought that the presence of designated hitters in the line-ups would speed up the games. The proposal was approved by the Senior Circuit, but it was rejected by the Junior Circuit at a combined meeting of the owners in both leagues. In 1928, agreement by both leagues was required for the proposal to become a rule of major league baseball.

Commissioner Bowie Kuhn was concerned about the current lack of offensive punch, reflected by the 1972 composite batting average of both major leagues, which was .244. He was pro-designated hitter, and he didn't want the American League to miss an opportunity to implement the DH during the 1973 regular season. On December 20, Kuhn called the club owners and general managers of both leagues to a two-day meeting in Chicago beginning on January 11. The purposes of the gathering were to reconsider the proposal for a designated hitter which had not been approved by the Rules Committee, and a to consider a proposal for the use of a pinch-runner for a player on base without that player having to leave the game. The commissioner also wanted the team representatives to explore a limited interleague schedule for 1973. The interleague proposal would only provide for games in geographic areas that had a pair of teams such as the New York Yankees and Mets, the Chicago Cubs and the White Sox, the Dodgers and Angels, and the Giants and the Athletics.

Kuhn, aware of the few rules changes that had been allowed in baseball, wrote:

My respect for the wisdom of this restraint [very few rule changes] did not deter me from wondering if the designated hitter concept could help baseball out of its hitting doldrums. The consideration of such a change was certainly very much in our interest, if only to demonstrate that we had some oil lubricating our imaginations. I freely talked in press conferences about the hitting problem and the possibilities of the DH. On more than a few occasions, owners asked if I could avoid public discussions of our problems. My answer was that I was not going to isolate myself from the public and press. That meant I was going to have to answer questions and my answers would be honest. We were not going to solve our problems by the ludicrous pretense that they did not exist.[3]

On January 11, with the clubs' owners and general mangers in attendance, the American League representatives voted 8–4 to allow for designated pinch-hitters (DPH) to hit for the loop's pitchers as part of a three-year experiment. The usually slow-to-change National League did not go along with the designated hitter experiment. When the votes of the two leagues were combined, it was clearly a minority decision, considering that four of the American League clubs did not vote in favor of the change. However, this was not 1928, when the Senior Circuit had approved the use of the designated hitter and the Junior Circuit had not, and the idea was put to rest because the leagues had not agreed on the question. In 1973, the Junior Circuit was going to proceed on its own with the rule change.

The Junior Circuit also approved the plan for limited interleague play, but, once again, the Senior Circuit rejected the proposal and killed the idea, which required the approval of both leagues.

National League president Charles "Chub" Feeney was not convinced that designated hitters would add significantly to run production. The probability that the best pitchers would go deeper in games, because they would no longer be pinch-hit for in key situations, would serve as a counterbalance to the presence of DH in the lineups. Feeney explained the National League's position and offered some of its owners' rationale for their vote against the use of designated hitters, saying, "Our league doesn't believe in change for change's sake.... I think this new rule is going to hurt fan interest. The people know when a tight situation is coming up and it's fun to sit back and try to figure out who the manager is going to hit for the pitcher. The baseball fan likes to second-guess the manager. This is going to take an important second guess away."[4]

An editorial in *The Sporting News Official Baseball Guide* (1974) disagreed with Feeney and the National League's position:

Feeney also decries the loss of moments in pinch-hitting situations, when fans implore the manager to bring on Willie Mays, for instance. Actually, the DH rule would give the fans four or five chances to see Willie Mays hit instead of one or none.

Neither does Feeney like the prospect that "moves and countermoves of managers will be radically affected." We hope Chub is right in forecasting sharp changes in this area. Let us pray for far fewer pitching changes which seldom produce high drama but invariably cause long interruptions in the action.

Back in 1969, the International League used the DH rule and some

American League president Lee MacPhail (1974–1984), left, and National League president Chub Feeney (1970–1986). They were close friends with very different views about the designated hitter. (National Baseball Hall of Fame Library, Cooperstown, NY.)

managers claimed they disliked it because it reduced their maneuverability in the use of relief pitchers. The same managers, however, rebutted their own argument. They didn't have to use the DH, which was optional. But everyone did. The DH could hardly get a stronger endorsement.[5]

After the American League's approval of the DH for the 1973 season, Milton J. Shapp, the governor of Pennsylvania (a state with two National League clubs), weighed in on the subject. In a letter to the editor of the *New York Times*, he wrote:

I look upon the American League decision to place a pinch-hitter in the place of the pitcher as only one step — and a minor step — along the road to rejuvenating baseball to make it once again the most thrilling and scientific sport of all.[6]

Shapp may have viewed the change as "a minor step," but the approval of a designated hitter was one of the few revisions of the game's playing rules in the 20th century. In 1901, the National League had ruled that a foul strike on a two-strike count would not result in a strikeout, and the American League accepted the same change in 1903. In 1920, the spitball and certain other pitches had been declared illegal. Readers of the *New York Times Magazine* were reminded that baseball fans often believe that the rules of the game "were dictated to Moses on Mount Sinai. They consider them Holy Writ and are as zealously protective of them as fundamentalists are of the King James Bible."[7]

The new rule provided that a pinch-hitter who is designated before the game would bat for the starting pitcher and any subsequent pitchers who might replace him in the game. A replacement could be used for the designated pinch-hitter. The designated pinch-hitter could not play a defensive position and could not serve as a pinch-runner. A replaced designated pinch-hitter could not reenter the game in any capacity.

It was not long before the term "designated pinch hitter" was dropped and "designated hitter" was introduced since that player was considered to be a part of the regular lineup in American League games.

Before the start of the season, a change was made in the rule so that designated hitters could play a defensive position in the field. Should that occur, the team would, however, lose its designated hitter. The pitcher would then hit in the place in the lineup where the player the DH had replaced in the field had batted.

One concern that was voiced about not allowing designated hitters to become a defensive player had to do with second-string catchers. Back-up receivers might not be used as designated hitters in order to the avoid the possibility of teams being caught short-handed if the starting catcher were injured.

Jim Campbell, the Tigers' general manager, was bothered by the change in the rule from the way that it had originally been approved:

> Look, ... we voted to accept this rule with the understanding that the designated hitter will *not* be used on defense. Are we now going to have to go out and explain a different kind of rule to the public? ... The worst thing we can do if we want to get this one off is to further confuse the fans.[8]

It had been agreed between the two leagues that a designated hitter would not be eligible to play in the World Series and in All-Star Games. The National League was still considering whether or not to allow the use of a DH in spring training exhibition games. On March 9, the National League, by a vote of 8–4, vetoed the use of a DH by the Junior Circuit's clubs in games involving Senior Circuit teams. Not everybody was happy with the decision.

Three days later, Boston Red Sox' manager Eddie Kasko blasted Kuhn for not requiring the National League to at least allow the use of a DH in the interleague exhibition games that were to be played in the American League team's ballpark. An angry Kasko, who had his lineup card refused by umpire Bill Deegan before a home game against the Phillies, said, "Here we have a rule, we're playing the game in our own park and we're not allowed to use our rule.... We've got a stupid rule that nobody wants to make a ruling on."[9]

Questions were being asked about some of the implications of the new rule that was going to be a part of the American League game beginning in 1973. They indicated some of the strategic moves that were being imagined. The following are examples of the questions:

Q. Does this (the DH rule) mean that in every American League game there will be 10 men in the line-up instead of nine?

A. No, the manager may elect to use the designated hitter on any given day or he may not. In fact, one manager in a game may start with one and the rival manager may go without one....

Q. If a team starts a game with a designated hitter, can the pitcher ever bat for himself that day?

A. Under the liberalization announced last week, he may. Suppose the Yankees open with Ron Blomberg as the designated man and he bats for the pitcher two or three times. Then, in the eighth inning, Ralph Houk wants the pitcher to bat for himself — maybe to bunt. That's legal now, but Blomberg is out of the game at that point and the Yankees must complete the game without a designated hitter.

Q. Suppose Norm Cash is Detroit's DH. Manager (Billy) Martin decides in the eighth inning that he wants to maneuver things with one goal in mind: to bring his pitcher up to bat in the ninth inning in order to pinch-hit for him. Can he do it?

A. One way is to remove Ed Brinkman, the shortstop, and replace him with Tony Taylor. But he puts Taylor into the batting order in place of the designated hitter, Cash. This means the pitcher bats in Brinkman's spot. So, in the ninth, the pitcher comes up instead of Brinkman — and Martin can pinch-hit for him, leaving Taylor at shortstop.

Q. Suppose Fritz Peterson is pitching for the Yankees and Ron Swoboda is batting for him as the designated hitter. But Manager Houk makes a slick move during an inning to retire one batter. He shifts Peterson to first base momentarily, lets a relief pitcher retire the batter, then moves Peterson back to the mound. Is that legal?

A.   It's legal and always has been. But now there is this difference: Once Peterson moves to first base, he stops being a pitcher, even though the move is temporary. Consequently, he no longer rates a designated hitter. So he instantly forces Swoboda out of the game as the "DH." Swoboda's vacated spot in the batting order is taken by the relief pitcher (and later by the new first baseman).[10]

As the 1973 regular season approached, at least three groups were trying to anticipate the effects of the new rule: managers; some hitters; and pitchers. The men in the dugout who would make out the lineup cards before every game were considering whether to settle on a single player to fill the role, or to spread out the job as a way of providing some time off for defensive players. Managers were seeking the player or players who were best suited to fill the new role — the role that was supposed to get the offenses going in the American League. Many discovered that the spring training limitation of being able to only use a DH in games against other American League clubs was making it difficult to formulate their plans.

An article in *Sports Illustrated* mentioned a number of players who might be ideally suited for the new role:

> There are some pretty fair bat swingers to noodle around with. Of the six American Leaguers with lifetime averages of .300 after five years of experience, at least five [Rico Carty, Tony Oliva, Al Kaline, Frank Robinson and Matty Alou] seem certain to see some DPH service, as do the league's top home run hitters of the past season — Harmon Killebrew, Dick Allen and Bill Melton.
>
> New leaseholds on playing life will abound — one of the most wondrous being that accorded to Old Fair Catch Rico Carty. Mark him down as DPH-in-chief for Whitey Herzog's Texas Rangers. If nothing else is accomplished, the rule will enable the fans to name at least this Ranger.[11]

Managers and players were wondering about the dynamics of being a "permanent" designated hitter. There could be problems connected with expecting someone who had been a full-time player to become a full-time designated hitter. What would it be like to be a player who was once good enough to put on his glove and take a position in the field, but who now believes that his manager no longer values his defensive skills?

However, other players who possessed certain valued offensive skills and decreasing defensive abilities saw the designated hitter role as an opportunity to extend their careers in the game and to stay on the payroll. If every team had one of those players there would have probably been 12 happy skippers!

Most pitchers secretly — and sometimes, not so secretly — dream of getting the big hit to win the close game. While they were growing up, many of them were the best players on their teams and also were among their team's best hitters. Although their hitting skills in professional baseball had not been developed and had not been valued, many of them still dreamed of delivering the key hit in the critical situation. Some had done it in their careers, and now the bat was going to be yanked from their hands. The Baltimore Orioles' ace Jim Palmer had gotten seven game-winning hits in 1972. The Athletics' Jim "Catfish" Hunter had pounded 36 hits for a .350 average in 1971 and added 23 more the following season for a .219 mark. Charles O. Finley, the A's owner, had included a $5,000 hitting bonus in Hunter's $50,000 contract. An angry Hunter, who believed that he could hit and that his ability at the plate gave his team the edge over the opposing pitcher, said, "I can hit the long ball. I can bunt. I take my hitting seriously. I didn't have such a good season last year — only .219. But the season before I hit .350. I'm good for a couple of home runs a year. This thing kinda hurts my pride."[12]

Hunter recognized the potential negative and positive factors about having a DH in the other club's lineup. He said, "It means I'll have to face another good hitter, and what's good about that? But maybe he won't feel he's in the game. The pressure will be on him real strong. If he goes 0 for 4, he's a failure. If, some days, a fine fielder doesn't get a hit he can still feel he's done a job."[13]

In 1972, A's reliever Rollie Fingers got six hits in his limited plate appearances for a .316 average. A disappointed Fingers commented, "half the fun of pitching is being able to hit."[14]

For pitchers who might have been pinch-hit for, their complete game numbers and their innings pitched had a chance to increase.

Managers were considering having smaller pitching staffs in the regular season since there did not promise to be as much use of the bullpens as there had been. That made for more spots on American League rosters for position players, but the tradeoff would be that there would be fewer openings for pitchers.

There promised to be many more questions asked and opinions expressed about the place of the DH in the game. But, ready or not American Leaguers, here come the designated hitters!

THREE

The Designated
Hitter Arrives

Major League Rule 6.10(b), which set the guidelines for the use of the designated hitter (DH) in the American League, was in place for the 1973 season.

The designated hitter must be "designated" before the beginning of the game. He can bat in any of the nine spots in the lineup, and his name must appear on the game's lineup card when it is presented to the umpire-in-chief prior to the start of the game.

The designated hitter can only bat for the starting pitcher and any subsequent pitchers who enter the game. The DH can be replaced during the game by another player(s) who then serves as the designated hitter.

Should the designated hitter take a defensive position during the game, a DH is no longer available to the team. The previously designated hitter continues to bat in the same spot in the order, and the pitcher(s) or a pinch-hitter(s) for the pitcher(s) bat in the spot that was previously occupied by the defensive player who was replaced. If a pitcher takes a defensive position, the designated hitter's position is no longer available for the remainder of the game.

A pinch-runner can be substituted for the DH once he has reached base, and the runner becomes the designated hitter.

Finally, the lineup does not need to include a designated hitter. A manager can choose to have the game's starting pitcher bat for himself. (This is part of the rule that has yet to find its way into a game!)

The advent of the designated hitter took place on Opening Day, April 6, 1973, when the New York Yankees' Ron Blomberg stepped to the plate in Fenway Park, Boston, to face the Red Sox' Luis Tiant.

The names and positions of those players who appeared on the Yankees' lineup card that was presented to the umpire prior to the game on April 6 were:

Clarke	2b		F. Alou	1b
White	lf		Munson	c
M. Alou	rf		Michael	ss
Murcer	cf			
Nettles	3b		Stottlemyre	p
Blomberg	dh			

In the top of the first inning, with the bases loaded, Tiant issued Blomberg a free pass, forcing in Matty Alou. The Yankees' DH became the first designated hitter to appear in a game, the first to reach base, and the first of the new breed to have a run batted in. As Alou crossed the plate, an observer was heard to say, "See, it's added offense to the game already."[1] Blomberg singled, flied out, and lined out in his other at-bats that day.

Blomberg was the first designated hitter in major league history, but he wasn't the most used DH for the Yankees in 1973. He was in the lineup as the DH in 55 games and was at first base in 41 others, hitting .329 for campaign. Early in the season, the Yankees acquired Jim Ray Hart from the San Francisco Giants, and he proved to be a good fit for the designated hitter role. Hart, in his 11th major league season, had been a power hitter in his earlier years in the majors, but he was nearing the end of his career. He had seen only limited action as a third baseman in recent years with the Giants. Manager Ralph Houk installed Hart as the club's primary DH. He was the "10th man" in 106 games, batting .256 with 12 home runs and 50 RBI.

Houk had chosen Blomberg as Opening Day's designated hitter even though he hadn't been in the role during any spring training game. There were a couple of reasons why Blomberg was the DH in the opener. He had come up with a slight hamstring injury near the end of spring training, and Houk wanted to keep his left-handed bat in the lineup against the Red Sox' right-hander Tiant. With Blomberg penciled in as the designated hitter for the opener, Houk was able to put hot-hitting Felipe Alou at first base, Blomberg's primary position.

After the top of the first inning, Blomberg experienced a strange feeling. He was not going to pick up his glove and go to first base. He was going back to sit on the bench and wait to hit again. Had he only been a traditional pinch-hitter, he would not have gone to the plate again that day.

Blomberg spoke about sitting next to coach Elston Howard. "I asked him, 'What do I do now?' It's 45 minutes between at-bats. It's very, very hard to sit there. You have to discipline yourself to be a DH. It took me awhile to develop a routine. It's difficult to condition yourself to be a DH."[2]

The New York Yankees' Ron Blomberg was the American League's first designated hitter (National Baseball Hall of Fame Library, Cooperstown, NY).

Years later, the first designated hitter in the game noted, "People like it, they hate it, or whatever. But it's going to be there for a while."[3]

Pinch-hitters were often "good hit, no field" players who were only valuable on a roster when they could deliver in a pinch. Throughout the years, there had been few players who had been able to glorify the designation.

Casey Stengel, the successful and memorable Yankees' and New York Mets' manager who had retired in 1965, spoke about the new DH role in his special "Stengelese":

> But maybe there is a difference between guys who could hit in the clutch, like Jerry Lynch, who they used to say was a bigger threat to his own manager catching a fly ball than he was to the other fellows swinging the bat, so they made him a pinch hitter, and these new guys who are gonna be like regulars who don't have to play defense.[4]

Forrest "Smoky" Burgess, who had played for five clubs during his 18 years in the majors, had been a pinch-hitter "par excellence," especially toward the end of his career. The 5'8", 195-pounder, who retired in 1967, pinch-hit in 543 games, and hit safely 144 times for a major league record. Burgess also played in 1139 games as a catcher.

Former Cincinnati Reds' pitcher Brooks Lawrence remembered Burgess and thought that he would have made an ideal designated hitter:

> Smoky wasn't a good catcher.... Smoky would do things to protect himself. He couldn't throw very well. If someone was on base who could run, every time I looked down at the catcher, I saw one finger. Fastball. But Smoky could hit. It was his one attribute.[5]

When Burgess arrived in Chicago in 1964, at age 37, to play for the White Sox, manager Al Lopez told him, "All you have to do for me is hit.... I don't need your glove, just your bat. Sit around and be ready.[6]

Burgess could hit, but he couldn't run. When he got on base he expected to see a pinch-runner coming into the game to replace him:

> I tell you, Ace, here would be Al Weis poised on the top step. He was a good fielder and a great runner. Couldn't hit much though. Anyway, I'd get a hit and he'd beat me to first base. One day I got a double and as I was chugging for second, I turn and Weis is matching me step-for-step. Now that hurt, Ace. That hurt.[7]

The New York Giants' Dusty Rhodes' three pinch-hits against the Cleveland Indians in the 1954 World Series were as exciting as it gets. His contributions in that Fall Classic certainly would put him in a "Pinch-Hitters Hall of Fame."

Rhodes' heroics in the series opener usually take a back seat to a defensive gem that happened late in the game. Willie Mays' back-to-the-plate catch, of Vic Wertz's long fly ball to deep center field of the Polo Grounds in the eighth inning with none out and the score tied, 2–2, rates as one of the most memorable moments in baseball history. The game would remain tied until the bottom of the 10th inning.

Rhodes' walk-off, three-run homer off Bob Lemon brought a 5–2 victory to the Giants. The next afternoon, pinch-hitting for future Hall of Famer Monte Irvin for the second straight day, Rhodes singled to center to tie the game, 1–1, in the fifth inning. He played the outfield the rest of the game and hit another homer run three innings later as New York took game two, 3–1. The journeyman, who was in his third major league season, pinch-hit and singled to drive in two runs in game three. Once again, he took the field for the Giants, and he made news when he struck out in his other plate appearance as the Giants went on to win, 6–2. Rhodes' pinch-hitting prowess wasn't needed the next day when the Giants beat the Indians, 7–4, to sweep the series.

Rhodes' approach to the game was simple. He said, "I ain't much of a fielder and I got a downright rotten arm…. But I sure do love to whack that ball. Pinch-hitting doesn't bother me. There's nothing to it. Just stand in there and swing."[8]

The designated hitter came too late for others whose work at the plate was of major league quality, but whose play in the field was difficult for a manager to watch. Babe Herman, who played with a number of clubs and had a .324 batting average during a 13-year career that began in 1926, would have been a "natural" in the DH role because of his defensive liabilities.

George "Showboat" Fisher, who had played in only 28 games in two seasons with the Washington Senators, hit .374 for the St. Louis Cardinals in 1930. He was so severely limited defensively that he took the field in only 18 other games after that season.

Smead Jolley hit .312 with 99 RBI with the Red Sox in 1932, but he was such a poor outfielder that his career was limited to four seasons. He once made three errors on one play when a ground ball in the outfield went through his legs, as did the rebound off the wall. When he finally got the ball, he threw it into the dugout for the third error on the play!

In more recent times, it was too bad that Dick Stuart was out of the game before the designated hitter made its appearance. The 6-foot-4-inch, 212-pound, power-hitting first baseman, who played for six different major league clubs during his 10-year career, was affectionately known as Dr. Strangeglove. That moniker poignantly described the defensive side of Stuart's game. He often led first basemen in errors, and he had been heard to say, "I know I'm the world's worst fielder, but who gets paid for fielding?"[9]

Although the designated hitter rule came too late for Lynch, Burgess,

Rhodes, and others whose ability to swing the bat far exceeded their ability to catch the ball, a new opportunity for those like them presented itself for the first time in 1973.

Pinch-hitting was one thing; would designated hitting be something else? On May 20, six weeks into the season, the *New York Times* published a report about the success of the designated hitter after 215 games. The report showed that the new hitters in the lineup were batting .235 as a group. American Leaguers as a whole were hitting .248 with the teams in each game averaging 7.32 runs. After a comparable number of games, the National Leaguers were batting slightly higher, at .250, and were scoring 7.39 runs per game while using baseball's traditional rules.[10]

The article concluded with an early evaluation of the new rule change:

> The conclusion seems to be: the designated hitter is doing no visible harm and is a popular innovation in many quarters, but if anyone is serious about restoring baseball offense to the standards of its more illustrious decades [1920 through 1960] he had better seek another mechanism.[11]

The Junior Circuit's season's figures represented an increase over the league's 1972 .240 composite batting average. That season had been abnormal because a strike had caused the cancellation of the first 10 days of the campaign. The American League's 1973 offensive numbers were back at about the same level as they had been in 1971. The anticipated explosive offensive surge had not yet been seen.

Although there had not been tremendous increases in the clubs' offenses, Houk noted that improved "entertainment content" had been a positive change in the games:

> It has certainly eliminated the dead inning with the pitcher coming to bat in the middle of it ... and it makes the games more exciting because a rally is more possible in any inning ... and it seems to give the team that falls behind early more hope and a better chance of getting some runs back.[12]

Blomberg was the first player to go to bat as a major league designated hitter. However, the Minnesota Twins' Tony Oliva went to bat the most times as a major league DH in 1973.

Before the opening of the regular season, Minnesota manager Frank Quilici had explained why a designated hitter in the Twins' lineup would help his club, saying, "I'd be a fool to oppose it with two $100,000 ballplayers, Tony Oliva and Harmon Killebrew, coming off serious operations.... It's a relief to know that if one of them doesn't respond to the point where he can play in the field everyday we won't lose his bat."[13]

Oliva was in the role on Opening Day, and he appeared in 146 games in 1973, with 142 of them as a designated hitter. He delivered the first home run by a designated hitter in his initial at-bat in the season's opener. The round-tripper came off the Oakland Athletics' Jim "Catfish" Hunter. Oliva made 564 plate appearances as a DH, batting .289 with 16 home runs and 91 runs batted in. The left-handed hitting, former outfielder had been with Minnesota since becoming a major leaguer in 1962. After brief appearances during his first two seasons, he was the Rookie of the Year in 1964, leading the league in hitting with a .323 average. Oliva hit .321 the next year and captured the hitting crown for the second time. He would go on to finish above .300 four more times during his major league career. A six-time All-Star, Oliva captured his third hitting crown in 1971 with a .337 average.

Oliva represented the type of player who, in the future, would benefit tremendously from the DH rule and would often become a club's primary designated hitter. Oliva had injured his right knee early in his career, and he underwent four surgeries during his major league playing days. He appeared in only 10 games in 1972 after surgery following a 1971 injury. Each injury and each surgery took its toll on the outfielder's speed and, in 1973, the designated hitter role gave him an opportunity to extend his career for a few more seasons.

Bob Fowler, writing in *The Sporting News Official Baseball Guide* (1974), noted Oliva's contributions in 1973:

> Thank you, American League owners, wherever you are. Thank you for the designated-hitter rule. Thank you for making the Twins respectable.
>   You see, without that rule, Tony Oliva wouldn't have been able to play. He was unable to run well enough to play in the field due to four past operations on his right knee and he performed the entire season as Minnesota's DH.[14]

Harmon Killebrew, in his 20th major league season, had much less success than Oliva that season Coming back from surgery, he was in only 69 games with 57 as a first baseman, nine as a DH, and six as a pinch-hitter. He hit .242 in the 69 games he played. The future Hall of Famer would be in 122 games (57 as the Twins' DH) in 1974, and he hit .222. He was with Kansas City in 1975, and was their designated hitter in 92 of the 106 games in which he appeared, and he and hit .199 to close out his 22-year career.

Quilici had mixed feelings about the DH. They had come as a result of having managed the Twins with their designated hitters from 1973 through 1975:

[The designated hitter] made managing easier handling pitchers and making out a lineup card with your everyday players.

You put your best nine out there and could manipulate your batting order easily. Pitchers could go longer if effective.

Naturally, [you would consider for DH those] hitters with little defensive skills and those getting older who couldn't take the grind of going both ways.

I don't care for it because it takes away the chess game that baseball is and tests the mettle of everyone from player, coaches to manager.[15]

Sometime later, Quilici added other thoughts about the designated hitter, writing:

After thinking about it further, it also changed some of the way the game was played.

Today, umpires are warning pitchers based on their assumptions on whether they were intentionally throwing at a batter.

The DH took away the fear of retribution by a pitcher who knowingly threw at a hitter and allowed the umpire to control the game instead of the unwritten rule in baseball that left it up to the players to decide when action should be taken.[16]

The Red Sox' Orlando Cepeda was not far behind Oliva in the number of plate appearances. Cepeda appeared in 142 games, all as a DH, and came to bat 550 times, hitting .289 with 20 homers, 25 doubles, and 86 RBI. He had played 15 seasons in the National League before he went to the Athletics of the American League in 1972. That move put him in the position to benefit from the designated hitter role when it came to the game a year later. Cepeda was the first player to be acquired specifically for the purpose of being a designated hitter. The Red Sox picked up the former National League MVP on January 18, 1973, shortly after the American League voted to use designated hitters in their lineups. The right-handed power hitter had played first base for the San Francisco Giants, Cardinals, and Braves. A seven-time All-Star, Cepeda had hit over .300 nine times, posting his highest average at .325 with the World Champion Cardinals in 1967. He had recorded his best power numbers with the Giants in 1961 when he slammed a league-leading 46 home runs and 142 runs batted in.

Cepeda was nearing the end of his career when he arrived in Boston. He had surgery for a knee injury in 1965 that cost him most of that season. His aging knees limited his playing ability late in his career, but he could still swing the bat. Cepeda was well-suited to be in the lineup as a DH, but he no longer had the ability to play effectively in the field. He played with the Red Sox in 1973 and then appeared in only 33 games in 1974 for the Kansas City Royals before retiring.

In 1973, the Boston Red Sox' Orlando Cepeda was the recipient of the first Outstanding Designated Hitter Award (Boston Red Sox).

Had things gone a little differently on Opening Day, 1973, Cepeda could have become an item of trivia. It was thought that Cepeda, who was batting third for the hometown Red Sox, had an excellent shot at becoming the major leagues' first designated hitter. However, Tiant was uncharacteristically wild in the top of the first inning, and Blomberg, the Yankees' sixth hitter, came to the plate and beat Cepeda into the history books.

The Baltimore Orioles' Terry Crowley was in the DH spot on Opening Day, but teammate Tommy Davis went to bat 532 times in 127 games as the club's primary designated hitter, placing him third in the number of plate appearances in 1973. Davis was another player who had spent the early years of his major league career in the National League, playing initially with the Los Angeles Dodgers in 1959. His other Senior Circuit stops had been with the Mets, Houston Astros, and Chicago Cubs. The Chicago White Sox, Seattle Pilots, and Athletics were the American League teams that the well-traveled, right-handed hitting outfielder had played with before joining the Orioles partway through the 1972 season.

Davis had been voted to the National League All-Star teams in 1962 and 1963 when he led the league in batting with .346 and .326 averages. During the early part of the 1973 campaign, he was the only Oriole hitting the ball consistently. He finished with a .293 average as a DH for the American League East (AL–East) champion O's. Besides his designated-hitting duties, Davis appeared in 10 other games as a first baseman and as a pinch-hitter. Those appearances helped him raise his season's batting average to .306, giving him six above–.300 finishes for his career.

Besides Blomberg, Crowley, Cepeda, and Oliva, the following players can say, "I was my team's first designated hitter:"

California Angels	Tom McCraw
Chicago White Sox	Mike Andrews
Cleveland Indians	John Ellis
Detroit Tigers	Gates Brown
Kansas City Royals	Ed Kirkpatrick
Milwaukee Brewers	Ollie Brown
Oakland Athletics	Billy North
Texas Rangers	Rico Carty

Some teams had one player, who for any number of reasons, fit the role of a DH. Other clubs used the extra batting spot in the lineup to give players a day of rest from defense while keeping their bats in the lineup. In 1973, a number of teams spread the DH around the roster, as would be the pattern in the years to come.

Athletics' manager Dick Williams used Deron Johnson, an early-season acquisition from the Philadelphia Phillies, as the designated hitter in 107 games, but he also tapped 18 other players to fill the role during the campaign. The White Sox gave game time to 14 designated hitters. Carlos May led the way with appearances in 75 games. May was the only DH in the league with 100 or more times at bat to hit above .300, finishing at .307.

The Royals had 14 players who served as a DH in at least one game. Hal McRae was one of them, and he would go on to become baseball's first long-term DH. McRae, another refugee from the National League, having come from the Reds in 1973, drew the most starts as a designated hitter for the Royals, appearing in the role in 37 games.

The Texas Rangers' Rico Carty did not turn out to be the quality designated hitter that some had expected him to be in 1973. He hit .242 and was in the outfield in 53 games and a DH in 31 games for the Rangers. He was traded to the Cubs after playing 86 games with Texas, and he was back for a short stay in the non–DH league where he had spent the previous eight seasons. Near the end of the campaign, he returned to the American League, going to Oakland where he played in seven games. Carty would be with Cleveland in 1974, and he would go on to have some successful seasons as a designated hitter with the Indians. He hit above .300 in three of the campaigns between 1974 through 1977.

During the 1973 season, the 12 American League clubs used 132 different players as designated hitters, and their combined batting average was .257. The Orioles' designated hitters, paced by Davis, lead the league at .286. Kansas City's lowly .217 average was the worst among the league's teams. With Frank Robinson hitting 30 homers and driving in 97 runs as a DH (127 games) and as an outfielder (17 games), California's designated hitters totaled 31 home runs and 100 RBI. Minnesota manufactured 102 RBI out of the designated hitter spot, and Boston followed with 101.

The Outstanding Designated Hitter Award was inaugurated in 1973. The award which was voted on by American League officials, beat writers, and broadcasters was to be given annually by *The Union Leader* of Manchester, NH, in cooperation with the American League. The initial ODH Award was presented to Cepeda for his performance as the Red Sox' DH.

Boston manager Eddie Kasko spoke about his experience with designated hitters and Cepeda's season with the Red Sox:

Eddie Kasko was at the helm for the Boston Red Sox during the first season of the designated hitter (Boston Red Sox).

I was managing Louisville of the International League in 1969 when it first came out. It was supposed to be an experiment for consideration.

My opinion was that it was great for the minor leagues because you were able to develop another hitter. You would develop five good pitchers and you just left them in. I had a reliever named Eddie Phillips and by July he had the most innings of all the pitchers in the bullpen with 22.

After the season, I wrote out an evaluation for Joe Cronin who was the American League president. I said, "I don't see the benefit of it in the major leagues except for extending the career of a good hitter. It takes all of the strategy out of the game such as when it's a close game and you have to decide whether or not to pinch-hit for the pitcher. It is not only the manager's decision, but the fans get involved as well. They might say, 'Why isn't he going to take him out?'" The experiment continued in the league the following years, but by then I was managing the Red Sox.

At the time I was managing the Boston Red Sox in 1973 it was an experimental issue. Orlando Cepeda was the designated hitter on the 1973 Red Sox. He was an excellent designated hitter in that he couldn't run and yet he could hit, and hit he did. He also had great fan appeal. He was an experienced type hitter and that helped him to prolong his career.[17]

Baltimore and Oakland won their division titles and were in the 1973 American League Championship Series (ALCS). The Athletics won the series, 3–2. Davis hit .286, going 6–for–21, in the five-game set. He and the A's Mike Andrews, Pat Bourque, and Johnson were the first designated hitters to appear in the postseason. Bourque and Andrews were hitless in brief appearances in the role, and Johnson was 1–for–10.

Although the Orioles found success with the extra hitter, veteran manager Earl Weaver wasn't a cheerleader for the new rule:

I think baseball is a very good game and has been successful and I don't think it has to have any changes. I might be from the old school but I don't think baseball needs saving. I'd like to keep the game just as it is.[18]

Baltimore's first baseman Boog Powell, who possessed the type of offensive skills that might lead to him becoming a designated hitter in the future, was less than enamored by the possibility and said, "I've worked hard on my fielding and I don't want to see all that work go down the drain. I'm not an old man. I want to play in the field."[19]

In the first season with designated hitters in their lineups, the American League clubs raised their composite batting average from .240 in 1972 to .260 in 1973. Run production in the American League went from 6441 in 1972 to 8314 in the first season with the DH, and home runs followed the same trend, increasing from 1,175 to 1,552. The comparative numbers for the two seasons for runs scored and home runs were slightly affected because the teams had played 10 fewer games in 1972 due to the strike.

What were the differences when a DH was hitting and a pitcher was not? After the regular season, the designated hitters' statistics were compared with what pitchers had done in 1972. The DHs accounted for 12 percent of the league's total hits compared to 4 percent by pitchers a year earlier. The designated hitters registered one RBI every seven times at-bat, and the pitchers had one RBI in every 20 plate appearances. The "10th men" homered 227 times, at a ratio of one every 33 at-bats with pitchers in 1972 hitting a homer every 217 times they came to the plate.

During the first year with the DH, more American League pitchers posted 20 wins than ever before. Chicago's Wilbur Wood (24 wins) and Detroit's Joe Coleman (23 wins) led a group of 12 pitchers who reached the 20-win level. The previous record had been set in 1907 when 10 American League pitchers had won 20 or more games. That record had been matched in 1920 and 1971.

With designated hitters in the lineups, many pitchers went deeper into the games. They could increase their chances of controlling the outcomes themselves, rather than turning games over to relievers.

Eleven pitchers took their swings in 1973, with the Yankees' Lindy McDaniel being the only hurler to bat twice. Cy Acosta, a reliever for the White Sox, was the first to bat, going to the plate on June 20 in a game against the California Angels and striking out. Hunter, who had expressed his disappointment at being replaced as a hitter in the A's lineup, got one of the two hits by pitchers that season. Hunter singled for a perfect one-for-one season, and Milwaukee's Eduardo Rodriguez slammed a triple. Five of the 11 pitchers who went to the plate were used as pinch-hitters. The White Sox' Terry Forster, and the Athletics' Vida Blue, Ken Holtzman, Hunter, and "Blue Moon" Odom were their managers' choices to swing for a player in the regular lineup.

The American League made significant gains in attendance during the initial regular season with designated hitters. Because of the strike-shortened 1972 campaign, the figures for 1971 and 1973 make for a better attendance comparison between the Junior Circuit with and without the DH. In 1971, four clubs— Baltimore, Boston, Detroit, and New York — had more than a million fans attend their games. With the DH in use in 1973, eight teams— Boston, California, Chicago, Detroit, Kansas City, Milwaukee, New York, and Oakland — surpassed the million-fan mark. Detroit was at the top of the list with 1,724,146 people coming through its gates. Chicago posted the season's greatest gain as 468,636 more fans came to Comiskey Park in 1973 than had done so two years earlier. Kansas City, with a 434,557 increase in attendance, was not far behind.

The American League welcomed 13,433,604 paying customers to its ballparks in 1973, which was 1,564,044 more people than had attended their games in 1971. In 1973, the National League's total attendance was 16,675,322, and that was 649,534 fewer admissions than they had in 1971. The Senior Circuit was still drawing more fans than its younger counterpart, but the Americans had closed the attendance gap in the initial season of the designated hitter. In 1971, with each league fielding 12 teams, the National League held a 5.5-million fan advantage; in 1973, the lead had been narrowed to 3.2 million.

Because the new rule didn't allow designated hitters in the World Series, six of the Athletics' pitchers took bats to the plate against the Mets, going 3–for–17 for a .176 average. Holtzman led the way with a 2–for–3 series, and Hunter went hitless in five at-bats. The Mets' pitchers, who had gone to the plate during the regular season, had a 2–for–16 World Series mark. Oakland took the seven-game set, hitting only .212 as a team, while the losing Mets hit .253.

The Junior Circuit had played a season with the DH, but its offensive and attendance statistics were not convincing enough to cause the owners in the other league to change their minds on the subject. The Senior Circuit decided to play without designated hitters in 1974. Following the NL meetings in September, president Chub Feeney said, "We will continue to play by baseball rules in 1974.... Unless there's a big change before the winter meetings, we'll probably do no more than just review the comparative figures then."[20]

The American League's executives took the season's statistics, which they believed indicated that the presence of designated hitters in their lineups had improved their brand of baseball, to the early December winter meetings in Houston. Their goal was to convince the National League owners that one year of the DH experience was enough to show that the new rule should become universal in major league baseball. The National League executives, who were not convinced by the American League's selling job, argued that tight pennant races in the Junior Circuit had spurred the increased attendance figures. The National League's rationale sounded plausible, but a close look at the American League's standings at monthly intervals throughout the season fails to show the existence of close and exciting pennant races beyond early August. Baltimore finished eight games in front of Boston and 12 ahead of Detroit in the Eastern Division. Oakland topped Kansas City by six games and Minnesota by 13 in the West.

There weren't any changes made in the designated hitter rule during the winter meetings. The National League followed its action at the league meetings in September and decided to continue to play without it. The

Senior Circuit's owners also rejected a request from the Junior Circuit to be able to use designated hitters in All-Star Games and in the World Series when those games were played in American League parks. Even after capturing the World Championship without having designated hitters available to them, the American Leaguers believed that the prohibition had been detrimental to their game. The American League did take action on its own. The Junior Circuit voted to make the "three-year experiment" a permanent part of their game after only one season.

There was change in the American League office. President Joe Cronin, who had been in the position since 1959, retired at the end of 1973. For some time, he had been encouraging the owners in his league to support his commitment to bring the DH to baseball, but he met resistance from some of them who didn't think that such a drastic change was necessary to remedy the loop's ills. He was persistent in his view and was able to get the support necessary for the rule change on an experimental basis.

Lee MacPhail, who had spent many years working in various capacities in the Yankees' organization and who had been general manager and president of the Orioles from 1960 to 1965, was elected to take Cronin's place on January 1, 1974. Along with Cronin, MacPhail had been a longtime supporter of the designated hitter. He had been in administrative positions with American League clubs and had experienced their offensive and attendance struggles. He was hoping to build unity on the rule with the National League.

During the 1974 spring training, the American League clubs were again forbidden to use designated hitters in games against National League teams. A year earlier, Kasko, the Red Sox' manager, had blasted commissioner Bowie Kuhn for not supporting the American League in its effort to play by its rules; in 1974, Milwaukee manager Del Crandall was outspoken about the American League officials for giving in to their National League counterparts. He called them a "bunch of weak sisters. It's a part of our game and we should have the right to use it when we want to."[21]

Although the National League didn't want anything to do with the DH, an ex–National Leaguer spoke in favor of it. Mays, who had spent 22 seasons in the Senior Circuit before retiring in 1973, believed that he could have extended his career a few more years had his league adopted the DH rule. Recalling his final season with the Mets, he said, "But after I pinch-hit for the pitcher, I was through for the day.... If the National League had the DH rule, I could have played every day as a hitter. That would have been great."[22]

Charles O. Finley, the maverick owner of the Athletics who had brought multi-color uniforms to baseball and had suggested the use of orange baseballs to help hitters see them better, had been one of the earliest and most outspoken advocates of having a designated hitter in the American League teams' lineups. Years later, he would say, "At first they thought I was nuts.... But after continuously harping, I finally woke them up."[23] Finley had another "designated" player on his roster in 1974. He had signed sprinter Herb Washington to be the A's designated runner. Without any baseball experience, Washington was learning the nuances of base stealing on the job. He was gunned out in four of his five attempts, but he then reeled off five straight stolen bases before he was caught again. Washington appeared in 92 games in 1974, scoring 29 runs and swiping 29 bases in 45 attempts. He was called on to be a designated runner in 13 games the following season. He stole two bases in three attempts, and his major league career was over without him ever going to the plate with a bat in his hand or throwing a baseball in a game.

Sportswriter Red Smith, who was a strong opponent of the designated hitter, found Oakland manager Alvin Dark's suggestion of having a designated runner available to take over for the designated hitter anytime he reached base an added insult to the game:

> In the American League, the designated hitter now bats for the pitcher, who remains in the game.... Dark could use a Herb Washington four of five times without being deprived of the services of the man Herb replaced. If the goal is to deface the game of baseball beyond recognition, this is the logical way to go about it.[24]

During the 1974 season, 143 different players, an increase of 11 over 1973, went to bat as designated hitters. The vast majority of those players made a only few appearances while they were being given a day off from playing defense. There were 24 players who had over 100 at-bats as a DH. Davis, who picked up the second annual ODH Award, led the list with 623 appearances, hitting .289.

The availability of the DH had extended the career of Detroit's Al Kaline's, who was in his 22nd season with the Tigers. Kaline, who retired after 1974, followed Davis with 557 at-bats and a .262 average. The long-time outfielder appeared in 147 games, 146 as the club's DH. He added 146 hits to his career total, giving him 3007. He became the 12th major leaguer to pass the hallowed 3000-hit mark, and he was the first to do it as a designated hitter. There would be more to follow. In 1980, Kaline became the first player who had spent time as a designated hitter to be elected to Baseball's Hall of Fame. Kaline made it to Cooperstown the first time that his name was on the ballot.

The Rangers' Mike Hargrove had 110 at-bats, and he posted the highest average for a DH at .327. The Royals' McRae hit .305 in 321 at-bats.

Designated hitters batted a combined .256, which was a single point lower than it had been in 1973. Cleveland's Oscar Gamble hit .291 in 115 games in the role as the Indians' designated hitters topped the league with a .296 average. The Angels were at the bottom of the DH standings with a .222 average. No team collected 100 or more RBI from its designated hitters. Baltimore, with 89, finished closest to the century mark. California, despite its lowly DH batting average, led the league with 23 home runs from their DHs, with Robinson blasting 20 before leaving for Cleveland near the end of the season.

For the second straight year since the inception of the DH, American League hitters topped those in the other league in batting average. The American Leaguers hit .259 and the National Leaguers finished at .256. The Junior Circuit registered 17,062 hits and 1,369 home runs compared with 16,907 hits and 1,280 homers in the Senior Circuit. The Nationals did hold an 8,070 to 7,976 advantage over the Americans in runs scored.

American League pitchers didn't register as many complete games in the second season with designated hitters. Nine pitchers won 20 or more games in 1974 with Oakland's Hunter and Texas' Ferguson Jenkins topping the list with 25 victories.

In 1974, the Baltimore Orioles' Tommy Davis became the second winner of the Outstanding Designated Hitter Award (Jerry Wachtr and the Baltimore Orioles).

In 1974, attendance fell by 383,310 in the American League. California, Milwaukee, and the World Champion Athletics, who had each welcomed more than one million fans the previous season, were unable to remain above the million mark. Cleveland and Texas made impressive gains of approximately 500,000 admissions to pass the million-fan mark. The National League clubs posted a 302,992 increase in attendance and stretched their advantage to 3,931,020 over the American League teams.

The Yankees welcomed 1,273,075 fans in 1974, which was 10,972 more than had come through the turnstiles in Yankee Stadium in 1973. In 1974, they did it in the Mets' Shea Stadium! Following the 1973 season, the Yankees headed to Flushing while venerable Yankee Stadium was undergoing a two-year, $100-million facelift. The Mets played before 1,722,209 fans in 1974, a 190,181 decrease for them. Had those fans decided to give a "looksee" at the American League's "10-man game" at the expense of their National League Mets?

In 1975, the third season of the designated hitter, which was originally to be the final year of the experiment before the rule was made permanent after the 1973 campaign, 164 batters appeared in lineups in the DH role. That was the largest number of players to be designated hitters in the first three seasons of its existence. Five players were in 100 or more games and 14 had 100 or more plate appearances.

Detroit's Willie Horton (615 at-bats, .275), Oakland's Billy Williams, an ex–National Leaguer who had been with the Cubs for 16 seasons, (500 at-bats, .244), Baltimore's Davis (456 at-bats, .283), Milwaukee's Hank Aaron (450 at-bats, .238), and Minnesota's Oliva (445 at-bats, .265) were the most frequent designated hitters in 1975. The batting average for all designated hitters fell two points to .254, four points below the average for all hitters in the league. Horton was chosen the outstanding DH and given the ODH Award.

Boston rookie Jim Rice, who played 99 games in the outfield and 54 as a designated hitter, hit .309, stroked 22 home runs and drove in 102 runs. Rice finished fourth in the MVP voting, an eye-opening finish for someone who had been in the DH role for a significant portion of the season.

Frank Lucchesi, who managed in both leagues and was Horton's skipper in Texas in 1977, commented about the ODH Award winner and his experiences with the designated hitter:

> Horton was an excellent person to be a designated hitter. He couldn't move much anymore and he wasn't fast enough in the outfield if he had to play there, but he cold still put his bat on the ball.
>
> It was certainly easier to manage in the American League. There weren't the double-switches to make and it wasn't as hard to make decisions about pitchers.
>
> My thought for the future is either have designated hitters in both leagues or don't have them in either. These are the major leagues and they should do things the same way.[25]

For the second consecutive season, no team's designated hitters produced 100 or more RBI with Detroit leading the list with 93. Ninety-two

Willie Horton swings away for Detroit (Detroit Tigers).

of those RBI came from Horton's bat. Cleveland's designated-hitting corps led the league with 30 home runs. Carty, who was in 72 games as a DH, 26 as a first baseman, and 12 as an outfielder, banged 18 homers for the Tribe.

Baltimore's designated hitters topped the league with a .278 average. That was below their .286 league-best average in 1973 and Cleveland's .296 average in 1974. However, the Orioles' designated hitters banged only six homers, which was the fewest for a team in the loop. California's DHs, who had been at the bottom of the league with a .222 average in 1974, were there again in 1975 with a .225 mark.

The designated hitters had not been able to match the composite batting average of all American Leaguers in the first three years that they were in the lineups.

	Designated Hitter Average	*Composite Average*
1973	.257	.260
1974	.256	.259
1975	.254	.258

In 1975, the two leagues posted identical .258 composite batting averages. That would be the only year through at least 2003 that the National League wouldn't trail the American League's hitters in the composite averages.

The fewest number of pitchers since the inaugural season of the DH reached the 20-win level. Hunter, who had moved to the Yankees as a free agent, and the Orioles' Jim Palmer both posted 23 victories to lead a group of five 20-game winners.

For the first time, nine American League clubs had more than one million fans in their seats. Chicago, Cleveland, and Minnesota were the three Junior Circuit clubs to draw fewer than one million paying customers. The National League had nine clubs above that mark for the first time in 1970. There were 11 clubs with more than one million in attendance the following season, and 10 teams exceeded it in 1974. The 1975 campaign was the first time since 1970 that the National League had fewer than nine teams with one million or more admissions. Atlanta, Houston, Montreal, and San Francisco had fewer than one million customers in the 12-team league.

The American League posted a small gain of 142,129 in total admissions in 1975, and the National League fell by 377,824. The Senior Circuit still held a 3,411,067 advantage in attendance numbers, but there were signs that the Junior Circuit was gaining on them. Perhaps the designated hitter had something to do with it, but only time would tell whether or not the American League would catch the other league and if the designated hitter would be a major factor in the accomplishment.

During the first three years with the DH, there were some changes in pitching statistics in the American League. With another legitimate bat for pitchers to face in the lineups, it was expected that their earned run averages (ERA) would rise, and they did. In 1971, American League pitchers posted a composite a 3.47 ERA, and a season later it was 3.46. In 1973, the Junior Circuit's pitchers had a composite 3.82 ERA; in 1974, it was 3.62; and in 1975 it was 3.78.

More pitchers in the Junior Circuit were going the distance now that a DH was in the lineup hitting for them. No longer did a manager have to make a choice between using a pinch-hitter or having a pitcher bat for himself in a crucial situation. In 1971, under the old rules, American League pitchers completed 537 of their starts. In 1973, 614 pitchers went the distance, and that number climbed to 650 in 1974 and it was 625 a year later. From 1973 to 1975, National League pitchers, who were hitting for themselves, averaged 438 complete games.

Bruce DalCanton, who pitched for the Royals from 1971 through 1975, described the varied effects of the DH on baseball:

The Kansas City's Bruce DalCanton pitched in the early years of the designated hitter (Kansas City Royals).

It let you concentrate on your pitching and not worry about the hitting or bunting or running the bases. Plus you could rest up between innings.

The designated hitter in the opposing team's lineup made you work harder when you were on the mound. You didn't have the easy out that having the pitcher in the lineup usually gives you.

The original idea of the DH was to score more runs to get the fans interested which I think has been done. It also enabled some of the veteran players to stay around longer by not having to play a position and risking injury in the field. It also has given some American League pitchers a few more wins by staying in a game when down by a couple of runs instead of getting pinch-hit for. The down side of the DH is it takes away from the strategy of the game by not making the manager decide to take a pitcher out of a game for a pinch-hitter or not [to do so] when down by a few runs.[26]

Sonny Siebert, who finished a 12-year career pitching for Oakland in 1975 after playing with five other clubs, including St. Louis and San Diego in the National League, had a different view of the DH era:

Having a DH in my lineup did not help me as a pitcher. It hurt the complete pitcher who could hit, hit and run, bunt and help himself with the bat. The DH hurt the careers of the pitchers who worked out of the bullpen because there was less chance of a pitching change during the game. The owners wanted more scoring in the game and unless you are a true baseball fan a 1–0 pitching duel is boring. The DH went along with the other changes like lowering the mound, making the strike zone smaller, making the ball livelier. Plus the umpires made it impossible to pitch inside. That's why Babe Ruth's HR record has been broken the past three years. That's my thoughts.[27]

Siebert also noted that he was the answer to a trivia question that might be a point of interest. He asked:

I hold an American League record that will never be broken. What is that record?
I was the last pitcher to hit 2 home runs in one game.[28]

He went on to say that he felt that the record was quite secure in the American League because of the presence of the designated hitter!

Sportswriter Leonard Koppett gave his three-year evaluation of the designated hitter and highlighted a specific contribution by the new men in the lineups. Although designated hitters had yet to register a combined batting average that was higher than the average for the league at large, they had been valuable contributors to the power game. Koppett wrote, "Almost the entire difference (since the arrival of the DHs) is the home runs hit by the designated hitters. This year they hit 222, last year 167, the first year 227. Since the American League's total of homers (in 1975) exceeded the Nationals by 231 (1,464 to 1,233), the effect is clear."[29]

A sportswriter from a different era had absolutely no use for designated hitters:

To the Sports Editor:
I find myself turning off Yankee games, and switching to the other league's games, mainly because the designated hitter is taking away still another nuance from the delicate game of baseball.
And I say this as an American League fan and sports writer, going back to the 1929 Philadelphia Athletics of Simmons-Foxx-Cochrane-Grove.
Three years is enough already.

Jack Orr
New York City[30]

Four

The American League Takes a Lead in Attendance

The designated hitter rule benefited a former career National Leaguer and one of the game's greatest players. Hank Aaron finished his major league playing days in 1976, appearing in 85 games for the Milwaukee Brewers, 74 as designated hitter. He played the outfield once and was a pinch-hitter in 10 games, and he hit .229 with 10 homers and 35 RBI. Aaron had come to the American League team in 1975 after 21 years in the National League, the final nine with the Atlanta Braves. He had previously been in Milwaukee from 1954 through 1965 as a member of the Braves. During 1975, Aaron was in 137 games, 128 as a DH, three as an outfielder, and six as a pinch-hitter. He hit .234 with 12 homers and 60 RBI. The opportunity to be the Brewers' designated hitter added two years to his career, and he added 22 home runs to finish with 755 homers, which still stands as the major league record.

In 1976, two other former National Leaguers and future Hall of Famers ended their major league playing careers almost exclusively as designated hitters. Frank Robinson had spent 10 years with the Cincinnati Reds and then played for the Baltimore Orioles from 1966 until 1971. He returned to the National League for one season with the Los Angeles Dodgers before joining the California Angels in 1973. He was the Angels' primary DH that season, hitting .266 with 30 home runs and 97 RBI. Robinson went to the Cleveland Indians near the end of the 1974 season. He became the club's manager the following year. As a player-manager, Robinson appeared as a DH in 42 games in 1975 and in 18 games in 1976, his final season as an active player.

Another long-time National Leaguer had answered the call to the DH league in 1975. Billy Williams, a sweet-swinging, left-handed hitting out-fielder, had spent 16 seasons with the Chicago Cubs in the National League before coming to the Oakland Athletics. The career .290 hitter had a .244

average in 145 games in 1975 as Oakland's designated hitter, and he retired after the 1976 campaign when he hit .211 in 106 games as the Athletics' DH.

Another long-timer would appear in his team's lineup in 1976. Minnie Minoso, who had "retired" in 1964 after 15 seasons of major league service, returned to the Chicago White Sox and played three games as the club's designated hitter. The 53-year-old went 1–for–8, and he became the oldest DH to go to bat. That record should be one that isn't broken! When Minoso appeared in two games in 1980 at 57 years of age, they were as a pinch-hitter for the White Sox. He went hitless in the two games, but he became the second major leaguer to play in five different decades.

The Kansas City Royals' Hal McRae received the 1976 Outstanding Designated Hitter Award (ODH) after a very productive season. McRae appeared in 117 games as a designated hitter, 31 as an outfielder, and one as a pinch-hitter. He had a .332 batting average in 149 games, and he produced the league's highest on-base-percentage, .412. His .329 average in 117 games as a DH was the highest average to date for a player who was in the role in more than 100 games in a season.

After two summers in Shea Stadium, the New York Yankees were back in the Bronx in their newly refurbished and modernized stadium. The excitement of their return helped them become the first American League team in history to pass the two-million mark in attendance, as 2,012,434 people passed through the turnstiles. Boston, with 1,895,846 admissions, was right behind New York. The Junior Circuit's total attendance increased by 1,468,379 admissions, and that closed the gap between themselves and the Senior Circuit to just over two million, the closest the two leagues had been since 1968.

The biggest news on the designated hitter front was made on August 2, 1976, at the owners' summer meetings, when commissioner Bowie Kuhn cast the tie-breaking vote to allow for the use of designated hitters in the 1976 World Series. As expected, the American League was unanimously for the move, and the Nationals remained dead-set against it. Kuhn's vote meant that the National League champions would have the opportunity to put a DH in their World Series lineups in the fall. The new World Series rule included a compromise. It provided that after 1976, the DH would be used only in alternating years. No change took place regarding designated hitters during spring training, and the DH would be active only in games between American League clubs. Eddie Kasko's and Del Crandall's earlier complaints about the unavailability of the DH in their clubs' lineups in spring training games against National League clubs, even in American League parks, had not brought about change. These two managers, as well as others, felt that the existing arrangement penalized the Junior Circuit's teams.

Shortly after Kuhn's vote regarding the DH in the World Series, Joseph Durso, in the *New York Times*, reminded his readers of the accomplishments of the 1975 World Champion Reds, the "Big Red Machine," who had banked 2,315,603 paid admissions to Riverfront Stadium during the regular season:

> They didn't use or need "the 10th man" last summer but, in one blistering 50-game stretch, they won 41 times, Pete Rose got 70 hits, Joe Morgan reached base 97 times, Johnny Bench hit 12 home runs and knocked in 47 runs, their three best pitchers went 17 and 0, and the defense played 152 innings without making an error.[1]

Manager Sparky Anderson, who led the Reds through their outstanding season and the memorable seven-game World Series victory over the Boston Red Sox, was not a cheerleader for the opportunity to have another bat in his lineup:

> We'll be there if they use 9 men or 10 or 12 on a side. But from the fans' point of view, I can see only two places where the designated hitter might create interest — in spring training, where they might see the odd player go to bat more often, and in the All-Star Game, where extra hitters always go to bat for the pitcher anyway.[2]

Anderson did have a DH in his lineup come mid–October when the Reds faced the Yankees in the 1976 Fall Classic. He chose first baseman/outfielder Dan Driessen, who had hit .247 as a part-timer during the regular season, to be the National League's first-ever "10th man." The 25-year-old Driessen, in his fourth major league season, responded with a 5–for–14 series (.357), with a home run, two doubles, and two walks to help the Reds sweep the Yanks in four games. It is interesting to note that aging Tony Perez, the Reds' long-time regular first baseman, was in a Montreal uniform the following season, and Driessen, coming off his World Series performance, became a fixture at first base.

The Bronx Bombers were limited to a .222 series average by the Cincinnati pitchers compared with the Reds' .313 mark. The Yankees' trio of designated hitters— Carlos May, Elliott Maddox, and Lou Piniella— didn't help the sputtering offense, going a combined 1–for–16 for the series.

In December 1976, the National League owners, by a vote of 8–4, once again rejected a proposal to adopt the designated hitter rule. The proponents of the DH had not gained any ground. They would take the same action, by a 10–2 vote, the following August at the major league summer meetings. The gains that the American Leaguers were making in their offenses and at the turnstiles had not convinced the Senior Circuit's executives to change the way baseball was played in their league.

Stagnant attendance figures and a continuing losing streak in the battles for fans with the National League had been one of the American League owners' major concerns when they approved the designated hitter rule in 1973. They believed that more offensive baseball would draw more people to the parks. Since that time, the Americans had narrowed the attendance gap and, finally, in 1977, the Junior Circuit reported having had more paying customers in its seats than the Senior Circuit. The American League had 19,639,552 fans attend their games, and the National League reported 19,070,228 people in their ballparks. However, the 569,324 advantage for the Americans was a bit misleading, since in 1977 the league was operating for the first time with 14 clubs, having added Seattle and Toronto through expansion. Both of the new teams played before more than a million fans in their home parks. The 12-team National League averaged 1,589,186 fans in each of its ballparks, and the larger American League had an average of 1,402,825. The Dodgers, who welcomed nearly three million fans (2,955,087) to Dodger Stadium, led the Senior Circuit in attendance while the Yankees, with 2,103,092 admissions, were at the top of the Junior Circuit.

When Seattle and Toronto joined the American League in 1977, two more players received the distinction of becoming their franchises' first designated hitters. The honor went to the Mariners' Dave Collins and to the Blue Jays' Otto Velez.

In 1977, California Angels' manager Dave Garcia had Joe Rudi and Don Baylor as two of his outfielders. At one point in the season, when Rudi was hurt and couldn't play, Garcia put Baylor in left field. When Rudi healed, he was sent back to left field, and Baylor was installed as the DH. Baylor wasn't enamored with the role, and he said that he had trouble getting loose to go to the plate to hit. Garcia recalled talking to Frank Robinson, his hitting coach, about Baylor's reaction to being used as the designated hitter in a game in Yankee Stadium:

> Baylor will DH, and he might say something. You tell him if he has to get loose, when Joe Rudi goes to left field, he can go right with Joe Rudi, but he goes right on into the bullpen. And when the inning's over, he comes back. He does everything that Joe Rudi does except he doesn't have to catch flyballs.[3]

In summary, Garcia said, "He didn't like it. But it made him a millionaire."[4]

The Red Sox' Jim Rice was voted the season's Outstanding Designated Hitter. Rice was a different type of DH in that he was not a veteran who was finishing a major league career by serving in the limited offensive

Boston's Jim Rice was chosen the Outstanding Designated Hitter in 1977 (Boston Red Sox).

capacity provided by the new rule. In 1977, the powerful right-handed hitter was only in his third full season with the Red Sox, and he was the DH in 116 games and played the outfield in 44 others. He led the league with 39 home runs, had a .593 slugging percentage, hit. 320, and drove in 114 runs in an All-Star season. Carl Yastrzemski was the Red Sox' regular left fielder, and Rice was waiting to take over for him. In the meantime, he was serving as the club's primary designated hitter and practicing taking fly balls off Fenway Park's Green Monster.

Orioles' rookie Eddie Murray was the DH in 111 games, at first base in 42 games, and in the outfield in three others, and he hit .283 with 27 home runs and 88 RBI. He was the first player to spend significant time as a designated hitter and be selected as the league's Rookie of the Year.

The American League topped the National League in almost every offensive category in 1977, both in terms of total numbers and in terms of averages for the clubs in the leagues which had an unequal number of teams. The Americans posted a .267 batting average compared with a .262 mark in the other circuit. They also produced 20,572 hits, 2,013 homers, and 10,247 runs scored while the National League had 17,465 hits, 1,631 home runs, and 8,556 runs scored.

When the number ".406" is noted, many in the American League recall Ted Williams' historic batting average in 1941. In 1977, .406 represented two other accomplishments. One of them was positive and the other was negative.

The American League had its first slugging percentage of the DH era that exceeded .400. The Junior Circuit's hitters posted a composite .406 average, which was the league's highest since 1940. It had been .369 in 1969 and .343 in 1972. Slugging percentage is an indicator of the level of power hitting. It is the numbers of singles, doubles, triples, and home runs divided by the number of at-bats. (The number of singles times one, plus the number of doubles times two, plus the number of triples times three, plus the number of home runs times four gives you the total bases that you divide by the number of at-bats.)

For the first time, the American League's rising earned-run average passed the 4.00 mark when it reached 4.06. The similar numbers in slugging percentage and earned run average were related to the increasing offensive output. Hitting had increased in the league, and the pitchers were feeling its effects in their personal statistics.

The ERAs were in the National League's favor, but the number of complete games was solidly in the American League's column. The Junior Circuit's pitchers, who were staying in games longer because they had designated hitters in their lineups, were far outdistancing those in the other league in the number of complete games. American League managers no longer had to remove them for pinch-hitters in situations when scoring runs became more important in terms of strategy than keeping an effective starter on the mound. In 1977, pitchers in the Junior Circuit posted 586 complete games while those in the other league had 321. Interestingly, National League hurlers had 121 shutouts while those in the American League tossed 117. Was it possible that the Senior Circuit's pitchers had learned that their best chance to go the distance was not to allow the opposition to score a run?

The American League had become the hitters' league. In 1978, the American League hitters had a composite .262 batting average while those in the non–DH league hit .255. Their batters recorded 19,952 hits, 1,680 home runs, and 9,509 runs scored. The National League's hitters posted 16,556 hits, 1,276 homers, and 7,742 runs scored.

The Detroit Tigers' Rusty Staub, another refugee from the National League, won the 1978 ODH Award. He had come to the Tigers in 1976 after 13 years with the Houston Astros, Montreal Expos, and New York Mets. He was the DH in all 162 games for Detroit in 1978, batting .273 with 24 home runs and 121 RBI. Rice, who won the award the previous season, saw more time in the outfield in 1978, playing only 49 of his 163 games (remember the one-game playoff with the Yankees) as a DH. Rice picked up the league's Most Valuable Player Award, coming off a .315 average with 46 home runs and 139 RBI. He would become the club's regular left fielder in 1979 when Yastrzemski moved between first base and the designated hitter role as he approached the latter years of an outstanding career.

Left-handed pitcher Bill Lee, who had a 14-year major league career, spent 1969 to 1978 with the Red Sox. He played from 1973 to 1978 with designated hitters in the Red Sox and the opposing teams' lineups. He finished his career in the National League, pitching for the Montreal Expos from 1979 until 1982. Lee had no use for designated hitters:

> He added the word "Sucks" to "Designated Hitter" which was the heading at the top of the questionnaire he answered. Lee estimated that the presence of designated hitters in the oppositions' lineups "Cost me 50 home runs." He did not see any way that the designated hitter has had a positive effect on baseball, and he quoted Buckminster Fuller, writing, "Specialization Breeds Extinction."[5]

The designated hitter was back in the World Series in 1978 on the alternating-year plan. The Yankees beat the Dodgers, 4 games to 2. During the regular season, Reggie Jackson, who would be in the DH role during the postseason, had played 104 games in the outfield and was the designated hitter in 35 others, hitting 27 homers and driving in 97 runs for New York. Jackson had played in the outfield during the non–DH Fall Classic a year earlier and had hit .450 with five homers and eight RBI. He continued his October excellence when hit .391 with two homers and eight RBI in the World Series. "Mr. October" had become a Fall Classic force, but the trio of DHs used by Dodger manager Tommy Lasorda — Lee Lacy, Rick Monday, and Vic Davalillo — went a combined 4–for–18 — and failed to duplicate Cincinnati's Driessen's offensive output in the series two years earlier.

In 1979, American League DHs hit .262 collectively, with 298 home runs and 1,280 RBI. Willie Horton, who had won the ODH Award in 1975 when he was with the Tigers, was the league's Outstanding Designated Hitter for the second time in 1979. After 15 seasons with Detroit, Horton had joined Seattle in 1979 after short stints with Texas, Cleveland, Oak-

The Detroit Tigers' Rusty Staub was given the 1978 Outstanding Designated Hitter Award (Detroit Tigers).

land, and Toronto. He, like Staub the previous season's winner, was his club's DH in all 162 games. Horton hit .279 with 29 home runs and 106 RBI. He played one more season before retiring after an 18-year major league career. Baylor repeated Rice's 1978 accomplishment by winning the Most Valuable Player Award while spending some significant time as the club's designated hitter. Baylor was in the role in 65 of his 162 games with the Angels and hit an overall .296 with 36 home runs and a major league–leading 139 RBI.

Horton recalled his career and the role of the designated hitter in it:

[The DH] helped me to look and watch the game a little closer and get a different perspective from a coach's and managerial standpoint.

Earlier in my career the designated hitter didn't help my career because I felt that I could still contribute in the outfield, but that was a managerial decision. Later in my career it helped me tremendously because I was out of the game for a year and I was given a chance to show that I could still hit and contribute to my team.

I retired at the end of the season in 1978, with a serious injury. Thanks to the Good Lord Above, I was able to come out of retirement to resume my career, with good health, with Seattle in 1979–1980.

Injury and being out of the game for a year led to being the comeback player of the year and the designated hitter of the year. In 1975 it was strictly a manager's decision even though I was very capable of playing the outfield.

To me, [the DH] has helped the game as well as some players. For the game I think it offers excitement and offense, and it also has prolonged some careers.[6]

The Junior Circuit recorded a .270 batting average in 1979, which was tops for the decade and nine points higher than the Senior Circuit's composite average. American League hitters also hit 2,006 home runs compared with an output of 1,427 in the National League. During the season, 10,527 American League baserunners crossed home plate, which was the highest total by a league in history. The league's slugging percentage climbed to .409.

In 1979, the American League pitchers' composite ERA also climbed, ballooning to 4.22, the highest in baseball history. As the hits and runs kept coming, the league's earned run average kept rising. In 1972, the season before the arrival of the designated hitter, the Junior Circuit's pitchers had posted a 3.06 ERA, and the Senior Circuit's pitchers registered a 3.45 ERA. In 1979, the Senior Circuit's hurlers allowed 3.73 earned runs per game.

By the end of the decade, fewer American League pitchers were going to the plate. While 11 pitchers had batted in 1973, only one, the Indians' Jim Kern, did so in 1978. The more usual number of those who would get to swing in a game in most years was three or four.

Let us examine the contributions of a DH in place of a pitcher. I will use a very limited sample, and draw from statistics from three offensive categories in 1979 — hits, home runs, and runs scored.

In 1979, the American League clubs averaged 1,477 hits, 143 home runs, and 752 runs scored. A designated hitter is one of nine batters in each club's lineup and can be credited with one-ninth of the team's offensive output. That would mean that each club's DH would be credited with producing 106 hits, 16 home runs, and 84 runs scored — the same as each of the eight other batters in the lineup. However, were a pitcher or a pinch-hitter for the pitcher to go the plate (as was the case in the National League) they would make a contribution to the offense as well, although it would be much more limited. To represent pitchers' contributions to the offensive part of the game, I will assign them credit for one-quarter of the offensive production of a designated hitter. The DH would now be credited with three-quarters of the numbers above and would produce 80 hits, 12 home runs, and score 63 runs.

When the differences in these numbers are subtracted from the league's club averages (1,477 hits, 143 home runs, and 752 runs scored) we are left with 1,451 hits, 139 home runs, and 731 runs scored.

How do these American League statistics compare with the average figures in these three categories in the National League in 1979? The National League clubs averaged 1,436 hits, 119 home runs, and 682 runs scored. Even with the adjustment for an estimated contribution from pitchers or pinch-hitters for them, the American League's offensive numbers exceeded the other circuit's in each of the three offensive categories The offensive accomplishments of designated hitters would have provided a significant contribution to the American League's edge.

Positions about the designated hitter had solidified by 1980. Proponents of the DH rule believed that it had been responsible for the increased offense that had brought additional excitement and more fans to the American League's games. In 1980, the American League registered 20,958 hits, which was the largest number for a league in the history of the game. More hits and runs had helped to resurrect a previously stagnant Junior Circuit, and the DH had been instrumental in greasing the turnstiles so that they spun more often than in earlier seasons. Opponents of the rule charged that the designated hitter was basically proving to be a junkyard for broken-down hitters so that they could extend their careers and pad their salaries. For those who disagreed with the DH rule, the addition of the DH had changed the game as they believed it was intended to be played. It had taken away occasions for some important managerial strategy, and it had removed opportunities for fans to approve or criticize the strategic moves that managers made.

Some opponents of the designated hitter were suggesting that the rise of interest in American League baseball and the resultant increase in attendance figures had to do mainly with an influx of good, young ballplayers about the time of the inauguration of the designated hitter in 1973. There were a number of players who became major contributors in the early and mid 1970s, adding offensive spark to the American League clubs. Players such as Rice, Fred Lynn, Carlton Fisk, and Dwight Evans in Boston, John Mayberry and George Brett in Kansas City, Thurman Munson in New York, Robin Yount in Milwaukee, Jeff Burroughs and Mike Hargrove in Texas, Baylor in Baltimore, and others were added to crowd pleasers such as Reggie Jackson, Lou Piniella, and Rod Carew, who were in the midst of their careers. To claim that an exciting new group of American League players was the major reason for the Junior Circuit's increased offensive statistics, and the narrowing of the gap in the attendance battle with the other league, is difficult to support. The National League also had its crop of young stars and stars-to-be who were arriving in the majors at the same time. Mike Schmidt, Dave Parker, Gary Carter, Al Oliver, Dusty Baker, Dale Murphy, Andre Dawson, Ken Griffey, Sr., Dave Kingman, Keith Hernandez, Steve Garvey and others were on the same timeline as those in the Junior Circuit. The National League also had the " Big Red Machine," with Pete Rose, Joe Morgan, Johnny Bench, George Foster, and Perez, powering its way through the league, creating excitement, and making its way to numerous postseason appearances throughout the 1970s.

How had the presence of the DH affected the managers' role in the American League? The strategy in the National League involved more decision-making on the part of managers, and, in the opinion of some, added its own degree of excitement and anticipation to the games. Should a manager pinch-hit for the pitcher at a time in the game when a run on the scoreboard would be more important than keeping a starter who is doing a credible job in the game? That one move would involve at least two choices; who to send up as a pinch-hitter and who to bring in from the bullpen. Those decisions appeared to be a bigger issue for managers and coaches in the National League than for those in the other circuit.

Baltimore manager Earl Weaver, who hadn't been a strong advocate for the DH, came to welcome the additional bat in the Orioles' lineup. Weaver's primary offensive strategy was to play for the "three-run homer." He and other skippers in the DH league waited expectantly for the "big bopper" (not always the DH) to do his work and clear the bases with one swing of the bat. For Weaver and others, the designated hitter meant that there was an additional batter in the lineup who was capable of helping to produce the big inning. They viewed the presence of a pitcher in the National League's lineups as generally leading to an unproductive out.

American League manager Bobby Winkles, who was a skipper for the

Angels (1973–1974) and the Athletics (1977–1978) after a long career in college coaching, was not enamored of the DH:

> There are pros and cons to this fact of the game. The fans [in most cases] want the DH. They like to see runs scored and we all know the pitcher doesn't put runs on the board with RBIs.
>
> I'm not a big fan of the DH. The pitcher is in many cases 90 percent of a baseball game. I feel he should take his turn at bat. I don't feel it's fair for a pitcher to intentionally hit a batter and not have to worry about getting hit himself. We know there are very few pitchers who hit .200. On the other hand, the bunt is a weapon and every hitter should become proficient at bunting.
>
> Managing in the National League is tougher. You have to deal with double-switches and using up your extra men can become a problem in a high-scoring game. Several pitchers are used and you have to pinch hit when it's his turn to bat. If you double-switch, you have to take out one of your regular players.
>
> [The best potential DHs are] those at the end of their careers. Those who are detrimental to the defense. Those who can hit but can't run anymore.[7]

The American League had become the power league, while the Nationals continued to play what was often called "small ball" or "little ball." "Small ball" involved methods of "manufacturing" runs, such as being patient at the plate and welcoming a base on balls as an offensive gift, moving baserunners with a well-placed bunt, employing the hit-and-run or the run-and-hit (whatever your preference is for naming the strategic move), the double switch, being ready to take an extra base on a single or double in the power alleys, and stealing bases. The sacrifice bunt was one of the pitchers' primary offensive duties. In the Senior Circuit, there were other occasions when skippers called for a bunt as an offensive weapon to move a player or players into scoring position. In the American League, after the DH joined the lineups, the bunt was rarely employed as a regular part of the offense.

The American League increasingly valued the bat over the legs and gradually became more of a hitting league and less of a base-stealing league. In the seven years prior to 1973, the Senior Circuit led the Junior Circuit in the number of stolen bases in five of the seven seasons. From 1973 to 1976, the first four seasons of the designated hitter, the American League clubs out-stole the National League's base runners in three of the four years. However, the Nationals took off in 1977, 1978, and 1979, and they built a significant edge in the theft statistics. The per-club average in the National League, which fielded 12 teams to the American League's 14, significantly outdistanced the stats from the other league, and that increase was just beginning. In 1977, the Nationals averaged 130 steals per team and the Americans averaged 104. In 1978, it was 128 to 105, and the following season it was 124 to 107, all in favor of the National League.

In 1980 and for the remainder of that decade until 1989 — even with an unequal number of teams — the Senior Circuit led not only in the number of thefts per team, but also in the total number of stolen bases. National Leaguers stole 1839 bases during the regular season in 1980. Montreal, Pittsburgh, and San Diego each had over 200 swipes by their players. In 1987, the Senior Circuit was even more on the run, stealing 1851 bases. In 1989, the National League continued to hold the per-club average, but they fell slightly behind the Americans (1,587 to 1,529) in the total number of steals.

There was increasing anticipation about the National League's vote on the designated hitter rule that was scheduled to take place at the summer meetings in August, 1980. Along with the Junior Circuit's dominant offenses, attendance figures continued to improve in the DH league. In 1979, the American League passed the 22 million mark for the first time in major league history with 22,371,980 admissions while the National League had 21,178,416. The Nationals still held a slight lead in the per-team attendance average because of the uneven numbers of clubs in the leagues, but that lead was becoming smaller with each passing season. Boston, California, Kansas City, and New York went over the 2 million mark, joining Cincinnati, Los Angeles, Montreal, and Philadelphia in the National League. The Yankees, with 2,537,765 admissions, and the Dodgers, with 2,860,954 admissions, were at the top of their league.

Thomas Boswell, writing in *The Washington Post*, described the situation facing the two leagues:

> A dramatic shift in offensive fire-power toward the American League in the last two seasons has made the days of an asymmetrically split sport obsolete and unnecessary.
>
> Conditions are finally right for reuniting the two leagues; play the game one way.
>
> With either all–DH or no–DH, the leagues would be in nearly ideal offensive balance.
>
> As matters stand now, however, the two loops are as unbalanced as they were eight years ago when the AL adopted the DH as a drastic restorative measure. Now, the tables have turned. The American League has suddenly and unexpectedly become the vastly higher-scoring league. New statistics show that even without any DH rule, the AL would now score more runs than the NL.
>
> The summer meetings in two weeks would be a perfect moment to begin getting baseball back on one track again.
>
> If there is movement, it will be from the National League, which is

now the worried league. Hitting is the baseball equivalent of heroin: fans get hooked on it. How long can the AL monopolize this DH connection?[8]

Boswell went on to present statistics to support his view:

> Over the first five seasons of the DH rule, the two leagues were in almost absolute run-scoring balance, with the AL — thanks entirely to the DH — actually scoring a tiny 1.6 percent more runs during the '73–'77 period…
>
> In 1976, the AL scored an infinitesimal 0.1 percent more runs. In 1977, the figure was 2.6 percent. Then, in 1978, it jumped to a significant 5.3 percent.
>
> Finally, last season, the big change was becoming obvious. The AL out-scored the NL [per team] by 10.3 percent with AL clubs averaging 143 homers and 752 runs scored compared with the NL's 119 homers and 682 runs per club.
>
> This season [1980], the gap had widened even more. The AL has scored 10.7 percent more runs per team, almost as great as the 12.7 percent NL superiority that precipitated the DH rule in the first place.[9]

Kuhn was also concerned about the leagues going in different directions, and he remarked, "It bothers me very much to see the game divided on the DH…. I see no need for me to push hard either way, though my personal preference is for the DH. Let time take its course. But I would hate to leave the game in a condition where it is permanently split."[10]

At the time of the National League vote at the summer meetings, their owners and other executives were reminded that they and the Central League in Japan were the only professional baseball leagues that were playing without the DH. The minor leagues in this country had joined the American League in using designated hitters, although in some leagues the pitchers hit when clubs with National League affiliations were playing.

Once again, on August 13, 1980, the Senior Circuit rejected the designated hitter at the summer meetings. With a simple majority vote of 7–5 needed to pass the proposal, the vote was four clubs in favor, five opposed, and three abstentions. Atlanta, New York, St. Louis, and San Diego voted for the proposal, and Los Angeles, San Francisco, Chicago, Montreal, and Cincinnati cast votes against it. Houston, Pittsburgh, and Philadelphia abstained.

The proponents of the DH were optimistic that they were getting close to approval. As reported in the *New York Times* on August 17:

> The National League moved perilously close last week to joining the American League in this designated daffiness. A proposed rule change adopting the designated hitter failed by one vote. But those in favor of the designated hitter promise to keep reintroducing it until it is accepted.[11]

Bill Giles, the Phillies' executive vice-president in 1980 (Philadelphia Phillies).

John Claiborne, the general manager of the St. Louis Cardinals, who was in favor of the change, promised, "Every six months I'll put it on the agenda, until it gets passed."[12]

The Philadelphia Phillies' executive vice president, Bill Giles, said, "Philadelphia is in favor ... but after finding out that we could not get it effective until 1982, we decided to wait until the winter meetings."[13]

Giles told a story about just how close the National League had come to having the designated hitter as part of its game:

> We had a personnel problem on our team. Keith Moreland and Greg Luzinski were both good hitters, but neither was strong defensively. The player personnel people wanted to be able to get both Moreland and Luzinski in the lineup, and they wanted the Phillies to vote in favor of the designated hitter proposal.
>
> Although club president Ruly Carpenter and I were philosophically opposed to the DH, Ruly instructed me to go to the league meeting and to vote "for" the DH. He would not be attending the meeting because he was going on a fishing trip.
>
> There was a lot of discussion about the proposal. The issue about not being able to begin using designated hitters before 1982 had to do with the Players Association. [The owners believed that if they gave the

MLBPA a one-year notice about the DH change, it represented a rules change and did not need the MLBPA's approval].

If we had approved the proposal at the August meeting for implementation in 1981, the Players Association would have had to approve it. I doubt that they would have approved it. So, I did not know which way to vote when I knew there would be a year delay in the implementation.

This is an interesting story. Before the vote, I tried to get in contact with Ruly, but I couldn't reach him because he was out in the middle of the ocean fishing. So I abstained. Pittsburgh was going to vote the same way we did, and if I had gotten Ruly's approval to vote for the proposal, they would have voted in favor of it also. I tell people, "If Ruly hadn't been out fishing the National League would have the designated hitter."

My father Warren Giles, who was National League president from 1951–1969, was an ultra conservative and he opposed the idea of designated hitters from day one.

One of the reasons that National Leaguers were opposed to the designated hitter was the economic aspect of it. Teams would have had to spend more money for a designated hitter than for an extra pitcher on the roster. There was also the strong belief that there was more strategy in our league than in the other league where managers sit and wait for the three-run homer.[14]

FIVE

The Designated Hitter
Is 10 Years Old

The American League continued its offensive dominance over the National League in 1980 when its hitters combined for a .270 batting average, 10 points higher than the National League's mark. The Junior Circuit's batters hit 1,844 home runs compared with the Senior Circuit's output of 1,243, and they also accounted for more runs scored, 10,201 to 7,852.

The 1980 World Series was the third time, on the alternating-year plan, that the teams were playing "the 10-man game" with designated hitters in the lineups. The Philadelphia Phillies, who beat the Kansas City Royals in six games, used Greg Luzinski, Keith Moreland and Lonnie Smith in the DH role. Luzinski and Moreland had been in Ruly Carpenter's and Bill Giles' grand plan if designated hitters had been approved by the National League in its August meetings. Moreland was the only one of three designated hitters used by the Phillies to contribute to the offense. He went 4–for–12 in the three games that he played. Luzinski and Smith combined for a 0–for–11 series. The Royals' Hal McRae went solo and hit .375 in a 9–for–24 series. McRae, who had won the league's Outstanding Designated Hitter in 1976, won it for the second time in 1980. He appeared in 124 regular season games, with 110 of them as the club's DH. He hit .297, with 39 doubles, 14 home runs, and 83 RBI.

McRae was a "professional hitter" who was able to adjust to what pitchers were doing to try to get him out. Philadelphia discovered what the American League clubs already knew:

> Hal McRae of the Kansas City Royals is one of those hitters on whom opposing teams have no real how-to-stop book. Even Philadelphia's best scouts couldn't come up with a World Series strategy that hadn't already been tried and found ineffective by most American League teams.
> This means that if an opposing pitcher is fortunate enough to get McRae out on a curve ball low and away his first time up, he would

probably be wise not to throw that pitch again. Hal is what they call an adjuster — that is, he's not apt to get fooled the same way twice in the same game…

Basically what McRae has learned is to adjust his stance so that he can pull the inside pitch to left, poke the outside pitch to right, and drive anything out over the plate up the middle. Good bat control has also allowed him to hit the ball in the gaps between the outfielders for extra bases.[1]

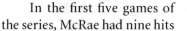

Hal McRae was the first of the long-term designated hitters during his career with Kansas City from 1973 through 1987 (Kansas City Royals).

In the first five games of the series, McRae had nine hits in 20 at-bats for a .450 average, and his hitting was an important factor in Kansas City's wins in the third and fourth games. In game five, his bid for a game-winning three run home run in the ninth inning just hooked foul at the last moment. He then grounded into a force play for the final out as the Phillies held on for a 4–3 victory. McRae went 0–for–4 in the series-ending sixth game to finish with a .375 average.

The former outfielder had adjusted to being an almost full-time designated hitter, something that some other ballplayers had difficulty handling. When he was asked about some of the problems that came with being a DH and some of his approaches to the job, he remarked:

> Most of the obvious ones, like staying loose between innings when you don't have a chance to run out to your position and back, you probably already know. The rest I won't talk about, and the reason is because I've had several years to perfect my role, and at this point I'm not sharing my knowledge with anybody.
>
> Maybe it would help opposing pitchers get me out easier if they knew what I was thinking…. I'm not sure. Maybe it would help players on the other clubs to become better designated hitters against the Royals if I told everybody what I do. I'm not sure about that either, but right now it's not for publication…
>
> During the three years Pete Rose and I were teammates on the Cincinnati Reds [1970–1972], I learned the value of thinking aggressively…. Although Rose and I sometimes talked hitting, Pete didn't really teach me what I know now — he showed me! I saw all the things that

worked for Pete because he was so aggressive, so I tried to make them
work for me, and I think I've done a pretty good job.

If you're making your living almost strictly as a designated hitter, the
way I am right now, you can't just be aggressive with the bat and earn
your salary, you've also got to be aggressive on the bases.... You've got to
try to stretch singles into doubles and force throwing mistakes by the
opposition.

Look at it this way.... A man who plays both ways can go zero for
four at the plate and still help his team by making a spectacular catch in
the outfield or by nailing a runner at the plate with a great throw.

But my situation doesn't provide those kinds of options. If I don't
get at least one hit in every game, I feel like I have let my team down.
And if I go two games without getting something going with the bat, I
really feel terrible.[2]

McRae added two more ingredients that are important in being a successful hitter. He said, "Well, assuming you've got big-league eye-to-hand
coordination, I think the most important thing is the condition of your
legs. Legs are what gives a batter his balance and they also generate the
speed in his upper body.... The reason Pete Rose has lasted so long is
because his legs are as well conditioned now as they were 10 years ago, and
I'm the same way."[3]

The 1980 December major league winter meetings in Dallas came and
went without any action on the designated hitter. The brief stir caused by
the National League's vote at the summer meetings in August didn't, as
some expected at the time, serve as the springboard toward acceptance of
the rule by the Senior Circuit.

The Phillies' Luzinski, who tasted the DH role in two games in the
1980 World Series and went 0–for–7 for the World Champion Phillies, was
dealt to the Chicago White Sox on March 31, 1981. The 30-year-old veteran outfielder brought a .281 career average with 223 home runs and 811
RBI to the American League club on the south side of Chicago.

After a quick start in Philadelphia in 1980, Luzinski had gone into a
slump, battled injuries, and had surgery on his knee in July. He returned
in late July, but didn't get much playing time the rest of the way. The trade
to the White Sox brought him to the DH league, and he was well suited
for it. In his first season in Chicago, which was strike-shortened, he was
in 103 games as the club's designated hitter and made one appearance as
a pinch-hitter in the White Sox' 104 contests. That was the first of four
seasons that he would be in Chicago's lineup as the club's primary DH.
"The Bull," as he was known, hit .265, banged 21 homers, and drove in 62
runs in his first year in Comiskey Park, and he was voted the American
League's Outstanding Designated Hitter.

In 1981, a 50-day strike shortened the playing season and brought a split season to the game. The American League outhit their rivals in other circuit, .257 to .256. The number of runs, hits, and home runs per club in each league also favored the American Leaguers. The Junior Circuit's teams averaged 437 runs, 930 hits, and 76 home runs while the Senior Circuit's clubs posted an average of 420 runs, 928 hits, and 60 home runs. The American League's on-base percentage topped the National League's, .335 to .323, and the AL led in runs scored, 10,201 to 7,852. Slugging percentage, which is an indicator of the power game, also went to the American League, .400 to .375.

On the pitching side, the American League almost doubled the National League in the total number of complete games, 334 to 176. While the Nationals trailed in that category, they led in earned run average (ERA), 3.50 to 3.66.

An example of the strategic differences between the two leagues was seen in the 1981 World Series, which the Los Angeles Dodgers won in six games over New York. In game two, Yankee starter Tommy John shut out the Dodgers through seven innings before manager Bob Lemon handed the ball to reliever Goose Gossage. Gossage preserved the shutout and nailed down New York's first victory. With the Yanks trailing in the series, 3 games to 2, John was on the mound again in the sixth game. With the score tied 1–1 in the bottom of the fourth inning, Lemon removed John for a pinch-hitter with two outs and runners on first and second base. That was the type of move Lemon had not had to make during the regular season when a designated hitter was in his lineup. Bobby Murcer, batting for John, flied out to end the inning. The Dodgers banged the Yankees' relievers for eight runs in the final five innings to pick up a 9–2 win and the World Championship. Lemon's decision to remove John so early in the game served as a prime topic for discussion during the "hot-stove league season." It wouldn't have been necessary had the clubs been playing in a DH World Series.

Dick Drago, who finished a 13-year career in 1981, commented about being a pitcher with designated hitters in the games:

> As a pitcher I would rather not had the DH. It made me one-dimensional. I liked being more involved in the game.
>
> I don't think it helped me that much. I would have much rather faced a pitcher in the 9th spot. I liked being involved in the game more — bunting, etc.
>
> It was equal for everybody. E.R.A. went up however.
>
> Fans like to see offense. More runs more excitement. It provided for longer careers for some players.[4]

In 1982, one of the game's elder statesmen settled into a nearly full-time designated hitter role. The Boston Red Sox' 42-year-old Carl Yas-trzemski, who had patrolled Fenway Park's left field area and had played ricochets off the Green Monster for the better part of his 22-year major league career, had been splitting time between serving as a designated hit-ter and being a two-way player since 1978. In 1982, which would be his next-to-last season in the majors, Yaz appeared in 131 games, with 102 of them as a DH, 14 as a first baseman, two as an outfielder, and 13 as a pinch-hitter. He made his 13th All-Star Game appearance, and hit .272, banged 16 homers, and drove in 72 runs during the season.

Yastrzemski commented about his career that was coming to an end and his changing role with the team that had been his home for all of his playing days. As a designated hitter, he had found it necessary to work to keep his focus on the game while it was in progress, and to be ready to hit when his spot in the lineup came around. He would sometimes go into the clubhouse to loosen up and focus on the upcoming at-bat:

> I'm getting keyed up, focusing on the pitcher, who was Goose Gossage. "Gotta get out there with the bat," I told myself. "Gotta get out there. He's gonna get it by ya. Be ready."
> I looked up and Wade Boggs was staring…. He had come into the clubhouse for something. I guess he thought I was losing my marbles.[5]

There was little difference in the age range of DHs from 1973 to 1982. (Total Baseball was the source for identifying those listed as the clubs' pri-mary designated hitters.[6])

Eight of the 12 primary designated hitters in 1973 had passed their 30th birthdays while 10 of the 14 in 1982 had passed that mark. In 1973, the California Angels' Frank Robinson, at age 37, was the oldest of the reg-ular DHs on Opening Day, and Cleveland's Oscar Gamble, at age 23, was the youngest. The average age of the primary designated hitters on the 12 clubs that season was 31. When the three youngest DHs were removed from the list, the average age jumped to 33. In 1982, Yastrzemski, at age 42, was at the eldest in terms of age, and Minnesota's Randy Johnson, who was 23, was the youngest. Johnson was in the second season of a two-year major league career! The average age of 1982's 14 most-often used desig-nated hitters was 32, and when the three youngest were removed from the group, the average age became 33.

McRae, who had made a career out of being a DH, received the Out-standing Designated Hitter Award for the third time that season. He had been the Royals' primary DH in 1973, and he was still in the role in 1982 at age 37. He had five more seasons to go before he would retire as an active player, after having played 1,427 games in the DH role. By that time he was already the batting coach with Kansas City, and he followed that with a managerial career. In 158 games as a DH in 1982, the All-Star McRae posted a .310 average, which was a DH record at the time. He delivered 189 hits, 27 home runs, and major league highs of 46 doubles and 133 RBI.

John Mayberry, one of McRae's Kansas City teammates, wasn't a great fan of the designated hitter. Mayberry had a 15-year major league career, beginning in 1968 with the Houston Astros. He came to Kansas City in 1972 and played in the American League the rest of his career. He was with the Royals from 1972 through 1977 and then went to Toronto from 1978 through most of the 1982 season. He finished his playing days with the Yankees at the end of the 1982 campaign. The left-handed hitting Mayberry was a two-time All-Star as a first baseman. He played the position in 1,476 games and was in the DH role in only 96 games. Mayberry's best offensive season was 1975 when he batted .291 with 34 home runs and 106 RBI. In 1972, his first season with the Royals, he hit .298 with 25 home runs and 100 RBI. He also led the league in bases on balls in 1973 and 1975.

When asked about the designated hitter, Mayberry said:

> I didn't like the designated hitter. It is important that players be totally involved in the games and I don't think that designated hitters could be. In between at-bats there wasn't much for them to do.
>
> People don't realize how exhausting and how much wear and tear there is when you play an entire season. I played 161 games one year [1976]. Designated hitters don't know what that wear and tear is like.
>
> I liked playing first base. I got to talk with everyone who got on base![7]

During the early years of the designated hitter, the number of pitchers who reached the 20-win level increased dramatically. In 1973, 12 won 20 or more games, and, a year later, nine reached the mark. Following that season, the range went from three to six 20-game winners. In 1982, for the second straight season, American League pitchers failed to have a 20-game winner in their midst. Prior to 1981, that hadn't happened since 1960. One of the major reasons for the difference appeared to be that more teams were using five-man rotations. That cut down the number of starts each member of the rotation made in a season.

Veteran major league pitcher George "Doc" Medich ended his career after the 1982 campaign. The right-hander, who had spent 11 years with a number of National and American League clubs, drew upon his experience and added his opinion about designated hitters:

The DH provided more offense for the team. [It] allowed pitchers to concentrate on pitching. [It] did not make a pitcher attempt to perform an activity for which they were not qualified [Hitting].

A pitcher had to concentrate more on getting the weaker hitters out. Did not have to worry as much about fielding, not as much about bunting. Strikeout totals were less. More innings were pitched per year. More complete games. Less relief pitchers needed on the roster.

DH has allowed older players with poor defensive skills to continue playing longer, and allowed younger players with poor defensive skill to get some time in the major leagues.[8]

Medich, who was pitching for the Yankees in 1973, had a inside view of what happened after Ron Blomberg became the major league's first DH. He recalled, "The 1st DH bat in the Hall of Fame is a surrogate bat. Blomberg, the 1st DH, shattered his bat and the Hall was given one out of the bat rack by (manager) Ralph Houk to get the HOF reps out of our dugout."[9]

In 1982, the American Leaguers outhit the National Leaguers once again. The Junior Circuit's composite batting average was .265 while the Senior Circuit posted a .256 mark, and the AL also led in slugging percentage, .403 to .373. Pitchers in the American League went the distance in 445 games compared with 289 games in the other loop. Once again, the National League's hurlers had a lower ERA, 3.61 to 4.08.

The American League had played for 10 seasons with designated hitters. A comparison with the National League in terms of composite batting average, slugging percentage, ERA, and complete games pitched shows some of the trends in the two leagues.

	Batting Average			*Slugging Percentage*	
	A.L.	*N.L.*		*A.L.*	*N.L.*
1973	.260	.255		.382	.376
1974	.259	.256		.372	.367
1975	.258	.258		.380	.370
1976	.256	.255		.361	.362
1977	.267	.262		.406	.397
1978	.262	.255		.385	.372
1979	.270	.261		.409	.385
1980	.270	.260		.400	.375
1981	.257	.256		.373	.364
1982	.265	.258		.403	.373

Earned Run Average

	A.L.	N.L.
1973	3.82	3.67
1974	3.62	3.62
1975	3.78	3.63
1976	3.52	3.51
1977	4.06	3.91
1978	3.77	3.58
1979	4.22	3.74
1980	4.04	3.61
1981	3.66	3.50
1982	4.08	3.61

Complete Games Pitched

	A.L.	N.L.
1973	614	447
1974	650	439
1975	625	427
1976	590	449

(There were 14 teams in the American League and 12 teams in the National League from 1977 through 1992)

1977	586	321
1978	645	389
1979	551	362
1980	549	307
1981	334	176 (50-day strike)
1982	445	289

During the 10 years, the regular season attendance in the American League had risen from 13,433,604 in 1973 to 22,080,448 in 1982. Attendance in the National League had risen from 16,675,322 to 21,507,424 over the same period of time.

The designated hitter was back in the 1982 Fall Classic. The St. Louis Cardinals took the seven-game series with the Milwaukee Brewers, and claimed the World Championship. The DH was expected to help the Brewers who had played all season with the extra hitter in their lineup. However, Roy Howell, who had been the Brewers most used DH, went 0–for–11 in four games in the series. Don Money had the other DH at-bats for the Brewers, going 3–for–13. The Cardinals' Dane Iorg, who batted .294 in limited duty with the Cards during the regular season, made the DH role his special possession. Playing in five of the games, Iorg went 9–for–17 with four doubles and a triple to help power the St. Louis offense.

The National League team had reaped more from designated hitters for the second time in the four seasons it had been in use in the Fall Classic. In 1976, the Cincinnati Reds' DH, Dan Driessen, hit .357 with a home run and an RBI while the Yankees' designated hitters went .063 and were without a homer or a RBI. Two years later, the Yankees' DH, Reggie Jackson, hit .391, blasted a pair of homers, and drove in eight runs while the Dodgers' designated hitters went .182 and were without a homer and added only a single RBI to the offense. In 1980, the Royals' McRae hit .375, without a homer, and with an RBI. In that series, the Phillies' DHs were an ineffective .174 without a homer and with one RBI. In 1982, the Cardinals' designated hitters, with Iorg leading the way, contributed significantly to the club's offense, going .429 with 3 RBI. The Brewers' designated hitters struggled to a .125 average and were without a home run and had only one run batted in.

There weren't any surprises at the 1982 major league winter meetings in Honolulu, Hawaii. On December 9, the National League owners once again voted down a motion to use designated hitters in the World Series and in the All-Star Games.

In 1983, the American League's combined batting average was .266 and the National League's was .256. The offensive per-team averages also continued to be in the Junior Circuit's favor. The clubs in the league averaged 727 runs, 1,476 hits, and 136 home runs compared with 666 runs, 1,398 hits, and 117 home runs in the Senior Circuit. On the pitching front, the Junior Circuit's pitchers averaged 34 complete games per team while those in the other league averaged 23 per club. However, the Senior Circuit's pitchers still held the upper hand in average ERA. They posted a 3.63 ERA while the Junior Circuit's hurlers were above four runs per game for the second straight season at 4.07. The league's ERA had been 4.08 in 1982, the fourth time it had been above the 4.00 level in the DH era.

Three designated hitters had outstanding seasons in 1983. The White Sox' Luzinski hit .only .255, but he put up power numbers with 32 home runs and 95 RBI in 139 games as a DH and two as a first baseman. He received his second ODH Award for helping lead Chicago to a first-place finish in the American League West. Perennial DH star McRae put together another strong season, hitting .311 in 156 games, but it was not enough to top Luzinski for the award.

It was the first time Chicago had been in contention for the division title during the designated hitter era. After finishing 20 games in front of

Greg Luzinski, the 1981 and 1983 ODH Award winner, delivers for the White Sox (Chicago White Sox).

the Royals, the White Sox met the Baltimore Orioles in the American League Championship Series. Luzinski hit .133 as the Orioles topped the White Sox, 3 games to 1.

The American League champion Orioles also had a designated hitter of some note. Ken Singleton, erstwhile outfielder who swung the bat from both sides of the plate, compiled a .276 average with 21 doubles, 18 home runs, and 84 RBI during the regular season. The 36-year-old, who hit .250 in the ALCS, was the man without a job in a non–DH World Series.

Baltimore manager Joe Altobelli spoke about the difficulty of finding a way to use Singleton in the series, saying, "We talked a couple of times. I don't want to do something that might damage Kenny's brilliant career. It's a tall order to ask a man to go out there in the Series after he's played about three games (in the outfield) in two years."[10]

Singleton was limited to a pair of hitless pinch-hitting appearance in the Orioles' five-game World Series victory over the Phillies.

Orioles' general manager Hank Peters, who was coming off a Fall Classic championship, was nevertheless angry about not being able to use a DH in his club's lineup:

> It's really wrong.... All AL clubs are constructed with the DH in mind.
> Would we have a third baseman [Todd Cruz] hitting .199? We offset them [him] with a DH. They're saying to us, "Unconstruct your team now." It's really penalizing the American League team. But we shall overcome.[11]

In 1983, left-handed pitcher Jim Kaat concluded a 25-year major league career. Like Medich, who had retired a year earlier, Kaat had pitched for both American and National League clubs. He gave the DH a mixed review:

> The DH allowed me to stay in games that were tied or close in the late innings. [The manager] didn't pinch-hit for me and it probably was worth 3–5 more wins. [The DH] gave me more wins— more innings.
> There was also a disadvantage [having a DH in other lineup]. I always thought I could help myself with the bat more than most pitchers. [Kaat had a .185 career batting average.]
> The designated hitter robs utility players of jobs. It also takes away from the strategy originally intended.[12]

Kaat also thought that having the leagues play with different rules was wrong, and he said, "It is absolutely ludicrous that we have 2 sets of rules— it dilutes the accomplishments of the great all-around players. It helps guys achieve Hall of Fame numbers by just hitting."[13]

As the American League's offenses continued to improve, so did their attendance figures. In 1983, with 23,991,052 paying customers, the American League once again outdrew the National League and it stretched its attendance lead to 2.44 million. It was the seventh consecutive season that the Junior Circuit had posted higher total attendance numbers than the Senior Circuit.

There had been an ironic twist in the Fall Classics since 1973, when designated hitters were first used in the American League. In the seven World Series to date in which DHs were not allowed (1973, 1974, 1975, 1977, 1979, 1981, and 1983), the American League teams held a 4–3 series advantage. The Oakland A's picked up championships in 1973 and 1974, the Yankees won in 1977, and the Orioles took the crown in 1983.

However, in the four World Series since 1976, when designated hitters were first used in alternating years, three National League clubs (Reds, Phillies, and Cardinals) picked up the World Championships. The 1978 Yankees were the sole Junior Circuit World Champion in the four DH–available Fall Classics.

For the American League clubs whose pitchers went to the plate in the Fall Classic after having designated hitters in the lineup for them during the regular season, only Ken Holtzman of the Athletics added significantly to his club's offense. He delivered a double and a single in three at-bats in 1973 and a homer and a double in four appearances at the plate the following year.

The series' totals for the moundsmen who took their bats to the plate were quite unimpressive. In 1975, the Red Sox' pitchers were 3–for–16. Two years later, the Yankees' hurlers were 0–for–13, and in 1979 the Orioles' pitchers were 1–for–15. In 1981, the Yankees' pitchers took the collar, going 0–for–14, and in 1983 the Orioles' hurlers followed suit with an 0–for–13 effort.

Over the same span of time, National League pitchers were 9–for–92 for a .098 average, but they went hitless only in 1981.

Since the inception of the designated hitter in 1973, one of the chief arguments against it was that it reduced overall baseball strategy. The belief on the part of many was that the National League continued to be the "decision-making" league and the American League was the "sit back and wait" league. However, not everyone was of that opinion. Bill James, a scholar and statistician of the game, disagreed with the belief that the DH had limited strategy.

James analyzed sacrifice hits and the use of pinch-hitters between 1968 and 1983, and he arrived at the opinion that the designated hitter rule actually increased managerial strategy. James believed that although the number of bunts and the use of pinch-hitters decreased in the American League after the arrival of the designated hitter, the decision to use these strategies became more complex. He wrote:

> I'm not an advocate of the Designated Hitter Rule; I'm only an advocate of seeing the truth and telling the truth. What the truth comes down to here is a question of in what does strategy reside? Does strategy exist in

the act of bunting? If so the Designated Hitter has reduced strategy. But if strategy exists in the decision about *when* a bunt should be used, then the DH rule has increased the difference of opinion which exist about that question, and thus increased strategy ... [the research shows] that there is *more* of a difference of opinion, not less, in the American League.[14]

In 1984, the American League had a new president at its helm. Dr. Bobby Brown was a former Yankee third baseman who had hit .279 during his eight years (1946 through 1952 and 1954) in the Bronx. He followed his Yankee days by pursuing a medical career as a heart surgeon before returning to baseball in an administrative capacity. Brown replaced Lee MacPhail, one of the leaders in the drive to gain approval of designated hitters in the league.

Near the end of the regular season, Brown took an action to benefit Oakland and its DH Dave Kingman. Kingman had been fined and suspended three games for charging the mound on September 10, after being hit on a 3–0 delivery by White Sox' pitcher Rich Dotson. A bench-clearing brawl ensued. Kingman appealed the decision, thus delaying its implementation. After the appeal was heard, Kingman's three-day suspension was upheld, and it was set to begin on the final weekend of the campaign. The A's were scheduled to play three games against the Royals, who were battling the Angels and the Minnesota Twins for the AL West's division title. Considering the importance of the final three games, Brown said, "At this juncture, it is neither practical or fair to contending teams in the American League West for the Oakland A's to be deprived of Kingman's services."[15]

The A's took two of the three games against Kansas City, and Kingman went 0–for–7 in his appearances. The Angels beat Texas in two of their three matchups, and the Twins dropped three games to the Indians. The Royals finished with a three-game lead at the top of the AL West.

Kansas City left-hander Paul Splittorff, who pitched for the Royals his entire 15-year career from 1970 through 1984, commented about how the designated hitter affected him:

> Early it hurt because I could hit pretty well [good contact & bunt, .225 in 1972] and we didn't have much for a DH. After Hal McRae developed in the mid–'70s we were solid.
>
> [There was] one more tough hitter in the lineup — more hits and runs allowed — fewer strikeouts.
>
> A higher ERA but also probably more IP [innings pitched] because no one pinch hit for the pitcher when losing a close game.
>
> It should be eliminated now. The offense has picked up and we would have fewer HBP [hit by pitcher].[16]

American League designated hitters posted a .256 average for the 1984 season, which was eight percentage points below the overall average for all hitters in the league. The DHs accounted for 16.3 percent of the home runs, 13.1 percent of the RBI, and 14.7 percent of the game-winning RBI. Considering that 11 percent would represent their part in the lineup (one out of nine hitters), they contributed more than their fair share to their offenses.

The Red Sox' DHs led the league with a .306 average and the Royals' designated hitters were a percentage point behind at .305. It was the first time that two clubs had registered above–.300 performances from their "10th men." The Orioles sat at the bottom of the league with an anemic .219 average. Singleton, who had hit .276 the previous season, struggled to a .215 average in 103 games as the O's primary designated hitter. Oakland's DHs, led by Kingman, totaled 37 home runs and 122 RBI. Don Baylor, with 25 home runs and 85 RBI, was the major contributor to the Yankees' total of 34 homers and 111 runs batted in.

Boston's Mike Easler's .330 average as a designated hitter led the other DHs on the club. It was also the highest average to date by any primary designated hitter. He also contributed 30 doubles, 23 home runs, and 79 RBI during the season. McRae, with a .309 average, had another strong campaign as the Royals' primary designated hitter. Neither hitter, however, was judged to be the best in the league. That award went to Oakland's Kingman. The 6-foot-6-inch, 210-pound, right-handed slugger had come from the New York Mets to the A's in 1984 after 13 years of service almost exclusively in the National League. He averaged .264, and added 35 homers and 112 RBI in power numbers.

The San Diego Padres reached the World Series in 1984, and they put 37-year-old Kurt Bevacqua in their lineup as the designated hitter. Bevacqua had spent time with four American League clubs as an infielder, outfielder, and DH before coming to the Padres. He had a number of at-bats as a pinch-hitter during the 1984 campaign with San Diego, but he knew from experience that duty as a designated hitter was different. He especially needed to keep loose between plate appearances:

> There's a gyro machine back there [in the clubhouse] that I used to stretch my back…. I'd go back there and get on that gyro that turned me upside down to stretch my back muscles. Now that I think of it, between my at-bats as a DH, I was literally upside down in the clubhouse.[17]

In the World Series, Bevacqua was well-prepared for his at-bats. He hit .412 (7–for–17) for the losing Padres. He hit two doubles, a pair of home runs, and drove in four runs during the series. Detroit topped San

Diego, 4 games to 1, but their DHs finished a distant second to Bevacqua. Barbaro Garbey (0–for–12) and Johnny Grubb (1–for–3) combined for an .067 average for the victorious Tigers.

A pair of managers spent their final seasons in their clubs' dugouts. Bill Virdon was the Montreal Expos' skipper in 1983 and 1984 after having managed the Pittsburgh Pirates (1972–1973), the Yankees (1974–1975), and the Houston Astros (1975–1982). Ralph Houk had managed 20 seasons with the Yankees (1961–1963 and 1966–1973), with Detroit (1974–1978), and with Boston (1981–1984).

Virdon, who had managed in both leagues, added his thoughts to the DH debate:

> I don't think it [DH] has affected my strategy. I usually put a good defensive player in the spot the player "DHing" would have played.
>
> I support the DH because it helps the defense, the offense and keeps the pitcher stronger as a pitcher. He isn't running the bases.
>
> It is harder to manage your pitching staff in the American League. The lineup does not dictate his replacement if you are behind. Pitchers ordinarily don't want to come out of the game so you have to make the move right now.
>
> I believe the leagues should be the same, either with or without the DH.[18]

Houk's managerial experience was limited to the American League, although he was on the job for 10 years before the designated hitter came to the league. He offered varied comments about the DH:

> I think it made the games closer. You could leave starting pitchers in longer, but you had to make the decision when to take him out. Without a DH, the bunt was almost automatic in some situations. There were many more lopsided games.
>
> It did not help or hinder me in the way I managed. It helped the older players and power hitters. It gave you an extra hitter in the line up. Few pitchers are good hitters.
>
> I think the designated hitter adds more offense to the game. Also more name players can stay in the game longer.[19]

Two years earlier, on November 1, 1982, at a major league meeting in Chicago, Bowie Kuhn had failed in his bid to gain a third seven-year term as commissioner, and he was scheduled to leave the job in August 1983. The owners extended his contract until March 1, 1984, and he was asked to remain in office until a successor was found. Some of those being considered for the position were James Baker (Ronald Reagan's chief of staff), A. Bartlett Giamatti (Yale University president), William Simon (former secretary of the treasury), and Peter Ueberroth. On March 3, 1984, Ueberroth was unanimously elected to be baseball's sixth commissioner. At the time of his election, the 47-year-old Ueberroth was heading the Summer Olympics in Los Angeles, and he was committed to work in that capacity until October 1. He said that he would only accept election to the post if the experienced Kuhn remained in office until he completed his Olympic duty.

Ueberroth took over in October, and Kuhn's work as commissioner was finished. He had been unable to unify the leagues with regard to the designated hitter question. Even though he had the power to cast the vote that would have broken the deadlock between the two leagues over the DH, as he had done in 1976 regarding the use of designated hitters in the World Series, he never took that drastic step as a way to settle the issue that had resulted in the two leagues playing different games for the past 12 seasons.

Resolution of the DH question was one of the most important items on the new commissioner's agenda. Ueberroth's plan included having fans express their opinions in a poll on the subject before taking action on the matter. On November 7, Ueberroth commented, "Too many times I hear somebody saying they're sure that all of baseball thinks X is right or Y is right…. Let's find out."[20]

The media provided input before the new commissioner had a chance to ask his questions. A *New York Times*/CBS poll conducted December 2–4, 1984, with 1340 baseball and sports fans responding, showed that those who said that baseball was their favorite sport approved the designated hitter rule by 52 percent to 31 percent. Among baseball fans 65 years of age and older, the breakdown was more even: 34 percent were in favor of the DH and 32 percent were opposed to it.[21]

In 1985, Thomas Boswell, writing in *The Washington Post*, expressed concern about the National League's sagging offenses. Only four National Leaguers in 1984 had hit more than 25 homers while 19 American Leaguers had reached the number. The Senior Circuit's top five home run hitters had fewer four-baggers than the top five on the Red Sox.

The National League's run-scoring numbers had sagged behind the American League's during the early 1980s. From 1980 through 1984, the Senior Circuit had averaged 8.1, 7.8, 8.2, 8.2, and 8.1 runs per game in successive seasons. During the same span of time, the Junior Circuit's runs-per-game numbers had been 9, 8.1, 9, 9, and 8.8.

According to Boswell, the 1985 season was starting in an even less productive manner for the Nationals. He reported some early-season statistics that showed the lack of offensive firepower in the Senior Circuit:

In last Sunday's averages, three NL teams—the Pittsburgh Pirates, Houston Astros, and Philadelphia Phillies—each had only one home run for
the season. That's in almost 1000 at-bats. Through the first two weeks of
the season, 20 percent of the NL games had been shutouts and the league
was averaging 6.9 runs per game.[22]

Boswell believed that baseball worked best at a one-run-per-inning
rate. He wrote, "When a league deviates too greatly from this nine-run
norm, we worry. If the offense gets the upper hand, we fret less. Fans don't
mind 10 runs in a game. In fact, many of the game's golden periods—
between 1920 and 1960—had patches of 10-runs-a-game seasons."[23]

A league average below seven runs per game had happened only twice
since 1920, and both times action had been taken to help the struggling
offenses. In 1968, both leagues plunged under the seven-run level with the
American League at 6.8 and the National League at 6.9. A smaller strike
zone and a lower mound greeted players for the following campaign. The
Junior Circuit's paltry 6.6 average in 1972 had been one of the factors that
had led to the introduction of the designated hitter.

Boswell worried that the American Leaguers had, in recent seasons,
been near the nine-run mark while the National Leaguers had been dan-
gerously close to the eight-run level.

Boswell's discussion of the National League's slumping offenses introduced a possibility that the stadium situation had come full circle. In the
1960s, when the American League was losing regularly in its battles with
the other league to put fans in the seats, it was suggested that the National
League's success in the attendance race was due largely to its foresight in
building new, modern stadiums that enticed fans to come to the ballparks.
Now, the big, symmetrical, artificial grass ballparks, with their fences a bit
too deep to aid the league's hitters, appeared to be hurting many of the
clubs' offenses. Boswell suggested:

> The true solution to the National League's dilemma probably would be to
> blow up all its ugly new parks, rip out every inch of AstroTurf in the
> league and spend the next 10 years developing the kind of athletes that
> God intended to play baseball.[24]

Boswell was not an advocate of the designated hitter, but he thought
that the time was rapidly approaching when the National League might
have to choose to accept it as a matter of competitive survival. Once the
change is made to "10-man" baseball in the Senior Circuit, Boswell said
that an asterisk should be affixed to the rule, saying:

"We did this sadly under duress," the footnote to the unified DH rule should read. "If we ever get our game straightened out again, we'll go back to the old way, which was the right way: nine men, nine innings, nine runs."[25]

It was announced on April 20, while the baseball world was waiting for Ueberroth to conduct his poll, that NBC had surveyed baseball fans by telephone during its television coverage of two games. Fans who were in favor of the DH were instructed to dial one number and those who were opposed to it had another number to use. There was a 50-cent charge for each call. Seventy percent of the respondents were tuned to the Mets and Phillies game and 30 percent were viewing the Red Sox and the White Sox. The results were different from the December *New York Times*/CBS poll that had come out in favor of the designated hitter. The NBC viewers had voted 38,432 to 27,676 against implementing the designated hitter in both leagues.[26] It appeared that more National League viewers were willing to spend their money to oppose the DH than there were American League fans who wanted to extend it to the other league.

In 1985, the American League had another successful year at the ticket windows and turnstiles. The Junior Circuit set an all-time major league attendance record when 24,532,220 people came to their parks to see their games. California topped the list with 2,567,427 admissions and Toronto trailed the leader with 2,468,925 people coming to SkyDome. Six American League clubs passed the two-million mark that season. The Dodgers had 3,264,593 paying customers to lead the National League. Although the American League still trailed the National League in per-team attendance, its total attendance surpassed the other circuit by 2.24 million.

The Yankees' Baylor was chosen the Outstanding Designated Hitter with Seattle's Gorman Thomas finishing in second place. Baylor, whose batting average was an unimpressive .232, put up important power numbers with 23 home runs, 91 RBI, and 205 total bases. Thomas' batting average was even lower at .215, but he also banged the ball hard for 32 home runs, 87 RBI, and 218 total bases. Thomas had come to the Mariners in 1984 after playing for the Brewers for most of his 12-year major league career. The former outfielder had been a primary designated hitter for the first time in 1985.

The overall batting average for designated hitters dropped from the 1984 numbers which had the Red Sox leading the league at .306, and with the Royals a single point behind them. The same two clubs led the league again, but, in 1985, Boston's DHs posted a .263 average and the Royals hitters were at .256. Easler hit .262 as the Red Sox' primary designated hitter. Seattle, with Thomas in the DH spot in 133 games, was at the bottom of the league with a .211 mark. The average for all American League DHs was .240 while the average for all hitters in the circuit was .262. That was nine points higher than the National League's average.

The 1985 World Series was another no–DH series. The Royals, who had the trusty McRae in the DH spot during the regular season, were forced to find pinch-hitting duties for him. McRae, who hit .259 during the campaign, was limited to three unsuccessful pinch-hitting appearances in the Fall Classic as the Royals defeated the Cardinals in a seven-game set. Kansas City's pitchers, who were unfamiliar with coming to the plate to hit, went 0–for–18 for the series. St. Louis' pitchers, who had been in the number-nine spot in the lineup during the regular season, didn't fare any better, going 0–for–12.

Perhaps that would be the final season that the World Series would be played without the presence of designated hitters. In October, there was discussion that Ueberroth was planning to offer a proposal that would allow for the use of DHs in American League parks and prohibit their use when a Fall Classic game was in the park of a National League club. That would end the alternating-year approach and introduce an alternating-park approach.

When the owners gathered in San Diego for the winter meetings in December, the topic of designated hitters was high on the agenda. Ueberroth's poll results proved to be inconclusive. The poll indicated that 42 percent of baseball fans were in favor of the designated hitter while 47 percent were opposed to it. Of the remainder of those who were polled, five percent were undecided and six percent didn't care.

The winter meetings passed without a vote being taken about the designated hitter in the National League or about the designated hitter in the World Series. However, Ueberroth had some thoughts about the future of both:

> As for the regular season.... I feel the commissioner should not change the way the game is played on the field.
>
> [With regard to the World Series], they decided not to do anything about it. But that's not to say I won't do anything about it. For sure, before the next season starts, I will decide on the use of the designated hitter in the World Series.[27]

SIX

A Changing Cadre of Designated Hitters

By 1986, three groups of players had appeared regularly as designated hitters. There were those who had been near the end of their playing days in 1973 when the DH became a fact of life in the American League, and it enabled them to extend their careers a few more years. Hank Aaron, Orlando Cepeda, Tommy Davis, Al Kaline, Harmon Killebrew, Tony Oliva, Frank Robinson, and Billy Williams were some of those who became DHs and then retired between 1974 and 1976. Some like Aaron, Cepeda, Davis, Robinson, and Williams had come from National League teams late in their careers and found the designated hitter role waiting for them. Others like Kaline, Killebrew, and Oliva were career-long American Leaguers who found a place in their club's lineups as designated hitters near the conclusion of their careers. Kaline used the extra seasons to reach the 3000-hit mark.

Players in the second group retired in the late 1970s and early 1980s. The list included Rico Carty, Greg Luzinski, Lee May, Bobby Murcer, and Ken Singleton, who had spent a number of seasons in the Senior Circuit before moving to the league where the opportunity to be a designated hitter greeted them. Others like Carl Yastrzemski and Willie Horton were career-long American Leaguers. Yastrzemski, like Kaline, reached the 3000-hit mark while he was primarily on DH duty.

The third group of designated hitters were those who were active in 1986, but who would hang up their bats in the near future and enter retirement. Dave Kingman, a former National Leaguer, and Gorman Thomas, a career-long American Leaguer, were playing their final season in 1986. Hal McRae, who had one more year to play, had served as one of the Kansas City Royals' designated hitters from 1973 to 1975, and would then become the club's primary DH from 1976 to 1987. He had made the DH role his sole occupation for longer than any other player. Reggie Jackson and Andre

Thornton would also retire with McRae, and Don Baylor and Darrell Evans would follow shortly thereafter. Evans and Thornton were refugees from the Senior Circuit who met up with the designated hitter opportunity near the end of their careers.

There had been at least four well-known players who had been in the designated hitter role at the start of their major league careers. Cecil Cooper, Kirk Gibson, Eddie Murray, and Jim Rice were primarily DHs before they picked up their gloves and went on to add defensive recognition to their offensive skills. Cooper was in and out of the designated hitter role with the Boston Red Sox from 1971 to 1975 before he became their first baseman. Gibson had a shorter apprenticeship with the Detroit Tigers, splitting time between DH and the outfield in 1983 before becoming one of the Tigers' regular outfielders the following season. Murray was a designated hitter for the Baltimore Orioles in 1977 and became their regular first baseman in 1978. Rice was primarily a DH from 1974 through 1977 before taking over the Red Sox' left-field job.

In 1986, there was a change at the top of the National League. Chub Feeney, who had served as president since 1970, left the office and was succeeded by A. Bartlett Giamatti, the former president of Yale University and a life-long Red Sox fan. He had often been seen wearing his favorite team's hat around the New Haven campus.

Feeney, a baseball traditionalist, had a number of owners in his league who, like him, had been dead-set against the DH from the very beginning. That group included the San Francisco Giants' Horace Stoneham, the Los Angeles Dodgers' Walter O'Malley, the Pittsburgh Pirates' John Galbreath, the St. Louis Cardinals' Gussie Busch, and the Philadelphia Phillies' Bob Carpenter. Feeney shared his thoughts about the DH:

> When the A.L. adopted it, Bowie [Kuhn] wanted both leagues to go by the same rules but the National League had a bunch of traditional owners then who didn't like it. The American League had some new owners like Charlie Finley who wanted to change things. Finley even wanted three balls and two strikes.[1]

Katie Feeney, Chub's daughter, who worked as vice president of Scheduling and Club Relations in the commissioner's office, reinforced her father's position in response to a series of questions about his thoughts regarding the DH, writing, "Thank you very much for your letter to my father. Unfortunately, he died several years ago so is unable to complete your questionnaire. I cannot put words in my father's mouth but I do know he was always opposed to the designated hitter and preferred the style of play in the National League without it."[2]

Ms. Feeney added her own thoughts about the designated hitter:

> Although I'm rarely asked, I definitely agree with him and would not want to see the DH rule added to the National League. I also do not see a problem with a difference between the two leagues on this issue. It generates conversations regarding the game and the players.[3]

Even though Giamatti had watched his Red Sox with designated hitters such as Cepeda, Rice, Yastrzemski, Mike Easler, and others since 1973, the National League appeared to be well protected against a DH insurgence while the former professor of Italian literature was in office. Early in his time as National League president, Giamatti gave a short and direct answer regarding the designated hitter, saying, "I'll soften my answer by just saying it's appalling."[4]

There was another change in store for 1986. Major league clubs opted to go with 24-man rosters in a cost-cutting measure. Lee MacPhail, the retiring president of the Player Relations Committee (PRC), management's negotiating arm, had reminded the owners that the Basic Agreement called for either 24- or 25-man rosters. With the average salary having risen to $371,157, one less player to pay was a noticeable saving.

The 24-man roster was not much of a challenge for the American League clubs. The designated hitter had cut down on the need for as many pitchers or pinch-hitters on their rosters. The National League clubs, however, were more dependent on deeper pitching staffs and longer benches. The availability of one more player was crucial in certain situations for them.

In 1986, the American League, with its designated hitters, continued to top the Nationals in batting average, .262 to .254. They also outdistanced the other league in several offensive categories. The American League clubs averaged 746 runs, 1,446 hits, and 164 home runs while the National League teams averaged 674 runs, 1,387 hits, and 127 home runs.

Baylor picked up the 1986 Outstanding Designated Hitter Award for the second time, and he became the first player to win it in consecutive seasons. He was named first on 70 of the 84 ballots cast. He was wearing a Red Sox uniform in 1986 after having been in New York Yankee pinstripes the previous season.

Baylor hit .239 with 31 home runs, and 94 RBI while helping Boston reach the World Series. The A's Kingman, with a .214 average, 35 homers, and 94 RBI, was the runner-up for the award. Designated hitters in the league posted a .256 average, and Texas' DHs combined for 30 home runs and 106 RBI while Detroit's "10th men" added 28 homers and 102 RBI to their offenses. Baltimore's DHs topped the league with a .298 average, and

Don Baylor won his second ODH Award in 1986, while playing in Boston; in 1985, he had been with New York (Boston Red Sox).

Oakland's designated hitters were at the bottom of the loop with an unimpressive .221 average. It is interesting to note that Kingman's batting average as the runner-up for the ODH Award pulled down his team's league-worst average for designated hitters.

American League pitchers registered 355 complete games compared with 224 in the National League. The American League's ERA was 4.18 and the National League's was 3.72. The DH had enabled the Junior Circuit's pitchers to go more innings in games and control their own destinies. However, the increased offensive output continued to force the ERAs higher. There was concern expressed about other effects of the pitchers' increased opportunities "to go the distance." Some thought that they were being expected to throw too many innings. The term "DH burnout" was being used to describe why more American League pitchers were coming down with tired or injured arms. Thomas Boswell wrote:

> AL pitchers have it tough. Fewer strikeouts. No breeze innings. No stress letup. As a concession, almost all teams now use five-man rotations and no longer have a machismo fixation with complete games. Going seven or eight innings in the AL may be as tough as nine once was.[5]

The Junior Circuit's attendance topped 25 million for the first time as 25,172,732 fans saw AL games. It was the first season that every team in the league drew more than one million people. The AL attracted 2.8 million more customers than the clubs in the Senior Circuit, but the AL still had not passed the other league in per-team attendance, trailing by an average of 63,071. The California Angels, with 2,655,872 admissions, led the American League at the turnstiles.

Although there had not been much movement by National Leaguers toward accepting designated hitters, perhaps experience with it would help to change their minds. That had happened to George Bamberger, the 1986 Milwaukee Brewers' manager. He had been the Brewers' skipper from 1978 through 1980 before taking the same position with the New York Mets in 1982 and 1983. He returned to manage the Brewers in 1985.

Bamberger spoke about his history with designated hitters:

> I didn't like the rule when it first came in. I was the pitching coach for the Baltimore Orioles at the time [1968–1977], and with [Mike] Cuellar, [Dave] McNally, and [Jim] Palmer we had pretty good hitting pitchers. At that time, the team ERA was about 2.68. There were not many runs put on the board. Also the idea of designated hitters was something that was new and I had never thought of that happening.
> In the National League everything is dictated in terms of when you remove a pitcher. What says that the pitcher you bring in is better than the one you took out? In the National League you have a six-inning game because the 7th, 8th, and 9th batters in the lineup are often easy outs.
> In the American League you take the pitcher out when your own two eyes tell you they need to be removed. I tell you, that's the most difficult thing a manager has to do.
> A designated hitter is usually a very good hitter whose legs or arm is gone. Larry Hisle was a very good all-around ballplayer. [He was a DH for the Milwaukee Brewers and was in 51 games in that role in 1978]. He was a good hitter and a great person to have on the team.
> I often used the designated hitter role as a way to get players in the lineup. We had a lot of good outfielders with the Brewers and I juggled them around by using the designated hitter spot as a way to get more of them in the games.

Sometimes a player would say, "I'm swinging the bat pretty good," and the designated hitter position was a way that I could keep him in the lineup and still give him a little rest on defense.[6]

Commissioner Peter Ueberroth, working through the Major League Baseball Rules Committee (MLBRC), had a change in store for the 1986 World Series between the Mets and the Red Sox. There was a new compromise on the DH rule for the series that produced the vivid memory of the Mets' Mookie Wilson's grounder sneaking through Boston first baseman Bill Buckner's legs in game six just when it looked as if the Red Sox were finally going to win their first World Championship since 1918. The Fall Classic featured the "rule of the park," which meant that the designated hitter was in the lineups in Series games in the American League park and not in the lineups in the games in the National League park— YES in Fenway, NO in Shea.

Baylor was in the lineup as the Red Sox' DH in the middle three games of the seven-game set, and he struggled to a homer-less, RBI-less, 2–for–11 series. The World Champion Mets spread their DH work between Danny Heep and Kevin Mitchell, and the duo also produced a 2–for–11 series. The Mets' pitchers, who went to bat in the first two games and in the final two games, outdid all of the designated hitters, going 2–for–8 in the series. The Red Sox' hurlers showed how rusty they were with the bat in their hands, finishing 0–for–10.

In 1987, another ballplayer who would later become a solid two-way performer got his feet wet in the majors as a designated hitter. Cecil Fielder, a 23-year-old first baseman-to-be, had been in 30 games in his first season with the Toronto Blue Jays in 1985. The right-handed power-hitter had been penciled in to be the Blue Jays' DH in 1986, but he ran into difficulty trying to adjust to the job. Fielder appeared in 34 games and was the designated hitter in 22 of them. He struggled to a .157 season's batting average. The more he struggled in 1986, the more difficult it had been for him to reach the expectations that the Blue Jays had for him. He put together a much more productive season in 1987, hitting .269. He spoke about his 1986 difficulties:

I put added pressure on myself.... Even that first series, I was all keyed up, and I wasn't sleeping well. I wanted to do so well, but I was gripping the bat so tight, and I was trying to hit the ball 900 feet. Cliff [Johnson] was here, and I knew if I didn't do well, I probably wouldn't start. Then I got into a rut and stayed there.[7]

As we have seen, some players who were inexperienced in the majors found the designated hitter role helpful as they worked to improve their

George Bamberger, manager of the Milwaukee Brewers, saw both sides of the designated hitter question during his career (Milwaukee Brewers).

defensive game and waited to take over a position when it became available to them. Rice was an example of this situation, as the younger player waited for Yastrzemski, the Red Sox' elder statesman, to relinquish his spot in left field. Others, who were near the end of their careers, found it a way to extend their time in the majors. Aaron and Kaline, two future

Hall of Famers, were stars of the game who benefited from being designated hitters at the conclusion of their careers.

Occasionally, a player came along for whom the DH role was an
affront, and no amount of reasoning could convince him otherwise. The
Blue Jays' George Bell fit in that category. The beginning of the conflict
between Bell and management took place in 1987, and it would also boil
over the following season. Bell, an outfielder who had hit .309 with 31
homers and 108 RBI in 1986, was beginning to have trouble with his knees.
In was the opinion of executive vice-president and general manager Pat
Gillick and manager Jimy Williams that Bell, who was in his sixth major
league season, would be able to significantly extend his playing career by
becoming a designated hitter. The move would protect his knees from the
pounding they would take over years of running on the SkyDome turf. It
was Gillick's and Williams' plan to slowly nudge Bell into the designated
hitter's role.

The opening shot was heard on April 29, 1987, after Williams posted
the day's lineup card which had Rick Leach listed as the left fielder and
Bell as the Blue Jays' designated hitter. Williams wanted to keep the right-
hander's bat in the lineup against Minnesota while giving him a day off
from defensive duties. Bell was angry when he saw the card and, during
batting practice, hurled a broken bat 15 rows up into the empty stands
behind home plate. Gillick and Williams huddled after the incident, and
the manager posted a revised lineup card. This one had Bell in left field.
He went 0–for–4 that day with one strikeout. Bell had won round one, but
the battle had a long way to go! Bell did serve as the team's designated hitter seven times during the season. It turned out to be a very productive
campaign for Bell, who hit .308 with 47 home runs and 134 RBI, and was
chosen the American League's Most Valuable Player.

Gillick said more about the role of the DH as he had experienced it:

> I have only been a General Manager in the American League so for me it
> has always been a part of our off-season planning.
>
> For the purist I would say "No," the DH does not have a positive
> effect on baseball. In today's society whatever the sport, offense is enter-
> tainment. Hockey, basketball, football, etc. So the DH does bring more
> runs and you are giving the fans what they desire — more runs.
>
> Pitching strategy is the most affected — removal of the pitcher. In the
> American League, in the 7th inning of a 1–0 game, you don't have to
> pinch-hit for the pitcher or make a double-switch.[8]

Cooperstown, the idyllic village in upstate New York where baseball
and John Fenimore Cooper reign supreme, was the unlikely site of a
squabble regarding the use of designated hitters. The dispute surfaced on

Saturday, July 25, during the annual Hall of Fame Induction Weekend. The New York Yankees and the Atlanta Braves had been designated to play that year's exhibition game at Doubleday Field on Monday afternoon. The designated hitter was ineligible when the game was a "home game" for the National Leaguers, which was the case in 1987. Yankees' owner George Steinbrenner said he would not allow the Yankees to play the game if a DH was not allowed in the lineup. He couched his opposition in terms of his concern for the safety of his pitchers, reasoning, "They haven't hit since the spring.... They could get hurt. We're in the middle of a pennant race. I didn't want to jeopardize any of my pitchers. If it were the World Series, they'd have a week to get ready. But they haven't had that now."[9]

Since it was too late to arrange for another team to take the Yankees' place, American League president Bobby Brown and Giamatti discussed the matter in an attempt to save the game for the 10,000 people who had purchased tickets to see major league players up close and personal in the tiny ballpark.

The leagues' presidents arrived at a compromise that allowed for designated hitters to be used in the game according to the wishes of the clubs. That was, in fact, what Rule 6.10 (b) allowed. A section of the rule states: "It is not mandatory that a club designate a hitter for the pitcher, but failure to do so prior to the game precludes the use of a Designated Hitter for that game."[10] The Yankees had a DH in their starting lineup; the Braves had their pitchers hitting for themselves.

Giamatti, speaking about the compromise, said, "I didn't want to make an episode out of it.... Fundamentally the game is for the Hall, the fans and the children. It's important that it be played."[11]

Steinbrenner was in Cooperstown for Catfish Hunter's Hall of Fame induction on Sunday. Hunter had closed out his major league career by pitching five seasons for New York after spending 10 years with the Kansas City and Oakland Athletics. Billy Williams and Negro League legend Ray Dandridge were also 1987 inductees. Both Hunter and Williams had experienced the designated hitter rule's impact on their careers. For Hunter, it changed the way he pitched and it took the bat out of his hands. For Williams, it put a bat in his hands when his playing career was nearing its conclusion.

A powerful hitting bug struck the major leagues in 1987. It was so powerful that Major League Baseball commissioned a study to see if the Rawlings balls that were flying out of the parks at an unusual pace were "juiced." Both the DH league and the non–DH league watched their hit and run totals soar.

The Junior Circuit's hitters blasted 344 more round-trippers than in

1986, and the Senior Circuit's corps added muscle to their games, hitting 301 more than they had the previous season. The American League's slugging percentage, which had been above the .400 level in seven of the past 10 seasons, reached its highest point to date when AL batters posted a .426 mark. The National League's .404 slugging percentage made it the first time that both leagues finished at or above .400.

Oakland rookie Mark McGwire hit 49 homers and Toronto's Bell banged 47 to lead the American League in 1987, while the Chicago Cubs' Andre Dawson, with 49, and the Braves' Dale Murphy, with 44, topped the National League.

The ERAs in both leagues also ballooned, and the Junior Circuit's hurlers saw their average ERA rise to 4.46. The Senior Circuit's pitchers had a 4.08 ERA, topping 4.00 for the first time since 1970.

Milwaukee's Paul Molitor, who played 58 of his 118 games as the Brewers' DH, put together the major leagues' fifth longest hitting streak, connecting in 39 consecutive games. During the streak, which was ended on August 27 by Cleveland Indians' rookie pitcher John Farrell, Molitor hit .415 to raise his average from .323 to .370. For the season, the DH/infielder had a .353 average, which was the second highest in the league. He added 16 home runs and 75 RBI to his offensive output.

McRae, who had defined the DH role during his lengthy career and had picked up three Outstanding Designated Hitter Awards, appeared in only 18 games—seven as a DH and 11 as a pinch-hitter—while also serving as the club's batting instructor. When manager Billy Gardner was fired on the same day that Molitor's streak ended, McRae was offered the position as Kansas City's manager. He turned the job down in order to spend more time with his family.

McRae's spot as the Royals' DH was filled mainly by seven-year major leaguer Steve Balboni, who had played first base in previous seasons with the Yankees and Royals. He batted only .207, but he added 24 homers and 60 RBI to the Kansas City offense. He had a successful year on the economic front. He had struggled with an injured back in 1986 and, by staying healthy all season, he earned more money in bonuses ($525,000) than 473 major league players made from all sources.

A new name appeared when the 1987 Outstanding Designated Hitter was announced, and it was a name that would continue to reappear for years to come. As McRae had defined the DH role in its early years, Harold Baines, the 1987 ODH Award winner, would carry the tradition into the future.

Baines had joined the Chicago White Sox as a rookie outfielder in 1980. He had been drafted and signed out of St. Michael's (MD) High

School in 1977. The sweet-swinging left-handed hitter had been on White Sox' owner and president Bill Veeck, Jr.'s, radar screen since he was a youngster playing in school and during the summers in St. Michael's, near where Veeck had a home.

Baines' batting average climbed in his early years with the White Sox, and it reached .309 with 113 RBI in 1985, which was the first of three consecutive years that he was selected to the American League All-Star team. He suffered a knee injury in a game in Cleveland in 1986 when he stepped on the foot of Indians' pitcher Neal Heaton on a play at first base. Until that time he had been a solid defensive outfielder, but the injury cut down on his speed and maneuverability, and he spent most of the remainder of a lengthy career as his club's primary designated hitter. He finished the 1986 season with a .296 average.

In 1987, Baines played in 117 games as a DH and batted .290. He also was in the outfield for eight additional games and raised his overall average to .293. He drove in 93 runs and posted a .479 slugging percentage.

Five teams (Detroit, 112; Seattle, 109; Chicago, 105; Boston, 105; and Texas, 100) got 100 or more RBI from players who served as their DHs. Designated hitters in the league had a .256 batting average (the league average for all hitters was .265), with California's DHs leading the way at. 278. Brian Downing, who was the Angels' designated hitter in 118 games, hit .272 and led the league with 106 bases on balls.

Attendance in the American League's parks continued to climb, and it reached another high-water mark in 1987 when 27,277,350 customers came to see one of baseball's most offensive seasons. Toronto led the league's attendance race with 2,778,429 fans coming to SkyDome. The National League fans also responded to their league's offensive explosion, and their total attendance rose to 24,734,156, which was a record for them as well. Two of their clubs— New York and St. Louis—finished above the 3 million fan mark. With increased offense in the air, and with fans responding to the excitement by making their way to the games, perhaps the Senior Circuit's owners would want to ensure the continuation of offensive baseball by finally welcoming the designated hitter into their league. They didn't alter their staunch stand.

The World Series was a seven-game set between the eventual champion Minnesota Twins and the Cardinals in which the home club won each game. The American League city hosted four of the matchups, and DHs were available in those games. Baylor, who was acquired from Boston near the end of the season, was in three games as the Twins' designated hitter and went 4–for–11, with a game-tying three-run homer in game six. Randy Bush and Gene Larkin were in the role in the second game, going a combined 1-for-4. Tom Pagnozzi, Tony Peña, and Terry Pendleton shared DH duties for the Cards and put together an outstanding 6-for-13 series.

In 1988, Bell continued to rebel against management's efforts to change him from an outfielder to a designated hitter. On January 16, 1988, in a meeting to set the parameters for the upcoming campaign, Bell was told by Gillick and Williams that he would play mostly DH, with perhaps 15 games in the outfield. Somewhere during the conversation the message became garbled. Following the session, Bell expressed his dissatisfaction with the decision, and he later claimed that he had been told that he would be mainly an outfielder with perhaps 15 games as DH.

Upon reporting for spring training, Bell, who hailed from the Dominican Republic, said, "I still think I'm too young to be a DH ... I'm only 28. I've played a pretty good left field all my life. They say it will make my career longer, but 10 years of DH I'd weigh 250 pounds from eating all those sunflower seeds sitting on the bench."[12]

Gillick was still concerned about the long-term effects on Bell of playing regularly in the outfield, especially on the artificial turf in SkyDome. The Blue Jays wanted to move Lloyd Moseby from center field to left field and put Sil Campusano in center. With the changes in the outfield and with Bell as the club's primary DH, Gillick reasoned, "He'll still get his at-bats and won't have to risk running into fences.... And considering we ARE a turf team, and will be for some time to come, it'll give us more team speed and make us a better club defensively."[13]

Williams, Toronto's manager, speaking about Bell's success in 1987 when he was named the league's MVP, said, "I think George Bell has the possibility of being the best designated hitter in baseball.... I don't know how he could possibly improve on his numbers in '87, but if anybody can do it, George Bell can."[14]

On St. Patrick's Day, March 17, Bell was hitting .417 in exhibition play, primarily as a DH, but that day he refused to be the designated hitter in a game against the Red Sox in Dunedin, Florida. Bell was fined $1,000 and was suspended for the rest of the day. The recalcitrant DH was in the lineup as the Jays' left fielder the next afternoon against the Cincinnati Reds in the Reds' home park, where designated hitters were not allowed.

In spring training, while Bell, Gillick, and Williams were doing their "DH shuffle," Giamatti was waxing eloquent about the game he loved and wanted to maintain. He was a traditionalist with regard to the DH, but, more than that, he was an idealist. At a breakfast gathering in Tampa, Florida, on March 11, the National League president fielded questions about baseball and its role, and said in part:

> It's the most perfect game ever invented.... It's symmetry. It's grace. It's beauty. It just gives me an enormous sense of pleasure.
>
> Baseball is basically not bound by the clock. It has the capacity to go on and on without resolution. Its mythical qualities are tremendous. The cerebral and strategic qualities are marvelous.[15]

Giamatti spoke about the past and mentioned a period when a DH might have made some sense:

> In the 1950s and '60s you had an extraordinary number of great pitchers, such that you had to lower the mound, bring in the DH.
>
> Earned-run averages were down to one-point something. Pitchers were so dominant that hitters couldn't get a break.
>
> The last 15 years, that hasn't been the case.[16]

Early in the regular season, Bell suggested that he might have a solution to Toronto's DH issue. In an interview clip that appeared during the April 10 Toronto-Minnesota game on NBC's Game of the Week, Bell commented, "If they pay me what I want (meaning extra to be the DH), okay."[17]

Bell didn't get the money, and Toronto didn't get their DH. Like the previous season, Bell was back in left field for the regular season, where he played 149 games. He was the Blue Jays' DH in only seven games. His offense tailed off from the previous year, and he hit .269 with 24 home runs and 97 RBI.

Yankees pitcher Rick Rhoden made history on June 11, when manager Billy Martin called on him to start the game against the Orioles as the club's designated hitter. It was the first time a pitcher had been given that duty since the designated hitter entered the American League in 1973. Since Ron Blomberg went to the plate for the Yankees in the season's opener that year, pitchers had only batted 65 times. Eleven had been used as pinch-hitters, and the remainder had been put in the DH slot later in a game.

Rhoden, who had pitched and lost to Baltimore the night before, was stunned when pitching coach Art Fowler told him that he would be batting #7 against the Orioles, right behind center fielder Jay Buhner and left fielder Gary Ward. Rhoden had pitched and hit in the National League for 13 years, and he had a .239 career average with nine home runs. In 1976, 1980, and 1984, he had hit over. 300.

Rhoden recalled, "Art told me I was DHing.... I thought he was kidding. Obviously, I was very surprised. Once the surprise wore off, I had to start thinking about not embarrassing myself. If I thought this was going to happen, I would have practiced all along."[18]

Martin had made the decision to use the right-handed hitting Rhoden because Yankee injuries had left him with mostly left-handed hitters to face Oriole lefty Jeff Ballard. Rhoden went to bat twice. In the third inning, he grounded out, third base to first. In the fourth inning, he hit a sacrifice fly to Joe Orsulak in right-field that scored Buhner. When right-handed pitcher Doug Sisk replaced the lefty Ballard in the fifth, José Cruz hit for Rhoden, and he became the Yanks' DH for the remainder of the game.

After 1988, Rhoden's name appeared on a list of pitchers who had batted during the DH era and who had accomplished something unique. He was the first pitcher to begin a game as a DH and the last to drive in a run. The Red Sox' Tim Lollar, on August 12, 1986, became the most recent pitcher to get a hit as a batter. Milwaukee's Eduardo Rodriguez had legged out the only triple by a pitcher as a batter on September 3, 1973, the designated hitter's first season in existence. On July 7, 1985, Chicago's Dan Spillner became the last pitcher to draw a walk. American League pitchers had not hit a double or a home run since designated hitters first appeared in lineups.

Molitor was elected to be the starting second baseman in the 59th All-Star Game, which was to be played in Cincinnati's Riverfront Stadium on July 12. The problem was that, in 1988, he was no longer a second baseman, having started 33 games as a DH and 45 at third base. Milwaukee manager Tom Trebelhorn gave Molitor a couple of games at second base before he headed to Cincinnati to fulfill the will of the fans. He was 0–for–3 in the American Leaguers' 2–1 win over the Nationals. There would have not been any place for him had he only been a designated hitter, since that breed was not yet welcome in the Mid-Summer Classic.

Baseball commissioner Peter Ueberroth brought the DH to every World Series and All Star Game under the "rule of the park" approach (National Baseball Hall of Fame Library, Cooperstown, NY).

That would change in 1989. On the day before the 1988 All-Star Game, Ueberroth announced that beginning the following season, there would be a DH in the game when it was hosted in an American League ballpark and there would not be one when it was in a National League park. The "rule of the park," which had become a guideline for the Fall Classics, was now the DH rule for the Mid-Summer Classics. The designated hitter would make its debut in both lineups in 1989 at Anaheim Stadium, the home of the Angels, but it would not be used in 1990 when the game was to be played in the Cubs' historic Wrigley Field.

In 1988, offenses in both leagues fell from their 1987 heights to levels that were generally below where they had been in 1986. The Senior Circuit's batting average dropped 11 points to .249, and the Junior Circuit's fell five points to .260. The number of runs, hits, and homers all dipped below the 1986 levels in both leagues.

Research done by *USA Today* focused on other aspects of the 1988 offenses:

> Comparison of 1988 American and National League team averages:
> Hits per game: AL 17.7; NL 16.8 Base runners: AL 24.4; NL 23.1
> Runs per game: AL 8.7; NL 7.7[19]

The average for designated hitters was .252, which was also below the previous season. Toronto's DHs, led by Rance Mulliniks, who hit .300 in 108 games as a DH and seven as a third baseman, led the league with a team .288 average. Texas' "10th men" were at the bottom of the loop with a woeful .197 mark. Larry Parrish was the Rangers' DH in 67 games before going to Boston. He hit .190 during his time in Texas that season, and those who followed him as the team's designated hitters didn't do much better!

The Outstanding Designated Hitter Award went to Baines for the second straight season. He was the White Sox' DH in 147 games, which was more than any other player in the role. His average was .285, and he led all DHs in hits with 160, in at-bats with 562, in RBI with 76, and in doubles with 39. The Yankees' Jack Clark, with

Chicago's Harold Baines won his second Outstanding Designated Hitter Award in 1988 (Chicago White Sox).

a .243 average, 21 homers, and 72 RBI finished second in the balloting. Clark was in his first season in the American League after splitting 13 years between San Francisco and St. Louis.

The expectations for the Junior Circuit's starting pitchers had changed since the introduction of the designated hitter. By the late 1980s, a 20-win season was becoming a much more difficult accomplishment than it had been back in the 1970s. Pitching rotations had been redesigned, bullpens were becoming more specialized, and new expectations were being developed for the starting corps.

The American League was producing many fewer 20-game winners than it had in the early days of the DH. In 1973, there had been 12. A year later, nine pitchers won 20 games or more. In 1988, Minnesota's Frank Viola, Oakland's Dave Stewart, and Kansas City's Mark Gubicza were the only pitchers to reach the mark. There had been only one 20-game winner in 1984, there were two in 1985, there were three in 1986, and there were two in 1987.

After the arrival of the designated hitter in 1973, there had been increased optimism that pitchers, who were now immune from pinch-hitters, were free to "go the distance." However, that pattern had not materialized as expected. There had been a gradual decline in two pitching categories—games started and innings pitched. Those changes had a direct bearing on the number of pitchers who racked up 20 or more victories. For example, the Orioles' four-man starting rotation of Mike Cuellar, Pat Dobson, Dave McNally, and Jim Palmer of the early 1970s had been expanded to five-man rotations on most clubs by the 1980s. That meant there were fewer starts in a season for most pitchers in the league.

Although the Junior Circuit's pitchers were no longer at the mercy of the manager in what used to be pinch-hitting situations in pre–DH days, their total innings pitched were decreasing, also due mainly to the five-man rotations. In 1973, the top five American Leaguers in innings pitched totaled from 359⅓ to 315⅔. The following season, the numbers for the top five were 332⅔ to 318⅓. A look at the comparable 1988 stats for the number of innings thrown by the top five pitchers showed totals of 275⅔ to 260⅔.

The Junior Circuit continued to increase its regular-season attendance numbers, putting a record 28,499,636 people in the seats. Minnesota became the first club in the Junior Circuit to welcome more than three million people, when 3,030,672 fans came to the indoor games in the Metrodome. The American League clubs outdistanced their rivals in the National League by four million admissions. The National League's lead in the per-team attendance average was cut to a mere 5,918 fans, the smallest it had been since the arrival of the DH. The Mets also had over three million in Shea Stadium during the regular season, posting a 3,055,445 attendance. The American League was but a short step from passing the National League in all aspects of the attendance race, a goal that was part of Joe Cronin's DH dream.

In 1988, the designated hitter was back in the lineup when games three, four, and five of the World Series were played in Oakland. The series opened on October 15 in Los Angeles, and that night Kirk Gibson, as a pinch-hitter, sent a charge into the Dodgers' offense when he pounded a two-strike pitch from the A's premier reliever, Dennis Eckersley, for a walk-off home run to win the game, 5–4. The next day, Los Angeles shut out the A's, 6–0, in the second game before the series moved to Oakland.

The injuries to Gibson's legs were such that a DH role was out of the question. That one at-bat was his only appearance in the 1988 World Series. Gibson had come to the Dodgers that season after nine campaigns with Detroit, where he had gained some experience as a designated hitter. The Dodgers called on Mike Davis and Heep, who had been in the Mets' lineup as a DH in the 1986 series, to be "the 10th man" in the three games in Oakland. Each of them went 1–for–4 in their appearances. The Athletics, who dropped the series to the Dodgers, 4 games to 1, countered with Dave Parker and Terry Steinbach. Steinbach was 2–for–3, and Parker, who had come to the A's in 1988 after 15 seasons in the National League, was 0–for–7.

In 1989, Bill White, who had played had played 13 seasons in the National League for the New York and San Francisco Giants, the Cardinals, and the Phillies, became the Senior Circuit's 15th president. The former first baseman and .286 career hitter succeeded Giamatti, who took over for Ueberroth as baseball commissioner on April 1.

Giamatti, and Chub Feeney before him, had strongly opposed the designated hitter. White was of the same persuasion, and any hope for a change in the National League's stance on the rule was slim. He was described as someone who "likes baseball the way it used to be. Outdoors. On real grass. Without designated hitters. And he likes balance. Leagues with equal numbers of teams. And order. No one touching the umpire, ever."[20]

White had broadcast Yankee games as Phil Rizzuto's partner for 18 years, but watching the American League's style of baseball had not converted him to the side of the designated hitter. Talking about the Junior Circuit, he commented, "Over there, all you got to do is be able to spell nine names, then sit around, maybe wail 'til the ninth inning and pinch-hit somebody. The DH is a no-brainer. American League managers will tell you the same thing."[21]

Kuhn and Ueberroth had been unable to unite the game either as total–DH or no–DH leagues. Giamatti, based on his clear statements while he was National League president, was not planning to move the game to a total–DH format as it had appeared at times that his two predecessors had wanted to do. Shortly after his election as commissioner, Giamatti had mellowed a bit on the subject, although his opinion about the designated hitter was still clear:

> It is a fan biggie. It's the most non-life-threatening controversy in baseball. You either like it or don't like it, but nobody's been endangered by it. It stimulates much discussion. I could argue both sides of it and doubtless will.
>   You just don't get up and wave a wand. It would have to be voted out by the owners.[22]

By the 1989 spring training, the new commissioner was fielding more questions about the future of the designated hitter. On April 1, his first day in office, Giamatti spoke on the topic, stating, "I'm not a fan of the DH, I've never hidden it, I was in the right league (as National League president for two years).... I could suggest one or the other, the DH or no DH. The day will come when I'll have some chats with some people and we'll see."[23]

Clark, a National Leaguer who had gone to the other league for one summer with the Yankees and had been their designated hitter, had returned to the Senior Circuit in 1989 to play first base for the San Diego Padres. Clark's experience as a designated hitter had not been a positive one. He had not felt that he was fully a part of the Yankees as a DH since he was only a one-dimensional ballplayer. He also had other observations about how baseball is played differently in the National League:

> National League games are more intense, there's more strategy.... In the National League, if you want to play hardball, if your pitcher knows the other team can come back and buzz a ball at his head, he's a little more careful. The pitchers in the American League take advantage of that. I always wanted to see Roger Clemens bat, but with the DH, he never has to.[24]

Early in 1989, Eugene J. McCarthy, the former United States senator from Minnesota who had made a run for the presidency in 1968, spoke about the greatness of the game even with some of the modern-day impositions on it:

> Another baseball season is under way. It will be a good season. Every baseball season is a good one. The strength of the game is proved year

after year, despite expansion teams, changes in rules and record-keeping. The designated-hitter experiment seems to have done no lasting harm.[25]

On July 11, there was another change in the game. For the first time, designated hitters were in the All-Star Game lineups. It was part of Ueber-roth's baseball legacy and, as usual, opinion about the change generally followed league lines. Oakland's Tony LaRussa, the American League manager, approved of its use in the Mid-Summer Classic. Los Angeles' manager Tommy Lasorda, the skipper of the Nationals, was not happy about having a DH in the game:

> I don't like it and I don't see where it brings anything better to baseball.... It takes away strategy, managing skills.... I really don't like it. With a DH it makes it simpler.... If you've got a 1–1 game [in the NL] with your best pitchers going, there are some big decisions to be made about whether to take him out and pinch-hit.[26]

There was a National Leaguer, however, who was pleased by the decision to have a DH in the All-Star Game. Pedro Guerrero, the Cardinals' first baseman, would be batting seventh as the designated hitter in the Senior Circuit's starting lineup. He had been in three previous All-Star Games as a pinch-hitter, and had gone 0–for–1 in each game. He expected to get several at-bats in his new role.

The American League picked up the victory, 5–3. Guerrero went to the plate twice, but remained hitless for his All-Star Game career. Pittsburgh's Bobby Bonilla followed Guerrero in the DH spot in the order and was 2–for–2 in his first experience with the American League's rule. Baines played the entire game for the Americans, going 1–for–3 with an RBI.

The Blue Jays had stumbled to a 12–24 start and fired Jimy Williams, replacing him with batting coach Cito Gaston. On August 10, the new manager, after watching Bell willingly play a game as the DH, spoke about his approach to the previously resistant Blue Jay:

> I believe if you communicate to a player what you are trying to do and why, the player feels respected and can accept it.... George just wants respect and [to be] dealt with straight up. He knows he'll play left field again for me. But my job is to match my team up against the opponent as best I can, and some days that might mean George is the DH.[27]

The kinder, gentler approach had not turned Bell into the club's regular DH, but perhaps it was a start for the future. Bell was in the role in 19 games and was in the outfield in 134. He batted .297 for the season.

Baines, who was 30 years old and in his 10th season with Chicago, had heard his name mentioned in trade rumors. The White Sox were sitting in the basement in the American League West, and general manager Larry Himes was trying to make deals for prospects. Baines was a very tradable commodity to teams who were making a push for the postseason. On July 29, the Texas Rangers became Baines' new team. The White Sox picked up shortstop Scott Fletcher and two minor league prospects— outfielder Sammy Sosa and left-handed pitcher Wilson Alvarez. At the time of the trade, Baines was hitting .321, sixth highest in the league, with 13 homers. The new Ranger finished second in the balloting for the 1989 Outstanding Designated Hitter Award. His batting average with the two clubs was .312 with 14 homers and 58 RBI.

Oakland's Dave Parker picked up the 1989 ODH Award. Parker, another former National Leaguer, had come to the A's in 1988 after playing 15 seasons for Pittsburgh and Cincinnati. An outstanding left-handed hitter, Parker had led the league in batting in 1977 and 1978 with .338 and .334 averages. A six-time All-Star, he had finished above the .300 mark six seasons.

In 1989, Parker appeared in 140 games, hit .265, and led all DHs with 22 homers and 97 RBI. The AL West champion Athletics and eventual World Series winners got 26 home runs and 107 RBI from its designated hitters. The Yankees, with 27 home runs and 106 RBI, also produced power numbers from its DH position. Balboni, who had come from Kansas City to New York in 1989 to replace Clark, contributed 14 homers and 52 RBI to the Bronx Bombers' total.

The batting average for all designated hitters was .255 compared with a .261 average for all hitters in the league. The National League hitters averaged .247 for the season. Minnesota, who finished in fifth place in the AL West, had the highest-hitting DHs at .295. Jim Dwyer, who was the club's DH in 74 games before he was dealt to the Montreal Expos, hit .316 to help the Twins' average. Toronto, whose designated hitters had posted the highest average the previous year at .288, plummeted to the basement with a .216 mark, as Mulliniks dropped from a .300 average the previous season to .238.

American League regular-season attendance took another jump in 1989, when 29,849,264 offense-minded fans made it to teams' ballparks. The National League also increased its attendance, and its clubs had had 25,323,834 fans in their parks. For the first time since the designated hitter came into play, the American League clubs' averaged a higher per-team attendance than the clubs in the National League. The American League's average-per-club advantage was 21,771. The DH league had finally passed the non–DH league in every aspect of the attendance race, and it had produced the happy results that the earliest proponents of the rule had imagined.

The baseball world was jolted on September 1, when Giamatti died suddenly from a heart attack. His tenure in office had been only five months, and he did not have the time to put his full imprint on the game.

"It will be a good season."[28] McCarthy's words of excited expectation didn't ring true in 1989. Giamatti's untimely death, just as he was beginning to display his leadership as a commissioner whose love for the game promised to touch all aspects of it, was followed by the massive earthquake in the San Francisco area on October 17, just as game three of the World Series between the Giants and A's was about to begin in Candlestick Park. Both tragedies shook more than the baseball world.

Fay Vincent, who had been deputy commissioner under Giamatti and had been elected on September 13 to succeed him, reminded the world that:

> Obviously there's been a substantial tragedy in this community.... Baseball is not the highest priority to be dealt with. We want to be very sensitive as you would expect us to be to the state of life in this community. The great tragedy coincides with our modest little sports event.[29]

SEVEN

The American League
Sits at the Top

Baseball experienced difficult times at the end of the 1989 season. Commissioner Bart Giamatti's sudden death, and the destructive earthquake in the San Francisco area that put the World Series between the San Francisco Giants and the Oakland Athletics on hold for 10 days, were a preview of the hard times that would follow early in 1990.

The negotiations between the Player Relations Committee (PRC) and the Major League Baseball Players Association (MLBPA) about a new Basic Agreement became bogged down, and the owners locked out the players from spring training for 32 days. The two sides reached a settlement on the seventh Basic Agreement on March 19. One of the issues at stake during the negotiations concerned the size of the teams' rosters. The MLBPA wanted club rosters returned to 25 players. According to the agreement, that requirement would not be in effect during 1990, but it would be in 1991.

When a shortened spring training was resumed, the question about the size of rosters at the start of the season became a central topic for the clubs. Managers and others believed extra bodies would be needed because players wouldn't have had the time necessary to get themselves in playing condition. Both sides agreed to allow teams to keep 27 players on their rosters until May 1. Another proposal would temporarily change the rule that required a starting pitcher go at least five innings to be credited with a victory. The change would allow a starter who pitched three innings to be eligible for a win.

On March 28, the commissioner's office announced that, because of difficulties that had arisen about the wording of the proposal, the 24-man roster and the five-inning requirement for starting pitchers to register a win would both remain as they had been. However, on April 2, it was announced that the major league teams had agreed to carry 27 players on their rosters during the first three weeks of the season. A few clubs, including the Philadelphia Phillies and the Toronto Blue Jays, were considering moving from the 24-man roster that had been in vogue since 1986 to 25-man rosters for the entire campaign.

A change at the top of Major League Baseball didn't promise any change in the designated hitter situation in the immediate future. Commissioner Fay Vincent, who had been elected in September following the death of Giamatti, held the same view about the designated hitter that his predecessor had. Like Giamatti, Vincent was a traditionalist:

> We don't know what it is that ties baseball so magically to the American soul. And to the extent you tinker with it without being able to predict what the result is, you do so at your peril. I'm against tinkering. I like it essentially the way it is— with the possible exception of the designated hitter rule.[1]

Vincent had been more explicit about his feelings regarding the DH immediately following his election as commissioner, when he said, "I don't like the designated hitter. I don't like aluminum bats.... I do like grass. I do like baseball as you and I knew it growing up."[2]

In 1990, the Milwaukee Brewers' Dave Parker was voted the Outstanding Designated Hitter. The former National Leaguer had also picked up the award in 1989 in his second season with the Athletics. During baseball's 1989 winter meetings, Parker, a free agent, had gone to the Brewers. The 38-year-old became the first free agent to sign with the Brewers in nine years, inking a two-year plus option-year contract estimated to be worth $3.8 million. Parker's contract was an indication of how, as the role of the designated hitter had become solidified in the American League, the DH's place on the economic ladder had risen. Designated hitters had become valued and costly members of their clubs.

Milwaukee hoped Parker would fill one of the Brewers' glaring needs. In 1989, they had gone 32–19 against left-handed starting pitchers, compared with a 49–62 record against right-handers. The difference in the records between when the Brewers were facing lefties and when they were facing righties was the largest in the league. Parker, a lefty, had been expected to give Milwaukee a more formidable lineup against right-handers. The new DH's contributions were not enough to lift the Brewers, as they finished 74–88 in 1990 compared to 81–81 the previous season.

Parker hit .281 as a designated hitter in 153 games (he was .289 overall) during his award-winning season in 1990. He led all DHs with 21 home runs and 89 RBI. Harold Baines, who moved from the Texas Rangers to Oakland during the campaign, was runner-up in the voting for the second consecutive season. He hit .287 in 125 games with 16 homers, 61 RBI, and 64 walks. Designated hitters averaged .251 compared with a .260 league batting average for all hitters. DHs didn't contribute 100 or more RBI to any club's offense in 1990.

The role of the designated hitter continued to differ from team to team, depending on personnel. Baines and Parker, like Hal McRae and others before them, were their club's primary DHs and didn't have a defensive role with their clubs. A number of teams, however, didn't have one person regularly in the role, but used it as an opportunity to rest a player on a given day. It also was a way to use more of the roster and keep bench players sharp. Managers would also draw from their pool of potential hitters to be a designated hitter in a particular game when it would be strategic to send a right-handed hitter against a left-handed pitcher and vice versa.

Designated hitters are often thought to be sluggers who managers put in the power spots in lineups. That often is the case, but a DH can be found anywhere in the batting order, depending on the team's need and the player's skills. A glance at box scores from 1990 show that DHs were most often in the third, fourth, and fifth spots in the batting orders, but there were others who were scattered throughout the lineups. There were games when the California Angels used Luis Polonia in the lead-off spot, and the Baltimore Orioles placed Randy Milligan second in the order. Felix José batted sixth as a designated hitter for the Athletics, and Gene Larkin was occasionally in the seventh spot in the Minnesota Twins' lineup. The New York Yankees also penciled in Matt Nokes in the number-eight place on their lineup card.

The American League's total attendance took another jump in 1990 as 30,332,260 people passed through the turnstiles. Toronto approached 4 million in attendance when 3,885,284 fans came to SkyDome. The National League's total of 24,491,508 represented a decline of close to a million customers from the previous season. For the second time since the arrival of the DH, the American League clubs averaged a higher per-club attendance than the teams in the National League. The AL advantage per club was 104,000 more than it had been in 1989, when it was 21,771.

The 1990 season offered some strange circumstances involving the designated hitter. First, the two leagues combined for eight no-hitters. One would have expected that the Senior Circuit, with their pitchers batting, would have been a more fertile field to produce a pitcher's masterpiece. However, six of the eight "no-nos" came in the American League, where a designated hitter graced every lineup and the "automatic out" in the ninth spot was not present.

Dave Parker moved from Oakland to Milwaukee in 1990 and picked up his second ODH Award (Milwaukee Brewers).

Second, there were mixed messages floating around about the future of the DH. In the September 4 edition of *The San Francisco Chronicle*, an article examining the possibility of having the DH in the National League reported:

> an inside source says that the idea [of having designated hitters] is gaining politically in high baseball circles, and is likely to be in the National League by 1995, earlier with expansion. Some of the staunchest oppo-

nents—former N.L. president Chub Feeney for one—are no longer on the scene and the "nay" vote is eroding.[3]

A little more than a month later, a report in the *New York Times* painted a far different picture:

> Vincent said he did not have a timetable for eliminating the designated hitter, but hoped the change would be made. With the influx of new owners in the American League, the matter may be brought up for discussion and vote at a league meeting, perhaps as early as December.[4]

If a majority of owners did vote for the DH's elimination, the next step would need to be the approval of the action by the Major League Baseball Players Association. Since the elimination of the DH would be considered a change in baseball's working conditions, the players' approval was required according to the Basic Agreement.

The saga of George Bell and the DH role finally ended in Toronto following the 1990 season. Once again, the Blue Jays had wanted to have Bell as their primary designated hitter, and, once again, Bell didn't want any part of it. He was a free agent and appeared to be holding the trump card in the negotiations involving club president Paul Beeston, assistant general manager Gord Ash, manager Cito Gaston, Bell's agents, and himself. General manager Pat Gillick, who had not made much headway with Bell in previous attempts to accomplish the DH placement, sat on the sidelines. Bell also wanted a longer contract than the one year that the Blue Jays were offering at $2.1 million, which was about the same amount he had made in 1990.

Ash summed up the situation from his and the club's perspectives:

> It's tough talking about George on a multi-year contract because of his physical condition. It's also tough not to say George would be a quality DH, but then other things come into the mix. If he's not going to do it willingly, then you've got other problems.[5]

On December 6, the Chicago Cubs signed Bell to a contract that guaranteed him $10 million during the next three seasons and could give him $15 million during the next four. It also provided Bell with the certainty that the DH would not be in his immediate future, and the annual discussion about it would be behind him. The designated hitter question was a dead issue for the present since he was now a National Leaguer—unless, of course, the Senior Circuit took an action that would be very different from the position they had clearly and strongly espoused since 1973.

Parker was on the move again before the 1991 season started, changing his Brewers' uniform for Angels' attire. After the trade in which the Brewers received outfielder Dante Bichette and a player to be named later, Angels' manager Doug Rader said:

> We needed left-handed power to balance our lineup.... I respect the man greatly for the way he projects himself and the positive way he has influenced the ball clubs he's been associated with.... I think Dave Parker could walk in the middle of the Grand Canyon and make his presence felt.[6]

Parker was with California for the majority of the season and then went to Toronto on September 14 after he was released by the Angels. He finished the season and his 19-year career with the Blue Jays. He played in 130 games as a DH with the two clubs and hit .239.

In 1991, the major league clubs returned to 25-man rosters as was required by the new Basic Agreement,. The National League welcomed the change because it gave their managers more flexibility in their strategizing.

A familiar name was added to the list of designated hitters. George Brett, the long-time Kansas City Royals' third baseman turned first baseman, was in the lineup as a DH. He had suffered knee injuries that restricted his range during the latter part of his career. Early in the season, Brett suffered a partial tear to a ligament in his right knee, and he was placed on the 15-day disabled list. When he was ready to play again, he suggested to the Royals' management that he become the club's designated hitter. It was not a totally new experience for the 38-year-old Brett, who had been in the role on a number of occasions during the previous five years.

The left-handed-swinging Brett was in his 18th major league season, all of them with Kansas City. He had led the league in batting in 1976 with a .333 average, and he had flirted with the elusive .400 mark in 1980, finishing at .390. When Brett led the league with a .329 average in 1990, he became the first major leaguer to capture batting crowns in three different decades. He had been an All-Star 10 times, and he was another player who would reach the 3000-hit mark with the help of the designated hitter's place in the lineup. Brett hit .255 in 1991 while playing 118 games as a DH and 10 as a first baseman.

Baines was making news early in the campaign. Near the end of June, Oakland's accomplished designated hitter was hitting .342, had eight homers, and had driven in 45 runs. The left-handed hitter was a disciple of Charlie Lau, who had been a coach with the Chicago White Sox early in Baines' career. Lau taught hitters about the action of the front leg, and he had them keep their heads down so that they could see the bat meet the ball.

Rick Burleson, Oakland's batting coach, spoke about what made Baines one of the game's top designated hitters:

> He never gets too high and too low, but just keeps working. It's kind of refreshing seeing a guy like that. So many guys get sky-high when they are going well and get too far down when they are not.[7]

Toronto's DHs were struggling mightily. Through the first 113 games, with Rance Mulliniks as their most often-used designated hitter, the Blue Jays' DHs were the least productive run producers in the league. Collectively, they had contributed only five home runs and 40 RBI to the club's offense. The lowly Cleveland Indians, who had scored the fewest runs as a team in the league, had eight homers and 42 RBI from their designated hitters.

Milwaukee sat at the top of the loop with a combined .300 batting average from its designated hitters. The Brewers' Paul Molitor put together a .325 average for the season while playing 112 games as the club's DH and 46 games as their first baseman. New York finished the season with the lowest DH batting average with a .222 mark. Kevin Maas, who was in his second major league season and had displayed an outstanding home-run stroke the previous year, struggled at the plate as the Yankees' DH in 1991, hitting .220.

Jack Clark had played for the Yankees as their primary DH in 1988 after 13 seasons in the National League. He had found it to be an unsatisfactory experience, and he returned to the Senior Circuit for the campaign. Clark was back in the DH league in 1991 with the Boston Red Sox, where he hit .249 with 28 home runs and 87 RBI in 135 games as their designated hitter.

Designated hitters averaged .257 for the campaign while the Junior Circuit's hitters batted .261. The offenses of Oakland (112), the Red Sox and the Orioles (105), the White Sox (103), and the Twins (101) each collected over 100 RBI from their designated hitters. Baltimore's "10th men" combined for 34 home runs.

Chili Davis, who was in his first season with the Twins after seven years with the Giants and three with the Angels, was voted the 1991 Outstanding Designated Hitter. He played in 150 games as the club's designated hitter and batted .277 with a career-high 29 home runs and 93 RBI for the division-winning Twins.

The White Sox' Frank Thomas hit .325 as a DH and .318 overall and finished second in the ODH voting. He delivered 32 home runs and 109

Chili Davis, the 1991 Outstanding Designated Hitter Award winner (Minnesota Twins).

RBI for the season. Thomas' numbers were such that his Total Player Rating was 5.5, which was the highest ever for a designated hitter. According to *Total Baseball*, Total Power Rating is "the sum of a player's Adjusted Batting Runs, Fielding Runs, and Base Stealing Runs, minus his positional adjustment, all divided by the Runs Per Win factor for that year — generally around 10, historically in the 9–11 range."[8]

In 1991, the American League continued to build on its attendance lead over the National League. Their clubs welcomed 32,117,584 fans, 7.4 million more than came to the other league's ballparks. The American League East champion Blue Jays, who lost to the Twins in the American League Division Series, were the first team in major league history to welcome more than 4 million fans in the regular season, with 4,001,527 paid admissions.

The 1991 Fall Classic featured two teams that had climbed from their division's basement the previous season to make it to the World Series the next year. The last-to-first Twins met the last-to-first Atlanta Braves for the right to proclaim themselves "the best in baseball."

The series opened in Minnesota, and Davis was in the lineup for the first two games. He was 1–for–6, with a run scored, in the pair of Twin wins. The Braves used outfielder Lonnie Smith as their DH, and he went 0–for–6 in the opening games. Smith became the first player to appear in the World Series with four different teams.

When the series moved to Atlanta for the next three games, the American League's top DH became a pinch-hitter and a part-time outfielder, and the Twins' pitchers picked up their war clubs. Minnesota's Scott Erickson, the scheduled starter in the third game, surveyed the situation and remarked, "It's kind of depressing, really.... When I was a kid, I could hit. I go out there now and it's a shame. I just lost it. I thought with Chili out, maybe I could hit well enough to help myself in a game."[9]

The third game, which was a 5–4, 12-inning victory for Atlanta, was an exciting, strategy-filled contest. Erickson, who pitched 4⅔ innings for the Twins, struck out in his only plate appearance. The teams used 42 players, with 23 of them taking the field for the visiting Twins. In the final inning, manager Tom Kelly was down to three players on his bench, and they were all pitchers! He sent reliever Rick Aguilera to the plate to pinch-hit for pitcher Mark Guthrie with the bases full and two outs in the inning. Aguilera sent a line drive to center field, but the ball was caught by Ron Gant to end the threat. The Braves scored the winning run off Aguilera in the bottom of the twelfth.

Kelly had raised some eyebrows when he announced that he was bringing a pitching staff of nine into the series and was adding an additional position player to the Twins' roster. Some questioned his decisions in the third game when he used relief pitchers and pinch-hitters early in the contest. The Braves held a 4–1 lead after five innings, and Kelly decided to try to get back in the game at that point rather than fall further behind. By the 12th inning, his bench had been decimated. The decisions he had to make in game three of the Fall Classic were not ones that he had faced during the regular season in the DH league. Kelly had called on eight pinch-hitters during the lengthy game, with four of them coming to bat for a pitcher.

The next day, Vincent said, "I think last night's Game 3 was the ultimate argument for baseball without the designated hitter."[10]

American League president Bobby Brown, when told about the commissioner's remarks, gave his own opinion, saying, "I agree that both leagues should be the same.... But what's wrong with using the DH in both leagues? Besides the Japanese League and the National League, tell me any other league that still makes the pitcher hit."[11]

Brown was correct that the designated hitter had been used in the minor leagues since 1973, but there is a slight variation in the rule as it applied to baseball at that level. The designated hitter is not used in Triple-A and Double-A when both teams are National League affiliates. In the Double-A Southern League, the pitchers hit if one of the teams is a National League affiliate.

The Braves took all three games in Atlanta, but the Twins took the series by capturing games six and seven in the Metrodome. The World Series followed the same script as it had in 1987, when the home team won every game.

Davis and Smith were in four games as DHs. Chili played in the outfield in one other, and Lonnie was in the outfield in the other three matchups. Neither player distinguished himself during the seven-game series, with Davis batting .222 and Smith hitting .231. It was a World Series when neither league gained an advantage by having an extra hitter in the lineup.

By 1992, there didn't appear to be any indication that the Junior Circuit's president and the clubs' owners were wavering on the value of designated hitters. Brown believed that the DH was safe in the American League. He said that the most recent secret ballot by the owners was 11–3 in favor of keeping "the 10th man." Both the loop's offenses and its attendance figures had increased dramatically since the pre–1973 period. There also didn't appear to be any movement by the National League's decision-makers toward bringing designated hitters to their games. For many, the major differences that it created had disappeared into the background, only to be resurrected for brief periods during All-Star Games and the World Series.

Others, however, pointed out that the designated hitter had created unacceptable differences between the leagues. They offered possible scenarios from other sports to make their point. Think, for example, of a National Football League in which the two-point conversion was used in the Eastern Conference but not in the Western Conference. For instance, when Philadelphia was playing a home game the two-point conversion was available following touchdowns, but it was not allowed when the Eagles went west to play in San Francisco. A more graphic example was drawn from the National Basketball Association, and it involved the three-point shot. What if a "home-team rules" approach was in place in the league? The teams in the Western Conference had the familiar arc painted on their floors, but it was conspicuously absent on the playing surfaces of the Eastern Conference's clubs. For those who drew examples from the other sports, the differences created by the designated hitter in baseball were equally as significant and unacceptable.

If there wasn't going to be a change with regard to the DH in baseball, might there be a compromise that would bring the two leagues under a single set of rules again? From time to time, suggestions were made about ways to increase the teams' offenses that fell short of having full-time designated hitters in the lineups. A couple of them surfaced for fans to discuss and critique.

The first appeared in an article in the May 18 edition of *The Houston Chronicle*. It was written by Larry Dierker, a 14-year National League pitcher, who had retired in 1977 and was a television-radio analyst in 1992. Dierker passed on a suggestion that had come to him by letter from a fan named John Thorn, who proposed the union of the designated hitter and the pinch-hitter:

> "A team may pinch hit for the pitcher one time in a game without the necessity of removing the pitcher."
>
> Thorn went on to say, "Actually, I would recommend this action could be taken twice during the first nine innings and once in extra innings."[12]

Thorn's ideas sounded quite similar to the approach that had been used in the Class AA Eastern League in 1969 and 1970.

Dierker had earlier made his own proposal as an alternative to the designated hitter, but he had a different purpose in mind:

> How about giving each team a legend spot on its roster? A place for a 26th man, who by virtue of say 7,500 at-bats or 2,500 innings pitched qualifies as a legend?

That way, the stars of the game could make their farewell tours without taking the roster spot of an up-and-coming youngster.[13]

The former Astros' pitcher was adamant against the designated hitter. He did not believe that a player who didn't play defense was a full player. Baseball was a game that previously had always had room for those who were less than spectacular fielders. After visiting the Baseball Hall of Fame in Cooperstown, NY, he wrote about his thoughts while he was there:

> First, the designated hitter doesn't belong here.... Oddly enough as I toured the baseball museum, I saw many boys and girls, some of whom were gazing upon Roy Campanella's uniform jersey. But I didn't see any evidence of a designated hitter. I began wondering whether a player who was primarily a designated hitter would ever be enshrined in the Hall of Fame.[14]

Retired left-handed pitcher Jim Kaat had become a TV analyst after a 25-year pitching career in the majors. He had played for the Washington Senators and the Twins when the American League was struggling offensively. He had been a decent hitter during his career, and, as a pitcher, he believed that he had the edge in the batter's box over the opposing team's hurler. Kaat spoke about the American League's answer to its woes:

> The American League was kind of a dull league and the National League was the league.... They had players like [Lou] Brock, [Joe] Morgan, and speed teams like the Dodgers. So the pressure to make a change was on the AL. Of course, we knew that if the AL was for it, the NL would be against it, because they never agreed on anything.[15]

In the National League a "regular" has to play in the field to earn the right to bat. In the American League, there can be one specialist in the lineup whose only job is to deliver at the plate. An article in *The San Francisco Chronicle* held up the skills of a couple of Senior Circuit players:

> We admire men such as Will Clark and Mark McGwire because they are exciting hitters. But our admiration for them increases exponentially because they are both great fielders. Both spend time before each game catching grounders and practicing throws, and each takes pride in being a complete player.[16]

The article also painted a picture of an American Leaguer who seemed satisfied to play one-way baseball:

> Our uneasiness with [José] Canseco is that he couldn't care less about fielding. He'll get his $4 million even if he's wretched in right field. This

is a man obviously on a career track to be a DH, and that makes us uncomfortable and gives us a sense of sadness and loss.[17]

For the first time since 1975, Brett's name would be missing from the All-Star Game ballot because the 10-time All-Star was no longer a position player. Write-in campaigns were the only way that a player who was primarily a DH could be elected to the Mid-Summer Classic. American League manager Tom Kelly could have selected Brett to fill out his squad, but he didn't.

As the 1992 season progressed, it became clear that besides the pennant races there was another battle was going on in baseball. A cadre of owners were making noises about wanting to remove Vincent from the commissioner's office. On September 4, 18 of the 27 owners who voted (the Reds' Marge Schott did not vote) asked Vincent to resign.

Some owners who voted against Vincent wanted the PRC to take a hard-line stance in the upcoming negotiations for a new Basic Agreement. They believed that Vincent had been conciliatory toward the MLBPA, and they didn't think he would stand firm against the players union during the negotiations. Others who opposed Vincent were upset that the $190 million in expansion fees for the new National League franchises in Miami and Denver, who were to begin operation in 1993, were not divided equally between the leagues. Vincent had announced that the American League, even though each of its 14 teams would lose three players in the expansion draft, would receive only 22 percent of the expansion money. The rub was that since the National League was operating at the time with only 12 teams, with each of them losing three players, the Junior Circuit would supply 54 percent of the personnel for the new Senior Circuit clubs and would receive only slightly more than one-fifth of the expansion fees. Vincent went on to say that in the future the leagues would split expansion fees equally, but that didn't help the American Leaguers in the near term. A third force, the Tribune Company, owner of the Chicago Cubs, was especially angry with the commissioner because of his attempts to reduce the impact of superstation broadcasts.

On September 7, after a long and contentious battle with some of the owners, Vincent, not wanting to turn the situation into a long legal battle, bowed to the will of the majority and announced his resignation.

Two days later, Allan H. "Bud" Selig, who had been among the group of owners voting for Vincent's resignation, was elected chairman of baseball's executive council. The position was a euphemism for "interim commissioner," but the owners didn't want to go there quite yet.

With Vincent out of the job, the commissioner's office was no longer a threat to outlaw the designated hitter in major league baseball. Whether Selig, who was the owner of the American League Brewers, would ever be in a solid enough position to foist the DH on the National League was yet to be determined.

Before the close of the 1992 regular season, Brett was back in the news. The Royals' designated hitter was closing in on 3000 hits. On September 30, while nursing a sore left shoulder and with five games remaining on the schedule, he hit safely in his first four plate appearances to become the 18th major leaguer to record 3000 career hits. He joined Al Kaline and Carl Yastrzemski as a player to reach the mark while he was primarily a DH. Brett hit .282 in 132 games as a designated hitter and had a .285 overall mark, which included 15 games at first base and several pinch-hitting appearances.

Bell had been on the move again. He had played the 1991 season with the Cubs, where he batted .285 with 25 homers and 86 RBI, before being traded late in spring training to the White Sox for Sammy Sosa and relief pitcher Ken Patterson. When asked about Bell's previous resistance to being a designated hitter, which was to be his major role with his new club, White Sox manager Gene Lamont said, "You tell George what you're going to do and stick to it."[18] A look at the White Sox' lineups showed Bell in them as the DH in 140 games. He batted .247 as a DH and had an over-all mark of .255 with an additional 15 games in the outfield. His power numbers included 25 home runs and 112 RBI. Bell finished second in the balloting for the year's Outstanding Designated Hitter.

The 1992 ODH Award went to the Blue Jays' Dave Winfield, who was in his first season as his club's primary designated hitter. He had been picked up by Toronto the previous December after the Angels did not re-sign him. In a season and a half as an Angel outfielder, Winfield had hit 47 home runs and had driven in 147 runs. Winfield initially seemed less than thrilled by Toronto's plan to use him in the designated hitter role. However, the 40-year-old settled into the position, although

Dave Winfield was the league's top DH in 1992 (Toronto Blue Jays).

he still hoped to get some time in the outfield where he had won seven Gold Glove Awards. Late in the season, he remarked, "I miss playing defense and having the ability to impact the game when you're out in the field. I know I can still do it. I've never been just a DH kind of guy. Hopefully, I'll get a chance to get back out there."[19]

Winfield hit .280 as the Blue Jays' DH in 130 games, and he raised his average to .290 overall after playing 26 games in the outfield. He hit 26 homers and had 108 RBI in helping lead Toronto to their first-ever World Series championship. He became the first "forty-something" player to drive in over 100 runs in a season.

Designated hitters batted a combined .259 in 1992, which was a point lower than the batting average of all hitters in the league. The National League's batters averaged .252. The Brewers' DH's led the league with a .290 overall batting average, with Molitor leading the way with a .320 average in 108 games as a DH and 48 at first base. The Red Sox' .235 brought up the rear, with Jack Clark hitting .210 in 64 games as the club's DH and 13 as a first baseman.

The "10th man" had been a part of the American League game for 20 seasons. Below is a list of the 15 highest seasonal averages by designated hitters with more than 300 at-bats.

Year	Player	Team	Avg.	Games	At-bats
1984	Mike Easler	Boston	.330	126	491
1976	Hal McRae	Kansas City	.329	117	417
1991	Frank Thomas	Chicago	.325	101	363
1991	Paul Molitor	Milwaukee	.321	112	476
1980	Richie Zisk	Texas	.318	86	302
1976	Rico Carty	Cleveland	.317	137	508
1977	Jim Rice	Boston	.316	116	468
1989	Harold Baines	Chicago-Texas	.312	115	414
1981	Richie Zisk	Seattle	.312	93	356
1983	Hal McRae	Kansas City	.311	156	588
1982	Hal McRae	Kansas City	.310	158	609
1984	Hal McRae	Kansas City	.309	94	307
1988	Rance Mulliniks	Toronto	.308	108	318
1981	Al Oliver	Texas	.307	101	420
1974	Hal McRae	Kansas City	.305	90	321

The Junior Circuit won the attendance race again, drawing 31,759,506 customers, a slight increase over the previous year. The Senior Circuit showed a slight decrease when it fell to 24,112,770 admissions. The Blue

Jays remained above the four-million mark, and the Orioles sat in second place, welcoming 3,567,819 fans to their newly-opened (April 6, 1992) Camden Yards, the beautiful baseball-only facility in the Inner Harbor section of downtown Baltimore. The American League's lead had now grown to 7.6 million. Since 1972, the season before the designated hitter, the league's attendance had exploded by 20.3 million fans, which was 4.8 million more than the growth in the National League. No one was claiming that the designated hitter was the total reason for the increase, but it clearly had played a part in the positive results.

In the Fall Classic, the Blue Jays defeated the Braves in six games. Winfield was in three games as a DH and three as an outfielder. Although he only hit .227 during the series, two of his three RBI came in his final at-bat in the top of the 11th inning of game six with the score tied, 2–2. His two-out double delivered a pair of runners to give Toronto a 4–2 lead. The Jays held on in the bottom of the 11th inning when the Braves scored once, and Canada had its first World Championship as a result of the Jays' 4–3 win. After being the Braves' DH in the 1991 Fall Classic, Smith was in the role again against the Blue Jays, although he didn't get any time in the outfield in the series. He hit .167 in the three games he played. He did not discover the Fall Classic magic that had been experienced by some previous National League designated hitters.

In 1993, change was a key word during the campaign. The two major leagues were equal in number for the first time since 1976. In 1977, the American League had added Seattle and Toronto, and the 14 clubs were playing in two seven-team divisions. The National League had remained with 12 teams until 1993 when the Colorado Rockies and the Florida Marlins joined the mix.

In June, the owners in the two leagues voted 26–2 to expand the playoffs in 1994 for the first time in 25 years. The owners' original proposal was to have the top two clubs in each of majors' four seven-team divisions face off against each other. The winners would then battle for the league championships before moving on to the best-of-seven-game World Series.

However, when the three-division format — Eastern, Central, and Western — in each league was approved for the 1994 season, the MLBPA's plan for the expanded playoffs was accepted by the owners. It had the winners of each of the three divisions plus the second-place club holding the best record making it to the postseason as a wild-card entrant. The format had the League Division Series (LDS) being followed by the League Championship Series (LCS) and concluding with the World Series. A possible ending date for the Fall Classic could be an evening in early November.

Some traditionalists let out a loud scream when they considered the possibility of a wild-card club becoming the World Champion!

Winfield had changed uniforms again for the 1993 campaign. Following his outstanding season as the World Champion Blue Jays' ODH Award winner, Toronto decided not to offer him salary arbitration, making him a free agent. In December, Winfield signed a two-year contract with the Twins. He was returning home, having been born and raised in St. Paul and having attended the University of Minnesota where he starred in baseball and basketball.

Winfield was in 105 games for the Twins as a designated hitter, 31 in the outfield and five at first base. He hit .271 with 21 home runs and 76 RBI. On September 16, he became another major leaguer to pick up his 3000th hit while he was in the DH role. He went 2–for–5 against Oakland, and he joined the exclusive club with a hit off Dennis Eckersley.

Another St. Paul native was in line to take Winfield's place as the Toronto DH. Molitor, who had played 15 seasons with the Brewers and had been a four-time All-Star, signed with the Jays as a free agent. Molitor went on to be more than an adequate replacement for Winfield. He picked up the 1993 Outstanding Designated Hitter Award, hitting .311 and driving in 107 runs in 137 games in the role. Molitor spent time at first base and raised his overall season's average to .332 with 22 homers and 111 RBI. Over the years it had been the case that a player who was his team's primary designated hitter often raised his average when he expanded his role and played a few games in the field on defense. Molitor finished second in the voting for the American League's Most Valuable Player.

The Angels' Davis finished second in the balloting for the ODH Award, coming off a .243 campaign with 27 homers and 112 RBI. Baines, who had hit .253 with Oakland in 1992, had become an Oriole in 1993, and he batted .313 in 116 games with 20 homers and 78 RBI. Brett played

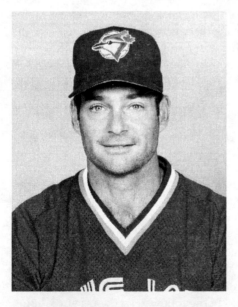

Paul Molitor followed Dave Winfield and picked up the 1993 ODH Award with the Blue Jays (Toronto Blue Jays).

his final major league season, hitting .266 in 140 games as Kansas City's primary designated hitter.

The league's DHs matched the overall batting average for all hitters at .267. Toronto's designated hitters, led by Molitor, were the best in the league with a composite .308 average. Chicago's .214 average, with Bell hitting .217 in 102 games, was the lowest in the league.

There was a stunning change in the attendance figures for 1993. With both leagues fielding 14 clubs, the Nationals forged ahead when 36,923,856 fans attended their games. First-year Colorado had 4.5 million people go through their turnstiles in Denver, and Florida welcomed 3.1 million in Miami. The Americans had 33,332,598 customers and were 3.6 million behind the other loop. In 1993, the excitement of new teams in new places appeared to make more of a difference than designated hitters!

The Blue Jays captured the American League pennant for the second consecutive season by defeating the White Sox in six games in the American League Championship Series. Molitor ripped the ball for a .391 average (9–for–23, seven runs scored, five RBI, a homer, a triple, and a pair of doubles) in the ALCS.

The Fall Classic opened in Toronto with the Blue Jays facing the Phillies, and Molitor was in his usual place in the lineup as the DH for the first two games. Molitor went a combined 3–for–7 in the opening games with a double and an RBI as the teams split the pair played in SkyDome.

Gaston faced some problems when the series moved to no–DH Philadelphia for the next three contests. His options were to put Molitor at first base, third base, in the outfield, or on the bench as a potential pinch-hitter. Each of the choices had its problem. The Blue Jays' first baseman John Olerud was the American League batting champ with a .363 average. A move to third base created possible defensive problems since Molitor had played only two games at the position since 1990. According to Gaston, a move to the outfield to replace a struggling Rickey Henderson, who had hit only .215 in 44 games for Toronto after coming from the Athletics during the season, was out of the question. The manager remarked, "Unless everyone else is dead you won't see Molitor in left field.... You'd be asking someone to play somewhere where he hasn't played in years and that's not really fair."[19] The fourth option, keeping Molitor on the bench, would be sacrificing one of the team's hottest bats.

In game three, with the Jays facing left-hander Danny Jackson, Olerud, also a lefty, was on the bench and Molitor was at first base. The move paid off early, when Molitor tripled home two runs in the first inning before an out had been recorded, and Toronto went on to win, 10–3. Molitor went 3–for–4 and added a homer, single, and another RBI to his series output.

   With Molitor in a hitting groove, Gaston had him at third base for
the final two games in Philadelphia, and his bat continued to sizzle. He
was a combined 3–for–8 in games four and five and banged another double and added two more RBI to his series total. Molitor played flawlessly
in the field, handling one chance in each game.

   Back at home for game six, Molitor capped his series with a 3–for–5
night with a single, triple, and home run. He scored what became the
series' winning run in the bottom of the ninth. He was on base when Joe
Carter hit his majestic walk-off home run off Philadelphia reliever Mitch
Williams.

   Molitor finished the Fall Classic with a phenomenal .500 average
(12–for–24, 10 runs scored, 8 RBI, two homers, two triples, and two doubles). He was named the World Series' Most Valuable Player. Not bad for
a 37-year-old designated hitter!

EIGHT

The Designated Hitter and Proposed Changes

In 1994, fans looked forward to "six-division, wild-card baseball" for the first time. The fans also worried about the possibility of a work stoppage caused by baseball's fourth strike. The season had begun on an unstable footing without a new Basic Agreement to replace the one that had expired December 31, 1993. As negotiations, which hadn't begun in earnest until March, continued between the Player Relations Committee and the Major League Baseball Players Association, management's proposal for a salary cap became the major stumbling block. Management believed that by putting a cap on salaries they could slow down the escalating player costs, which they believed were spinning out of control. Some owners also believed that there would be more competitive balance in the leagues with a salary cap in place.

With the negotiating fights just beginning, brawls at the pitcher's mound were in full force — so much so that players and executives were getting together to determine what was causing them and what could be done to stop them. More pitchers were throwing inside, more batters were being hit or brushed back, and the ugly confrontations between hurler and hitter had increased dramatically. Management representing both leagues and the MLBPA had watched the ugly scenes that were erupting much too often on the playing fields.

Gene Orza, associate general counsel of the Players Association, remarked:

> Obviously, the time has come for some heavy thinking to see what can be done to curtail the incidents.... Somebody's going to get seriously hurt one of these times. I'm concerned about players getting serious back injuries.
>
> We'll have discussions and get the players' input on this question.... It's a question we're concerned about. It's a multifaceted matter; it's not

as simple as saying don't charge the mound. There are a whole bunch of concerns to be taken into consideration. We want to do something about it. How to resolve it is another matter. It's a trickier question than anyone wants to acknowledge.[1]

The early season statistics regarding the number of brawls weren't released, but they were on the rise. However, other statistics were known, and perhaps they were related to the dramatic increase in the hitter-pitcher confrontations. In April 1994, a record number of home runs had been hit — 708. A year earlier, *only* 498 balls had "left the yard" by that point in the season.

Brawls had been occurring in both leagues. The first one had taken place on April 13 in the game between the Montreal Expos and the Cincinnati Reds. Expos' pitcher Pedro Martinez, who wanted to control the inside part of the plate, had a perfect game going until he hit the Reds' Reggie Sanders with an 0–2 pitch with one out in the eighth inning. Sanders charged the mound, and the two players ended up in an attack mode, rolling on the ground. A bench-clearing brawl followed. When the game was resumed, Martinez took a no-hitter into the ninth, but Brian Dorsett singled up the middle to start the inning. Martinez was removed from the game with a 2–0 lead, but reliever John Wetteland failed to protect the lead as the Reds scored twice in the top of the ninth. The Expos came back to win the game, 3–2, in the bottom of the inning.

In the National League, which had elected Leonard Coleman to succeed Bill White as president on March 1, the pitcher takes his turn in the batter's box, and the opposing team has an opportunity for "pay-back time." When a pitcher brushes back or plunks one of the opposition's players, he can become the target in one of his at-bats and sometimes gets an inside pitch from the opposing pitcher. Often that's enough to settle the score.

The presence of designated hitters in American League lineups removed the most direct method for settling disputes. Since 1973, pitchers in the American League have been protected from retaliation. A power pitcher like Roger Clemens and other American League hurlers like him believe they must control the inside portion of the plate, and that sometimes creates anger in opposing batters when they are hit or brushed back. Since these pitchers will never take their bats to the plate except for an occasional All-Star or World Series game, the retaliation can take a different form from what often happens in the National League. In the DH league, charging the mound is the most direct way to make the pitcher pay for his actions. Short of that, one of the pitcher's teammates will take the hit in his stead. That can sometimes lead to further retaliation.

Larry Dierker, who had pitched and managed in the National League, commented on this factor in his assessment of the designated hitter, saying, "I may be wrong, but I think the DH led to a lot of brawls. It is a lot easier to hit a guy if you know you don't have to step in the batter's box yourself."[2]

The American League's leadership was in transition as the issue of brawls was being addressed. President-elect Gene Budig, who was scheduled to take over for retiring Bobby Brown on August 1, said the on-field brawling would be one of the first issues he would confront. The former University of Kansas chancellor, who was elected on June 7, said, "Violence has no place in baseball. It must be dealt with before someone is seriously injured. When violence erupts, thousands of young people get the wrong message."[3]

On another topic of importance for American Leaguers, Budig, in one of his initial interviews with the media, backed the DH, saying, "it has enlightened the game and extended the careers of some of baseball's greatest hitters."[4] The Cronin-MacPhail-Brown linkage as designated hitter advocates was clearly going to continue under the leadership of the incoming league president.

As the season progressed, negotiations about a new Basic Agreement bogged down, and the season came to a halt on August 11. Many thought that if the players went on strike the owners would make every effort to reach an agreement so that the postseason with a new format that included an additional League Division Series could be salvaged. That did not happen, and the new league presidents had to wait a year to see how the expanded postseason worked.

The attendance race during the strike-shortened season went to the National Leaguers for the second straight campaign. They registered 25,807,820 paid admissions and the American League had 24,202,196. Every American League club had more than one million fans at their games, with Toronto leading the way with 2,907,933 customers. San Diego was the only major league club to fall short of one million admissions in 1994.

The Kansas City Royals' Bob Hamelin was chosen the American League's Rookie of the Year. Hamelin, who hit .282 with 24 home runs and 65 RBI, was the second designated hitter to receive the honor. The Orioles' Eddie Murray had captured the award in 1977. Hamelin was another player like Murray, Jim Rice, Cecil Fielder, and others before him who got their major league baptisms with bats in their hands and gloves in their lockers.

The bats in both leagues were alive during the 1994 season, and the home runs and other hits kept coming. While the pitchers weren't able to shut down the offenses, the strike did. The American League posted a record high .435 slugging percentage and the National League's hitters had a .415 mark for the shortened season. It was only the second time since 1973 that the Senior Circuit had finished over .400. They also reached the mark in 1987 when they registered a .404 slugging percentage. The Senior Circuit had done it twice since 1973 while the Junior Circuit had accomplished it 10 times. Both leagues would finish above the .400 level each year during the remainder of the decade.

After the season, the leagues chose their Most Valuable Players and their Cy Young Award winners, but the Outstanding Designated Hitter Award was not given. It is unlikely that Hamelin would have received it had it been voted on. The winner would probably have been Paul Molitor in a repeat of his 1993 achievement. Molitor was the designated hitter in 110 games and was at first base in five more for the Toronto Blue Jays, batting .332 for the season. He hit .339 as a DH, which was the highest average to date for a "10th man."

Designated hitters throughout the league posted impressive statistics. Their composite .273 average was the highest during the DH era, and the Blue Jays, with Molitor in the role for most of their games, led the way at .333. The .273 average for designated hitters matched the composite average for all hitters in the American League. The California Angels were second at .309, with Chili Davis hitting .314. Chicago's Julio Franco had a strong season, hitting .306 in the designated hitter role. The Texas Rangers' José Canseco, playing all 111 of his games as a DH, had a .282 average with 31 homers and 91 RBI. The New York Yankees were at the bottom of the league at .233, a full 100 points below the Blue Jays.

Based on the salaries of the players on the 25-man rosters and the disabled lists at the beginning of the strike, designated hitters led the way on the clubs' payrolls. A list by positions of the median salaries of all American Leaguers showed that full-time DHs were being paid $1,650,000 to do their jobs. The median is not the average, but it is the amount at which as many designated hitters earn more as earn less. The median for all major leaguers was $437,500. The median salary for starting pitchers was $736,667, for first basemen it was $650,000, and for catchers it was $237,750. Right fielders were closest behind designated hitters with a median $848,334 salary.[5]

Early in 1995, designated hitters were not the group of players drawing special attention. The focus was on "replacement players," that group of baseball hopefuls who were not on the clubs' 40-man rosters or, in some cases, not on any roster, but who might have an opportunity to step in and play major league baseball that summer. The strike had not been settled, and spring training camps were void of major leaguers and the top players in each club's farm system. The owners were committed to playing the season, and for some time it looked as if it would be played with replacement players. They played in the spring training games, and they appeared ready to begin the regular season.

With the talks between the PRC and the MLBPA in recess, the Federal Government's National Labor Relations Board (NLRB) was called into action. The union had filed an unfair labor practice charge with the NLRB that was based on the owners having ended salary arbitration, and not having followed the directives against collusion as they had agreed to in the expired Basic Agreement.

With April 2, the scheduled opening day of the regular season, rapidly approaching, Fred Feinstein, the NLRB's general counsel, sought to speed up the Board's consideration of the union's charges. Once the NLRB got rolling, there was no stopping it. Whereas the talks between management and labor had stopped and started and then plodded along, the NLRB raced to a decision.

On March 26, the NLRB voted 3–2 to seek an injunction against the club owners. The next step would be a hearing that was set for Friday, March 31, in United States District Court in Manhattan before Federal judge Sonia Sotomayor. The Government's wheels were in motion!

Sotomayor reviewed the two sides' briefs and came prepared for the March 31 showdown. After a 98-minute hearing and an 18-minute recess, the Federal judge read her 47-minute opinion in which she issued a temporary injunction against Major League Baseball's clubs. In the swift and stern ruling, Sotomayor instructed the clubs to reinstate salary arbitration, to participate in competitive bidding for the available free agents, and to follow the anti-collusion guidelines. She also warned against the imposition of any new work rules in the absence of a new Basic Agreement.

The ruling set the stage for the players to return to work if the owners would allow them to do so. The owners' first response was to seek an immediate stay of the injunction, but that request was denied. There were some brief discussions by management about locking out the players again, but that path was not taken.

During meetings in Chicago on April 2 — the 234th day of the longest strike in professional sports history and the day originally set for the New York Mets and Florida Marlins to open the 1995 regular season — management accepted the players' offer to return to the field, and opening day was rescheduled for April 26. The clubs would play a shortened 144-game schedule. Designated hitters would be back, but replacement players were gone from the scene. Hopefully, the season would be played to its conclusion, and the new and expanded postseason plan would come into play.

When the season opened on April 26, Major League Baseball was still without a new Basic Agreement. Although the agreement wouldn't be finalized until after the 1996 season, baseball continued to be played while the negotiations continued. Because of the shortened spring training, teams were allowed to have 28-man rosters until May 16 when 25-man rosters would again become the legal limit.

As the season progressed, it became apparent that the lengthy strike had hurt fan interest at the major league level. Baseball owners, in an attempt to increase fan appeal, adopted three recommendations aimed at shortening the length of the average game by about a half hour. Starting July 12, the day after the All-Star Game, umpires were instructed to prevent players from routinely stepping out of the batter's box. The break between half-innings would be shortened from two minutes, 25 seconds to one minute, 45 seconds, and public-address announcers were directed to introduce the first batter of each half inning one minute, 15 seconds after the previous out.

In 1995, another baseball great reached the 3000-hit mark as a designated hitter. On June 30, Murray, playing his second season with the Cleveland Indians, slapped a fastball from the Minnesota Twins' Mike Trombley into right field in the Metrodome for his milestone single. He became the first Cleveland player to reach 3000 hits since Tris Speaker accomplished the feat in 1925. Dave Winfeld was one of Murray's Cleveland teammates, and it was the first time that a pair of players with 3000 hits were on the same club. Winfield was a part-time DH and was in his 22nd and final major league season.

Interestingly, Murray was the first player to get 3000 hits who had begun his career as a designated hitter (111 games as a designated hitter with Baltimore in 1977). He soon became a solid defensive player. The DH role had helped him at both ends of his lengthy career.

Also, for the first time, a designated hitter was the American League batting champion. The Seattle Mariners' Edgar Martinez, like Hal McRae before him, would make designated hitting an almost full-time career. Early in his time with the Mariners, which had begun in 1987, he had been a third baseman. He was stuck behind fellow third basemen Jim Presley and Darnell Coles, and he didn't become a full-time player until 1990. After he battled hamstring and knee injuries in 1993 and 1994, it became clear that the DH role was well-suited for him. Martinez had been on the All-Star team in 1992 as a third baseman, and he also won his first batting title that season with a .343 average. In 1995, which was another All-Star season for Martinez, he hit a league-leading .356 (.350 as a DH) with 29 homers, 50 doubles, and 113 RBI while playing in 138 of his 145 games as the Mariners' designated hitter. The right-handed hitter, who made use of the entire field, was named the 1995 Outstanding Designated Hitter, capturing 82 of the 83 first-place votes. He went on to have an outstanding American League Division Series against the Yankees, which the Mariners won 3 games to 2. He was 12–for–21 for a .571 batting average. He also drove in 10 runs, and he contributed a grand slam homer to the Mariners' offense in the fourth game. In the American League Championship Series, which Seattle lost to Cleveland in six games, Martinez cooled off significantly, going 3–for–22 for a .087 average. Following the season, the Mariners picked up the one-year option on Martinez's contract that was set to pay him $3.6 million for 1996.

Canseco had moved from Texas to Boston where he took dead aim at Fenway Park's "Green Monster." In 101 games as the club's DH and one game as an outfielder, Canseco hit .306 with 24 homers and 81 RBI. Harold Baines, with the Baltimore Orioles, batted .299 in 122 games, and Molitor slumped from the previous season, hitting .270 in 129 games for Toronto. Hamelin, the 1994 Rookie of the Year, was back as the Royals' DH in 70 games and as their first baseman in 24 others, hitting .282 with 24 home runs and 65 RBI.

For the second consecutive season, the major leagues had a shortened schedule. The American League had 25,358,990 fans go through its turnstiles, and the National League welcomed 25,110,248. The Junior Circuit had regained the lead in the attendance race that the Senior Circuit had held the past two seasons. Baltimore led the way with 3,098,475 admissions.

Early in January 1996, discussions involving interleague play and the designated hitter were intertwined. The owners proposed to introduce interleague play in 1997 on a one-year trial basis in another effort to resurrect fan interest. Major League Baseball had received a "wake-up call" in 1995 when attendance fell approximately 20 percent after the game's longest strike. In 1993, which had been the most recent season with a normal 162-game schedule, teams in both leagues averaged 30,977 admissions per game. In 1995, when the strike shortened the season to a 144-game schedule, an average of 25,034 people came through the gates for each game.

The initial discussions about interleague play included the idea that the DH would be available for use in the American League parks, but not in the National League's. The approach was the same as the compromise that had been reached for the World Series and All-Star Games.

The Mariners' Edgar Martinez is on his way to becoming baseball's best-ever designated hitter (Ben Van Houten, the Seattle Mariners).

However, there were suggestions made by some that the introduction of interleague play would offer an excellent opportunity for the American League to eliminate the designated hitter. Their reasoning was that baseball would be balancing something new (interleague play) with a return to what had been normal for most of baseball's history, nine-man baseball.

John Harrington, chairman of the Boston Red Sox, who made the proposal to inaugurate interleague play, said, "We might be able to work out an arrangement by which the DH would be phased out over time."[6]

Atlanta Braves general manager John Schuerholz had worked for the Royals earlier in his career, and he had been involved with baseball in both the American and National Leagues. He spoke about the DH, saying, "I was a proponent of it when I was in the American League.... I thought it was good to keep popular aging star players around, but I don't think we need that now.... I think it's better for the esoteric nature of the game not to have it."[7]

In mid–January, the owners unanimously approved a plan for each club to play 15 or 16 games against teams from the corresponding geographic division in the other league. The MLBPA, which had watched the presence of designated hitters help generate income for players, had to approve the plan. The union gave different messages about where it stood with regard to interleague baseball and the DH. It indicated that it would not stand in the way of interleague play as long as designated hitters were not eliminated immediately. But there was an indication that the MLBPA might seek to have the DH used in all interleague games as a condition for approving the owners' plan.

Donald Fehr, the MLBPA's executive director, expressed concern that the unequal balance in the use of designated hitters could affect the outcome of the divisional races:

> Having the DH only in certain parks raises a whole host of questions. Since you're playing 15 games—six and nine or nine and six—that means some American League teams will have more games at home with the DH, and their rivals are going to have fewer games at home.[8]

During recent years, another factor had entered the DH debate. Some American League owners had come to view the presence of the designated hitter as a growing economic issue; the MLBPA saw it as a serious economic issue as well. The problem was that they viewed the DH from quite different perspectives. The owners saw the "10th men" as money "out," and the players saw them as money "in."

In 1995, figures for the average salaries by position (not median

salaries as was used in 1994) showed that the 10 full-time designated hitters in the league averaged $3.46 million, and they were second only to
first basemen, who were making $3.57 million per season.

Designated hitters had added significantly to club payrolls and, as
their salaries had risen, support for them among a number of American
League owners had dropped. Budig reported that in 1995 the league's owners had their most recent vote on the DH, and the result was a 7–7 tie.

Murray Chass, writing in the *New York Times*, examined part of the
National League's experiences without designated hitters:

> Do the devotees of hitting pitchers have Butch Henry and his .048 batting
> average last season in mind? Are they thinking of Mike Morgan and his
> .091 career average, Terry Mulholland and his .081 and Jeff Fassero and
> his .070 average? Or do they drool at the thought of watching Joey
> Hamilton strike out 38 times in 65 at-bats, Mark Leiter 33 times in 61
> times at-bat and Hideo Nomo 33 times in 66 tries? The futility of pitchers
> with bats in their hands is the most glaring argument in defense of the
> beleaguered designated hitter. While Seattle fans watch Edgar Martinez
> bat .360 [.356], hit 29 home runs and drive in 110 [113] runs as the Seattle
> Mariners' DH, Montreal fans watch Henry get 2 singles in 42 at-bats and
> Fassero 4 in 47....
>
> Of 51 pitchers who had 35 at-bats or more last season, 8 had averages
> that begin with a 0, 21 hit no higher that .111, 28 hit under .150 and 41
> didn't reach .200. Combined, the 51 pitchers had 407 hits and 990 strike-
> outs for a .153 batting average and a .373 strikeout average.
>
> All pitchers who batted struck out two and a half times for every hit
> they got: 609 hits for a .148 batting average and 1,569 strikeouts for a .381
> ratio.
>
> By comparison, the 180 players who served as designated hitters in
> the American League batted .276 with 2,118 hits and struck out 1,540
> times for a .020 strikeout ratio.[9]

There have been exceptions to Chass' portrait of pitchers, but they
have been few and far between. In 1995, Allen Watson, a left-hander for
the St. Louis Cardinals, had an outstanding season with the bat. He had
15 hits in 36 at-bats for a .417 average, with a .528 slugging average and
five RBI. Even with his success, he understood the problems facing some
hurlers when they are forced to go to bat. He said, "There are guys who
haven't hit their whole life.... Guys get traded from the American League
to the National League. They don't have a clue. It could be dangerous.
They could be standing there, not know how to react to a fastball in, get
hit and break their wrist or get hit in their face. It could happen."[10] Watson was with the San Francisco Giants in 1996 where his magic disappeared, and he hit .231. He was back in the American League with the
Angels the next season.

Shirley Povich, writing in *The Washington Post*, offered a different point of view about the DH:

> It was in 1973 that a new figure of speech crept into the language of baseball. Something called the "designated hitter." The game's vocabulary has expanded to allow for this new gimmick that has become a blight on the traditions of what for 134 years had been a nine-man game.
>
> The designated hitter obliterated what used to be one of the crisis points in the game. Would the manager lift the pitcher for a pinch hitter? Will he or won't he? Now, no more manager-on-the-spot. No more fan-surmise or speculation or second-guessing. The pitcher won't bat. He's now a eunuch in the batting corner. The DH will hit. That's it, the manager's refuge. Dullsville. Thanks also to the re-constituted role of the pitcher, the language of baseball has become an alien tongue.
>
> He is no longer a pitcher trained to go nine innings. He is (1) "in the rotation," meaning he's the starting pitcher; or (2) the "long relief" man [lowest in the game's new pecking order], who replaces the starter; or (3) "short relief," who ostensibly relieves long relief; or (4) the "setup man" [WOW!], who sets the stage for (5) "the closer" [the coup de grace executioner who is valued for his glower].[11]

Povitch also noted that the American League, where the designated hitter in its earlier days had enabled pitchers to stay in games and "go the route" more often, had also fallen victim to the new pitching pattern. He wrote, "In the American League last season, only every 13th game was a complete game. Tony LaRussa, last year with the Oakland A's and the manager most committed to the current pitching-surfing, used six pitchers in holding the Orioles to one run in a 3–1 game."[12] LaRussa was more often focused on going to the bullpen than letting his pitchers work out of jams. This was becoming a new trend in the DH league. It was an approach that many managers in the National League had lived by for a number of years.

The 1996 All-Star Game was played on July 9 in Veterans Stadium, Philadelphia. With the site being a National League ballpark, designated hitters were not in the lineups. Bobby Cox, manager of the Nationals, was dead-set against the DH, but he expressed a much different opinion about having it available in the All-Star Games—an opinion that had not been heard much from Senior Circuit skippers:

> I hate the DH. But for the All-Star Game it's a much needed tool for the manager because it's so much easier to manage with the DH. You don't have to do double switches, worry about this pitcher hitting, getting this guy in.... With the d.h., your whole plan can be laid out before the game starts.[13]

Budig was in Cox's corner, saying, "I think it [the DH] has special appeal for an All-Star Game…. I intend to raise it (the issue about using it in every All-Star Game). I'm going to talk to Len Coleman and Bud Selig about that possibility.[14]

During the season, the Orioles discovered that they had a potential DH for whom the role was not a smooth fit. Bobby Bonilla, who had come from the Mets during the 1994 season, was not pleased when it was suggested that he would not be a full-time defensive player. He said:

> The trouble is, I told the truth. I was asked about being the DH. I said I didn't like it. I didn't say I wouldn't do it. But I figured after hitting .190 for two months, it wasn't for me….
>   Molitor said he pretty much had to do it because of his arm. Edgar Martinez, if he picked up his glove he got hurt. They wouldn't let him pick up a glove anymore.[15]

Two of the major leagues' best outfielders had vastly different experiences at the end of their careers. Winfield had retired after the 1995 season with the Indians with a .283 career batting average. In the National League, another long-timer played his final season in 1996. Andre Dawson had made his major league debut on September 11, 1976, three years after Winfield. Winfield had played the final 14 of his 22 years in the majors in the American League, where the designated hitter had offered him the opportunity to extend his playing days. Dawson would finish a 21-year career, but would see action in the American League only in 1993 and 1994 when he was with the Red Sox. The rest of the time he played for the Expos, Chicago Cubs and Marlins. He would retire with a .279 batting average.

Both Winfield and Dawson came to the majors as excellent athletes. Both, over time, suffered the ravages from the pounding their legs and knees took while patrolling outfields and running the bases in major league ballparks. As their careers were coming to an end, Winfield found playing time with the Blue Jays, Twins, and Indians, and Dawson played out his days primarily with National League clubs.

For Dawson, there was something wrong with being in the lineup without playing in the field. He had tried it for two seasons with the Red Sox and it didn't feel right to him. He did not want "the few more years" that the designated hitter role had offered him. He said, "If I want to be a professional ballplayer, I want to do all the elements…. I would say eliminate it (the designated hitter) altogether. There's so much more strategy when a pitcher's hitting. And I don't think being a DH keeps you in the kind of physical shape you want to be in. Playing the game, you need that edge."[16]

Winfield, who estimated that 18 percent of his career would have been lost had the designated hitter not been available for him, commented:

> If you can keep good players around this game who for some reason or another are relegated to just hitting, that's an asset. What about Willie Mays? Willie McCovey? You can't tell me you wouldn't want to see them. When I was a young guy, I would have said, "Forget the DH," because I didn't know I'd be in a situation where it would be beneficial to me.[17]

A number of designated hitters had impressive campaigns in 1996. On September 16, the 40-year-old Molitor, who was now the Twins' DH after coming from the Blue Jays via free agency, joined the 3000-hit club when he tripled off Royals' rookie José Rosado in the fifth inning. He had set the stage for reaching the milestone when he singled off Rosado in the first inning. Molitor was in the midst of another excellent season in the designated hitter role. He was the Twins' DH in 143 games and was at first base in 17 other games. Molitor led the league in hits with 225, drove in 113 runs, and finished the season with a .341 average. As a designated hitter, he hit .340, with 200 hits, and 100 RBI. In December, he was named the Outstanding Designated Hitter for the second time.

Seattle's Martinez, the ODH winner the previous season, hit .327 with 26 homers and 103 RBI while playing as the club's DH in 134 games and being at first base in four and at third base in two other games. Baines, who was with the White Sox, having come from the Orioles for the 1996 season, had a .311 average and delivered 22 homers and drove in 95 runs, while Davis hit .292 with 28 homers and 95 RBI with the Angels. The Rangers' Juan Gonzalez repeated a feat accomplished by Jim Rice in 1978 and Don Baylor one season later when he was voted the league's Most Valuable Player while playing part of the campaign as a DH. Gonzalez appeared in 32 of his 134 games as the Rangers' designated hitter, and he batted .314 with 47 homers and 144 RBI for the season. The Red Sox' Reggie Jefferson was in the DH role in 49 games, played in the outfield in 45, and was at first in 16 others. The left-handed hitter put together a lofty .347 average, hit 19 homers and drove in 74 runs.

A pair of statistics from the 1996 season painted a picture about American League offenses. Hitters in the DH league posted a .445 slugging percentage, their highest to date. Pitchers in the league had a record of their own, but it was not one that they proudly extolled. Their composite ERA reached a lofty 5.00!

In October, the National League received a vote of confidence regarding its refusal to adopt the DH from a veteran of 14 seasons in the American League. Gary Gaetti, who was with the Twins from 1981 through 1990

and then played with the Angels and Royals, joined the Cardinals for the
1996 season and had been converted to the Senior Circuit's game. He said:

> I used to hate it. I couldn't stand to watch pitchers trying to hit, or when
> they would sacrifice with one out.
>   You can't believe how the offense of the game revolves around what
> happens with the pitcher and that ninth position in the lineup. I honestly
> think it's a better game.[18]

The plan for interleague play and the place of the designated hitter
in baseball's newest experiment was not finalized until the eighth Basic
Agreement was ratified by the owners and the MLBPA. The owners voted
to ratify the agreement on November 26, 1996, and the players did the
same on December 5. The new agreement was finally in place, more than
two years after the players walked off the job in August 1994.

The MLBPA's ratification came with a twist that promised additional
debate in the time ahead. The players' executive board gave the owners the
right to have interleague play in 1997 and 1998. They also said that the owners could increase the numbers of games in the second year of interleague
play, but only if they agreed to use the DH in all interleague games. The
"but only" addition to the plan promised to keep the two leagues in their
opposing places!

The 40-year-old Paul Molitor delivered his second ODH Award in 1996, this
time with the Twins (Minnesota Twins).

An article written about the 1996 season might have been titled "Interleague Play and the Designated Hitter." A sequel for the following season might have been: "Radical Realignment and the Designated Hitter."

In 1997, the major league owners engaged in lengthy discussions about the alignment of the two major leagues for the following season. The impetus for the discussions was the upcoming addition of two new teams—the Arizona Diamondbacks and the Tampa Bay Devil Rays—who would begin play in 1998. If one new team was put in each league, each league would be operating with 15 clubs, and that would create a scheduling nightmare. If that turned out to be the owners' final decision, the only way to accomplish it would be to schedule at least one interleague game each day. The owners were also searching for ways to control travel costs, which were an ever-increasing part of the teams' economic lives.

The first realignment plan had Arizona going to the National League West and Tampa Bay joining the American League East. During an American League owners' meeting on January 15, Texas and Kansas City executives voiced concerns about the plan. Texas wanted Arizona to join them in the American League West to provide another western franchise. Kansas City president Mike Herman wanted the owners to look at the big picture and consider a more massive restructuring approach.

A suggested radical realignment plan appeared early in the season, and it would have placed 14 teams in the American League and 16 in the National League. Teams would be grouped according to geography in an attempt to maximize rivalries and cut down on travel. The proposed geographical realignment offered a significant economic benefit for the Mariners, who were the majors' most distant travelers. It was estimated that they would fly 50,000 miles during the 1997 regular season.

There were a number of permutations this type of plan that attempted to meet the goals of maximizing rivalries and cutting down on travel. One approach divided the National League into two eight-team divisions—the National League West and National League Central. The Western division would include Anaheim, Arizona, Colorado, Los Angeles, Oakland, San Diego, San Francisco, and Seattle. The Central Division would include the two Chicago teams, Houston, Kansas City, Milwaukee, Minnesota, St. Louis, and Texas.

The American League Eastern I would have seven teams including Baltimore, Boston, Montreal, the two New York teams, Philadelphia, and Toronto. The American League Eastern II also had seven teams, and it would be made up of Atlanta, Cincinnati, Cleveland, Detroit, Florida, Pittsburgh, and Tampa Bay.

The subject of the designated hitter was central to the discussions about the realignment plans. As was the case with interleague play, the options for the DH were to eliminate it, use it in both leagues, or to retain it for use only in the American League. The third option appeared to be the most realistic if realignment was to take place for the 1998 season.

An examination of the four proposed divisions shows that 15 teams would have a new relationship with the designated hitter if it were to continue to be used only in the American League. Seven previously National League clubs would have designated hitters in their lineups as American Leaguers, and eight previously American League teams would be playing without them.

The current National League teams that would have designated hitters under the proposed realignment plan:

Atlanta Braves	New York Mets
Cincinnati Reds	Philadelphia Phillies
Florida Marlins	Pittsburgh Pirates
Montreal Expos	

The current American League teams that would not have designated hitters under the proposed realignment plan:

Anaheim Angels	Minnesota Twins
Chicago White Sox	Oakland Athletics
Kansas City Royals	Seattle Mariners
Milwaukee Brewers	Texas Rangers

Three of the current long-term designated hitters would find themselves in the non–DH league. Seattle's Martinez, Minnesota's Molitor, and Kansas City's Davis would all be National Leaguers under the plan. Molitor was already considering retirement after the 1997 season, but Martinez had a two-year, $4 million commitment remaining with Seattle, and Davis' career still had two years remaining before retirement would arrive.

NINE

Interleague Play

The 1997 season offered a number of National Leaguers an opportunity to be "the 10th man" in interleague games. When it was certain that interleague play would be on the schedule and designated hitters would be used in the American League parks, National League managers and others in the organizations began to examine their rosters to identify the players who were most suited for the role. Clubs took different approaches in the decision-making process.

The Philadelphia Phillies quickly identified Darren Daulton, a catcher and first baseman, whose mobility had been limited by nine knee surgeries but who still swung a good bat. The Atlanta Braves' Ryan Klesko was troubled by a bad back, and short respites from playing left field could benefit him. The Los Angeles Dodgers' Mike Piazza could move from behind the plate for a few games and still add offense to the lineup. The Colorado Rockies' Dante Bichette, who was returning from reconstructive surgery on his left knee, could find the DH role inviting.

Some clubs were looking to use players who brought some experience as designated hitters, having been in the role with teams in the American League. The Chicago Cubs had Dave Clark and the Montreal Expos could use Sherman Obando and Joe Orsulak. Although Jim Eisenreich had not been a DH in the American League, he had been a very successful pinch-hitter coming off the bench and that ability was translated into "DH time" by the Florida Marlins.

Managers of other teams were viewing interleague play as an opportunity to rest players from defensive duties on a day-to-day basis. Some skippers were planning to use "the 10th man" as an extra left-handed hitter in the lineup against a right-handed pitcher and vice versa.

The following players were the first designated hitters for their clubs during interleague play in 1997:

Atlanta Braves	Keith Lockhart
Chicago Cubs	Dave Clark
Cincinnati Reds	Eddie Taubensee
Colorado Rockies	Dante Bichette
Florida Marlins	Jim Eisenreich
Houston Astros	Sean Berry
Los Angeles Dodgers	Mike Piazza
Montreal Expos	José Vidro
New York Mets	Butch Huskey
Philadelphia Phillies	Darren Daulton
Pittsburgh Pirates	Mark Smith
St. Louis Cardinals	Dmitri Young
San Diego Padres	Rickey Henderson
San Francisco Giants	Glenallen Hill

American League managers had to deal with the flip side of the designated hitter situation. When an interleague game was played in a National League park, they had to decide whether to slip the DH into the regular lineup at a defensive position or find a place for him on the bench. Joe Torre, the New York Yankees' manager, was caught in a weighty dilemma for his first-ever interleague game on June 13 against the Marlins in Florida. He decided to bench first baseman Tino Martinez, his most productive hitter, and replace him with Cecil Fielder, the club's regular DH. The game went 12 innings before the Marlins won it, 2–1. Fielder was walked four consecutive times by the Marlin pitchers. After his fourth base on balls, Pat Kelly came into the game as a pinch-runner for him. Martinez finished the game at first base, going 0–for–2.

The 1997 All-Star Game was played on July 8 in Jacobs Field, Cleveland. In an interview, Torre, the manager of the American League club who had spent 18 years as a National Leaguer, saw the value of the designated hitter during spring training and in All-Star games, but he gave a greater vote of approval to the league without the DH:

> Without the DH, there's much more for the fans to second guess, and there are many more decisions for managers to make. That's what makes the game of baseball. This is not football, basketball or hockey, where you put in plays that have to be executed. This is more a game of strategy.[1]

Seattle's Edgar Martinez became the first designated hitter to be voted into the All-Star Game by the fans. He had been in three Mid-Summer Classics, in 1992, 1995, and 1996, but he had gotten to those games by being added to the roster by the manager. Now that "designated hitter" had a place in the lineup and appeared on the ballot, he was the fans' choice to fill it.

Martinez, who had been 0–for–5 in the three previous games, led off the second inning with a home run off Atlanta's Greg Maddux to give the Americans a 1–0 lead. He singled in his other at-bat as the American Leaguers went on to pick up a 3–1 win.

Discussions about realignment continued throughout the season. Interim commissioner Bud Selig was still pushing the radical realignment plan. On August 6, he said, "Nobody is more traditional than me. But this could be spectacular for baseball. You walk this very fine line between the history and the tradition of the game and the need to get the game ready for the 21st century."[2]

In late August, I found myself in the midst of the debate about radical realignment. At the time, I was doing research about the MacPhail family — Larry, Lee, and Andy — in preparation for writing *The MacPhails; Baseball's First Family of the Front Office.* I met with Selig in his Milwaukee office after having spent time two days earlier with Andy MacPhail, the Cubs' CEO and president, in Chicago.

Although examination of the realignment plan was not the purpose of the meeting with Selig, after we discussed his experiences with Lee and Andy MacPhail, he shared a few of his thoughts. He was especially excited about the opportunities to develop thrilling geographic rivalries that would result from playing 93 to 96 games each season against teams in one's own division. He also had a dream about developing a special type of competition in those places where two teams were in close proximity to each other, such as in Chicago, in New York, in San Francisco and Oakland, and in the Los Angeles area. He reminisced about the memorable rivalry that had existed in New York when the Brooklyn Dodgers went to battle against the

Baseball Commissioner Bud Selig was excited about the proposed "Radical Realignment Plan" (National Baseball Hall of Fame Library, Cooperstown, NY).

New York Giants, either in Ebbets Field or in the Polo Grounds. He envisioned the same excitement and competition developing in the rivalries between the Cubs and the White Sox in Chicago, between the Yankees and the Mets in New York, between the Giants and the Athletics in the Bay Area, and between the Dodgers and the Angels in the Los Angeles area.

My meeting with MacPhail took place the day before he was to be visited by Selig, who wanted to convince him about the benefits of the proposed radical realignment plan. MacPhail had been the general manager of the 1987 and 1991 World Champion Minnesota Twins. He was the son of Lee MacPhail, who had been one of the earliest proponents of the designated hitter while he was a Baltimore Oriole and Yankee executive and later the American League president.

There were a number of reasons why Andy MacPhail was not a proponent of radical realignment. Interleague play was in its first season, and he thought that it would be wise to see how that went before launching into another major change. He also was not enamored about having the Chicago White Sox in the same division as the Cubs. He certainly didn't buy Selig's excitement about that part of the plan. MacPhail asked, "How does it help the Chicago baseball fan if all the same teams come into Wrigley Field and then go play 9 miles south (at Comiskey Park)?"[3]

The Cubs' fans had not caught the thrill of a city rivalry. In the first season of interleague play, the Cubs played the White Sox in a three-game series in Comiskey Park. The schedule would be reversed the following summer when the White Sox would travel north to Wrigley Field for a three-game set. In 1997, the White Sox introduced a ticket package for the three games in Comiskey Park that was aimed at discouraging Cubs fans from going to the Sox' ballpark. The ticket plan, which was dubbed "Four Packs," required that anyone who wanted to purchase a ticket to one of the three games between the Cubs and the White Sox had to also buy three tickets to other games on the schedule that would be designated by the White Sox. Rob Gallas, the team's senior vice-president for marketing and broadcasting, said:

> The whole idea of this is to keep the Cubs fans out…. It's no big deal for White Sox fans to buy tickets for four games. Last year we wound up with a lot of Cleveland fans in the park for both series with the Indians. You could hear them, and we lost a little of the home-field advantage. We didn't want that happening with the Cubs.[4]

MacPhail, who had seen the DH in action during his seasons with the Twins, was no longer an advocate of the designated hitter, and he feared that it was possible that realignment might eventually bring the "10th man" to both leagues. MacPhail spoke about how he viewed the situation:

With radical realignment, the likelihood is you're going to have the DH in baseball in both leagues. This is not something that I personally or the overwhelming amount of our fans support. When my father [Lee] brought it in, his context and his day made it perfect. The leading hitter was batting .301, you had earned run averages in the ones, and you really weren't scoring enough runs. We've expanded, the parks are getting smaller, the players are getting bigger and stronger, and we have all the offense we need. The reason for bringing the DH is gone. We just don't have the problem we made the alteration for. In its time it served its purpose. I'm not advocating eliminating it totally. But what I'm advocating is keeping the leagues' rules separate.[5]

MacPhail also believed that Selig's plan carried realignment too far and too fast:

You need to preserve what you have, and Interleague play is O.K. on a regional basis, on a limited basis but not beyond that. To me, we have taken an historic step in the past year. There is no hurry to radically realign everything else now just because the initial reaction was good. Let's just let this play out and see what sticks and what doesn't.[6]

On August 29, the owners made a proposal regarding the designated hitter. Only time would tell whether it would bear any more fruit than the earlier proposals. Management negotiator Randy Levine told Donald Fehr, executive director of the Major League Baseball Players Association, that management wanted to eliminate the designated hitter in three to five years. The length of time before the action would be taken was a subject for discussion between the Player Relations Committee and the MLBPA. *The Houston Chronicle* reported:

in exchange for the union's agreement to eliminate the DH, owners would expand active rosters from 25 to 26. The DH would not be eliminated immediately; instead, it would disappear several years after the agreement so veteran DHs could complete their careers, and AL teams and pitchers could prepare.[7]

In response to the proposal, Fehr said, "Our position on the DH is well-known, and I see no reason to change it."[8] The players association found a significant problem with the proposal and ultimately rejected it. Although it would bring 30 more players from the minor leagues to the majors, those players would no doubt be on the low end of the economic ladder, with many drawing the minimum salary. They would have replaced a number of high-salaried designated hitters, and that change would provide a huge economic boost for the owners.

Sportswriter Bob Costas, who had been mentioned as a possible candidate for baseball commissioner, applauded the owners' proposal:

> A clue to the thinking that baseball needs more of can be found in the owners' innovative approach to eliminating the DH. The owners have proposed to the players association that the DH be phased out over time, with a permanent extra roster spot added in return. This offer is so fair and reasonable the players association ought to be embarrassed to reject it.
>
> It's further proof [as if any were needed] the players association, which once owned the moral high ground and fought for fair and honorable goals, is now committed to little more than greed. The players association is run by intelligent and honest people, but that's not the same as being reasonable. And it has become too easy to confuse stubborn self-interest with integrity....
>
> The owners are on the right track with their offer to trade jobs for concessions. The shame is they arrived at this approach so late. Had they divined this kind of solution for the DH four years ago, it might have led them to a larger vision that would have given them a chance to accomplish something significant in their last disastrous go-round with the players.
>
> So for the time being, the answers are direct: Don't make major moves with long-term implications just to address relatively minor problems. Make changes when the best chance exists to do so intelligently and permanently. For now, work on negotiating a phase-out of the DH, put major realignment on ice until the next round of expansion and keep interleague play as a limited but significant part of baseball's future.[9]

When it appeared that the radical realignment plan would not garner enough votes for acceptance, National League president Leonard Coleman presented a revised proposal. The Coleman Plan would require seven to nine teams to switch leagues rather than the 15 that would be moved under Selig's original proposal. The new approach also did away with same-city rivalries in New York and Chicago. The Yankees and the White Sox would remain in the American League, and the New York Mets and the Cubs would stay in the National League. According to the plan, the White Sox would play in the American League South, and the Mets would be the only National League team in the Eastern time zone. Coleman's proposal would bring about change in 1998, but it would not reach the level that had been envisioned in Selig's radical realignment plan.

Interleague play in 1997 — Advantage, the National League! American League teams took the lead after the first round, winning 48 of the 84 games played. However, by season's end, the National Leaguers held the edge with a 117–97 record. The Marlins and the Expos both had 12–3 records against their American League opponents, and the Texas Rangers'

10–6 mark led their league. The Senior Circuit had a .273 batting average in interleague games compared with the Junior Circuit's .260 mark. The Nationals led in runs scored, 1,007–994, and the Americans had the most home runs, 229–220. Martinez led both leagues in hitting with a .475 average, and the San Diego Padres' Wally Joyner batted .442.

Lou Gorman, a long-time Boston Red Sox executive, commented about the designated hitter and how interleague play had raised a concern about it:

> Yes, I believe the designated hitter has brought more offense to the game. It changed the strategy of the game for the managers of both clubs. The purists would say "yes" the leagues suffer by playing by different rules. In interleague play it impacts the A.L. clubs dramatically in a negative way.
>
> I don't think that the N.L. will adopt the DH. The A.L. may eventually give it up. Whether for better or worse I don't know, but it's only a matter of time.[10]

Seattle's Martinez picked up the 1997 Outstanding Designated Hitter Award for the second time in three years, having also won it in 1995. He batted .330 with 35 doubles, 28 home runs, 108 RBI, and collected 119 walks. Martinez received 71 of the 84 first-place votes, and Kansas City's Chili Davis, who was in his seventh season as a fulltime designated hitter, was the choice on the remaining 13 ballots. Davis batted .279 with 30 homers and 90 RBI.

Other designated hitters had productive seasons and were at the top of the list of those who had excelled in the role. Reggie Jefferson hit .319 for the Red Sox in 119 games as a DH and 12 games as a first baseman. David Justice, who was with Cleveland in his first year in the American League after eight seasons with Atlanta, was in the outfield in 78 games and was the Cleveland Indians' DH in 61 others. The left-handed hitter posted a .329 average to go along with 33 home runs and 101 RBI. Minnesota's Paul Molitor finished above the .300 mark again, hitting .305. The Rangers had Juan Gonzalez in the outfield for 64 games and put him in the DH spot in 69 others. His combined batting average was .296, and he smacked 42 homers and drove in 131 runs.

Harold Baines divided his season between Chicago and Baltimore, with a combined .301 average. A week before the July 31 trade deadline, White Sox' general manager Ron Schueler worked out a deal with general manager Pat Gillick of the Baltimore Orioles, but it almost fell apart before it happened. Orioles' owner Peter Angelos was in agreement with the trade, but his sons John and Louis, who trusted the astrological signs, were opposed. They said, "No, no, no. You can't do that. It's not in the stars."[11]

Fortunately, the stars aligned in time for the deal to be finalized and for Baines to head to Baltimore for a player to be named later.

Baines hailed from nearby St. Michaels, Maryland, and Schueler was giving him an opportunity to play in the postseason with his "hometown" team. Baines was the left-handed DH in the postseason, and Geronimo Berroa faced the left-handed pitchers, swinging from the right side of the plate. Baines hit .364 with two home runs and three RBI in eight post-season games with the Orioles, who won the American League Division Series but lost to the Indians, 4 games to 2, in the American League Championship Series.

Baines, who was in his 18th major league season, had received great acclaim for his conduct off the field and for the way he had played the game. Schueler's desire for Baines to play in the postseason was an example of that respect. Shortly before the trade, White Sox' manager Terry Bevington described Baines, saying, "He handles and conducts himself in a professional manner ... all the time and not some of the time. And as a manager, you appreciate that. And he's also a very good hitter. Possible Hall of Famer. That pretty much speaks for itself.[12]

Tom Grieve, who had been the Rangers' general manager when Baines was with the club, spoke about his qualities:

> The thing that's most impressive about Harold is how steady he is.... He's not flashy. He's not loud. You hardly know he's around. But when there's men on base and he comes up, you say, "Oh, no. Here comes Harold." You look up, and he's always hitting around .300 and getting a key RBI.[13]

Another designated hitter was near the top of another list. The Yankees' Fielder, who had hit. 260 with eight home runs and 81 RBI as the team's DH in 87 games and as the first baseman in eight others, was in second place on the 1997 salary list. Fielder earned $9,237,500, and he was topped only by White Sox' outfielder Albert Belle, whose salary was $10 million. The league's seven full-time designated hitters earned an average salary of $3,358,788, and they were surpassed only by first basemen, who earned $3.7 million annually.

American League batters topped the National League hitters once again, going .271 compared with the non–DH league's .263.

Attendance increased in the majors, although the leagues didn't reach the record-setting high of 1993, when 70.3 million fans had made their way into the ballparks. During the first season of interleague play, the National League had 31.9 million fans go through its turnstiles and the American League had 31.3 million people in their parks for a grand total of 63.2 million. Attendance averaged 33,407 fans during interleague play, a 20.2 percent increase over the intraleague average of 27,800.

Both leagues had three teams with more than three million admissions. The National League was topped by Colorado, Atlanta, and Los Angeles, and the American League was led by Baltimore, Cleveland, and Seattle. Attendance in Philadelphia (1,490,638) was the lowest in the Senior Circuit, but Oakland, Minnesota, and Milwaukee of the DH league posted lower attendance figures than the Phillies. The last place Oakland Athletics of the American League West, with 1,264,218 paid admissions, had the smallest draw in the major leagues.

Early in the postseason, Indians' general manager John Hart, a longtime advocate of the designated hitter, said that the first two games of the ALDS between the Cleveland and New York were what baseball was intended to be. In the opener in Yankee Stadium, the Yanks had an 8–6, come-from-behind victory, and the next night Cleveland won, 7–5, in the same fashion. An exuberant Hart said, "This is America. People want to see the ball bouncing around the ballpark. I think it says a lot about the DH vs. the pitcher hitting. In the National League series, you had the intrigue of watching the manager make a double-switch for the pitcher. I hope the right people were watching."[14]

The Indians beat the Yankees, 3 games to 2, to capture one of the division series, and then they topped the Orioles, the other ALDS winner, in a six-game set for the American League pennant. Justice went a combined 12–for–40 in the two series for a .300 average.

Going into the 1997 World Series, National League teams had benefited more than American League teams from the DH rule. The trend began in 1976, which was the first season that designated hitters appeared in the Fall Classic. That year, and for some years to follow, the DH was only in action in the World Series in alternating seasons. The Cincinnati Reds' Dan Driessen went 5–for–14, including a home run and a double in his club's four-game sweep of the Yankees. Since then, the Senior Circuit's "10th men" had batted .270 compared to .238 for the Junior Circuit's DHs.

That pattern continued when Cleveland met Florida in the 1997 Fall Classic. Designated hitters were now being used in every World Series, but only in American League parks. The Marlins, who had finished in second place in the National League East and had battled to capture the league's pennant, beat the Indians in seven games to become the first wild-card World Champions. They used a stable of designated hitters in the three games in Cleveland. Kurt Abbott, Alex Arias, Daulton (who had been acquired from the Phillies for the stretch run), Eisenreich, and Cliff Floyd all had DH after their names in the box scores. Eisenreich went 4–for–5,

Daulton was 2–for–5, and the others went 0–for–2. Their combined average was a lofty .500. Justice was in the outfield for four games and in the DH spot for three others for Cleveland. He struggled offensively, going 5–for–27 for a .185 average.

The major issues of the past two seasons came together in 1998 to form a triangle — interleague play, realignment, and the designated hitter. On April 4, management sent word to the MLBPA that they might eliminate the designated hitter after the 1998 season. The owners viewed this action as a rule change which they had the right to do as long as the union was given a one-year notice that it was going to happen. The MLBPA believed that the removal of the DH did not represent a rule change but was rather a change in working conditions that could not be effected without their approval. The courts could eventually become the arbiter on this significant difference of opinion.

Ken Singleton, who had retired from the Orioles in 1984 after playing 477 games as a designated hitter at the end of his career, weighed in on the question about the future of the DH, stating, "The DH is like a sad old veteran who hung around too long. It's time to retire it."[15]

Management's "shot across the bow" was greeted by a retaliatory strike from the players union. They took the opportunity to remind the owners that baseball was in the second and final year of interleague play, and a continuation of the "experiment" required approval of the MLBPA. Interleague play, especially those featuring geographic rivalries such as the Mets and Yankees, the Cubs and White Sox, the Dodgers and Anaheim Angels, and the San Francisco Giants and Athletics, had been cash cows for the owners, and they were intent on having them continued. The players' bargaining chip was retention of the designated hitter.

As so often happens in baseball, the final realignment changes were minimal. There was neither radical realignment nor even moderate realignment. There was neither the Selig plan nor the Coleman plan. The 1998 season would have the same three-division structure in each league that had been in place since 1994. Arizona joined the National League West and Tampa Bay was placed in the American League East. To avoid having two 15-team leagues, Selig took his Milwaukee Brewers from the American League Central to the National League Central. The move gave the National League 16 clubs. The American League remained with 14. Only one designated hitter was displaced as a result of the realignment. The Brewers' Julio Franco, who had finished the 1997 season in the role with Milwaukee, was out of a job. He retired after 15 major league seasons.

In 1998, two more players joined the list of those who had served as their teams' first designated hitters. Paul Sorrento was in the role in Tampa

Bay's opener against Detroit on March 31. Arizona's Kelly Stinnett had to wait until June 5 to be a designated hitter in the National League, when the Diamondbacks were in Oakland to play the Athletics in Arizona's first interleague game.

Phil Garner, the manager of the now DH–less Milwaukee Brewers of the National League, spoke in favor of the owners' right to eliminate the designated hitter. After having the DH at his disposal for the seven seasons while he was the manager of the American League Brewers, Garner raised the economic element, saying, "Why shouldn't management be allowed to cut costs? This is a business. They're in it to make money. Most teams would just take the money and spend it on another player, anyway, but why shouldn't owners be allowed to cut costs?"[16]

The owners kept the realignment question alive, and indicated that what they had in mind for the future was a major change in the makeup of the leagues rather than the cosmetic adjustments they had made for 1998. With some clubs destined to go to a different league, the designated hitter's place in the changing realignment scenery would become an important topic for consideration.

The 1998 All-Star game was held on July 7, in Denver's Coors Field, the home of the Rockies. With the game in a National League park, designated hitters were absent from the lineups. However, *The Denver Rocky Mountain News* used the occasion to ask the All-Stars whether or not the DH should be abolished. The vote of the players was 45–7, with six abstentions, to retain the designated hitter.[17] Clearly, the top players in both leagues stood on the side of the DH.

Two days later the owners voted 30–0 to remove the term "interim" from Selig's position, and he became baseball's ninth commissioner. They also approved a schedule for the 1999 season that that included a slight increase in the number of interleague games. The schedule was also "unbalanced," meaning that teams would play more games against teams in their own division and fewer games against the clubs in the other divisions in their league.

Martinez had another stellar season with the Mariners and picked up his third Outstanding Designated Hitter Award. He was in the DH role in 147 games, and he played first base in four of the interleague games. Martinez led the league with a .433 on-base percentage and batted .322 with 29 homers, 46 doubles, and 102 RBI.

Two players, Tim Salmon and Matt Stairs, were in the DH role for the first time because of injuries. The Angels' Salmon suffered a partially torn plantar fascia ligament in his left foot that limited him to playing only 19 games in the outfield and had him in the lineup as the DH in 111 games. He swung a good bat throughout the season, hitting .300 with 26 home runs and 88 RBI. Salmon's injury, which led to him becoming Ana-heim's DH, put Fielder, who had been acquired from the Yankees, at first base. Late in the season Fielder joined the Indians and played out the final season of his major league career.

Oakland's 5-foot-9-inch, left-handed swinging Stairs was in the outfield for 12 games, at first base for six, and in the DH role for 120 games. Stairs injured his right shoulder on April 21 in a collision with Molitor, and he was limited to DH duty most of the remainder of the season. He had a .294 average for the campaign, and he added 26 home runs and 106 RBI to the Athletics' offense.

The White Sox' Frank Thomas, who had played first base in 97 games and was the club's designated hitter 49 others in 1997, was the primary DH in 1998. He was back at first base for the interleague games in National League ballparks. For the season, the right-handed hitting Thomas batted .265 with 29 homers and 109 RBI.

José Canseco split the season between designated hitter (78 games) and outfielder (73 games) for the Toronto Blue Jays, batting only .237, but slamming 46 home runs and driving in 107 runs. Baines remained in Bal-timore and hit .300 in 80 games with the Orioles. Molitor batted .281 in 115 games as a DH and nine at first base.

Following the 1998 campaign with the Twins, Molitor retired with a career .306 average for 21 seasons. Looking back at his time as a designated hitter, Molitor said:

> My approach was the same [as a DH] in preparing for opposing pitchers, but I would prepare differently between at bats. There was time because of not playing defense.
>
> [Being a DH] took away risk of injury on defensive side. I was injury prone, but I could be a force offensively. [It] gave me time to concentrate on offense. [It] prolonged my career.
>
> [Did it help or hinder the quality of baseball?] [That is] always to be debated. Do you want offense or tradition?[18]

The American League hitters had a 10-point advantage on the National League that season. The Junior Circuit's batters hit a combined .272 and the Senior Circuit's posted a .262 average.

Jack McKeon, who came out of retirement during the 2003 season to manage the Florida Marlins to a World Championship, had managed the Cincinnati Reds in 1998 after having been at the helm of the Kansas City Royals, A's, and Padres. He was not a fan of the DH:

I like National League strategy. It makes the other manager make decisions. It makes pitchers learn how to hit and bunt in order to help themselves. Managing in the American League, I made less decisions, especially in pitching changes [do you pinch-hit for a pitcher in a close game?]. Do not have to double switch.[19]

Jack McKeon has managed in both leagues. Here the skipper of the 2003 World Champion Florida Marlins is shown during his time with the Royals (Kansas City Royals).

In 1998, Major League Baseball set an all-time attendance record of 70,339,808, but it took 30 teams to accomplish it. The addition of Arizona and Milwaukee to the National League's ranks helped them build a 6.5 million advantage over the DH league. The Senior Circuit's lead was the largest they had ever had over the Junior Circuit, whose gains during the DH era appeared to have run out of gas.

The Yankees and the Padres met in the 1998 World Series. Prior to the start of the Fall Classic, the annual debate was renewed about whether the National or American League team had more to gain or lose as a result of the designated hitter rule. Logic seemed to favor the Padres since they were used to playing without the DH, and their pitchers had experience going to the plate during the regular season.

Padres' manager Bruce Bochy wasn't sure they held an advantage over the Yankees when they played in their own ballpark. He noted that New York manager Joe Torre had played and managed in the National League:

> We feel we have a couple of good DH candidates in Greg Vaughn and [Jim] Leyritz and it's going to take a bat out of our lineup, too. [Yankee starter] David Cone has played in the National League and he's swung a bat before. So I don't know that it's going to give us the advantage that some people are talking about.[20]

The Yankees made short work of the Padres in the World Series, sweeping San Diego in four games. The Padres' designated hitters, Leyritz and Greg Vaughn, contributed nothing to their club's offense, going

0–for–8. The veteran Davis was the Yankees' designated hitter in the first two games of the series that were played in Yankee Stadium. The 38-year-old DH had made his way from Kansas City to New York in 1998 via free agency and had signed a $9.8 million, three-year deal with the Yanks. He saw only limited service (35 games) during the regular season because of surgery to reconstruct tendons and ligaments in his right ankle. He went 2–for–7 (.286) in the pair of games played in the American League park. The Padres' pitchers outperformed the Yankees' hurlers when they were in the batter's box. Both Sterling Hitchcock and Kevin Brown had 1–for–2 games for San Diego and only David Cone matched that for New York.

Red Sox general manger Dan Duquette added a number of new players to his club's roster prior to the 1999 season. Two of them were potential designated hitters, and they were in line to split time with Jefferson, who had filled the role and played some first base since 1995. The Red Sox paid José Offerman $26 million over four years. The 30-year-old Offerman, who had signed as a free agent, had led the Royals with a .315 average and had 45 stolen bases in 1998. He had played shortstop, second base, and first base in his major league career that had begun with the Dodgers in 1990. Offerman came to the Red Sox with seven games as a designated hitter on his résumé. Manager Jimy Williams' believed that Offerman's defensive skills made him a better candidate for first base or designated hitter than at second base or shortstop. The opening at first base had been created when Mo Vaughn took his eight-year Boston career and .304 batting average to the Angels by way of free agency.

Brian Daubach, who came to the Red Sox with much less experience than Offerman, was the second acquisition who was a possible designated hitter and first base candidate. He was a nine-year minor leaguer when he was called up by the Marlins near the end of the 1998 season. The power-hitting left-hander was batting .316 with 35 homers and 124 RBI at the time of his recall from Triple-A Charlotte. He played in 10 games with the Marlins at the end of the season. He went 3–for–15 in his short stint with Florida.

Like many clubs, the Red Sox had a history of using a number of players as designated hitters. They had begun the DH era in 1973 with Orlando Cepeda as the primary player in the role, but they had spread the responsibility around during many of the seasons that followed. That would be the case in 1999 when Jefferson was the DH in 58 games, Daubach was there for 48, and Offerman was in the role in 18 games.

As the third season of interleague play approached, a number of full-time designated hitters would probably miss the games played in the

National League parks. That could be as many as nine games. The list included:

Anaheim	Mo Vaughn (recovering from an ankle injury)
Baltimore	Harold Baines
Detroit	Gregg Jefferies
New York	Chili Davis
Seattle	Edgar Martinez
Tampa Bay	José Canseco
Texas	Rafael Palmeiro (recovering from an knee injury)
Toronto	Dave Hollins

Tampa Bay's Canseco was an interesting case. The 35-year-old much-traveled ex-outfielder had come to the Devil Rays via free agency from Oakland after the 1998 season when he hit .237 with 46 homers and 107 RBI. He had been signed to a one-year, $2 million, incentive-laden contract for 1999, with Tampa Bay holding options for 2000 and 2001.

Canseco and Mark McGwire had been Oakland's "Bash Brothers" during the latter part of the 1980s. Early in his career, Canseco added defensive prowess and speed to his power-hitting ability. In 1988, he became the majors' first "40–40 man" when he hit 42 home runs and stole 40 bases. Along the way, injuries, off-the-field problems, and defensive difficulties that were heightened by a diminished interest in playing in the field had turned Canseco into a one-dimensional player — a hitter. The DH role was invented for players like him. He had outdistanced all designated hitters in the number of home runs hit by a designated hitter. His immediate goal was to hit 500 career homers and then possibly have his ticket punched for entrance into the Hall of Fame. All 14 of the previous 500-home-run hitters had been inducted into baseball's shrine. Canseco's dream was loftier than that — he was reaching for 600. He said, "If I stay healthy for the next five years, there's no reason I shouldn't hit 600. But it's all about health. To me, health equals home runs. It's as simple as that."[21]

Canseco was 103 home runs short of 500 at the conclusion of the 1998 season. If he were to reach the 500 mark, it was estimated that half of them would have come while he was an outfielder and the other half would have been produced while he was a DH. That raised a question about how the 500-home-run test for Hall of Fame membership would stand up when the DH role had been so central to its accomplishment. Reggie Jackson's 101 homers from the DH spot in the lineup was the highest number that had been hit by a member of the 500-Home-Run Club.

Canseco was chosen by the fans to be the American League's designated hitter in the 1999 All-Star Game on July 13 in Boston's Fenway Park. It was the sixth time that he was slated to be in the Mid-Summer Classic, but it became the third time he ended up missing it because of injury. Just days before the game he underwent surgery to repair a herniated disk. At the time, he was leading the league with 31 home runs. Canseco returned later in the campaign and finished the season with 34 homers and 95 RBI. He appeared in 109 games as a DH and was in the outfield in six others.

Baltimore's Baines replaced the injured Canseco on the All-Star team, and he made his sixth appearance in the games. The 40-year-old Baines came into the game batting .345 with 19 home runs and 63 RBI for the first half of the season. He singled in his one plate appearance.

Baines changed teams again on August 27 when he was traded to the Indians for a minor leaguer and a player to be named later. Baines finished the season with a combined .312 average with 25 home runs and 103 runs driven in. He was 217 hits short of reaching a special goal — 3000 hits.

After the trade to the Indians, the much-traveled Baines, who had one-year contracts for the past 10 seasons, spoke about his goals:

> I could[n't] care less [about recognition]. Personally, I don't need it. The biggest thing to me is the respect of my peers, and I have that.
> I've always just tried to hit the ball where it is pitched and hopefully, when I hit it, nobody will be standing in front of it. There's no major science involved.[22]

Over in the National League, a long-timer was seeking to reach the 3000-hit mark without benefit of the DH rule. Tony Gwynn, who was in his 18th major league season — all of them with the Padres— registered his 3000th hit on August 6 in Montreal's Olympic Stadium. In his first at-bat, Gwynn lined a hit past second base on a pitch from Montreal rookie Dan Smith for #3000. He added three more hits before his work for the day was finished. Gwynn became the 22nd major leaguer and the first National Leaguer in 20 years to accomplish the feat. The St. Louis Cardinals' Lou Brock had reached the milestone in 1979. Gwynn had beaten a pair of American Leaguers— Wade Boggs and Cal Ripken — who were closing in on the 3000-hit mark. Both Boggs and Ripken had played in the field throughout their careers, but the last seven players before Gwynn to reach 3000 hits— Carl Yastrzemski, Rod Carew, Robin Yount, George Brett, Dave Winfield, Eddie Murray, and Paul Molitor — had all extended their careers as designated hitters.

Gwynn commented about the aid provided to American Leaguers, saying, "I'm not trying to downplay what guys have done in the American League, but if you've got a ding, you can always DH over there. I'm proud as heck of doing this in the NL. And really proud to be following a player like Lou Brock."[23]

Brock, who was in attendance when Gwynn hit #3000, added his thoughts, commenting, "The designated hitter has been the vehicle that allows many players nearing the end of their careers to maintain some longevity. They were not out there on a daily basis, subject to the aches and pains of playing in the field. In the National League, you have to do it the hard way.[24]

In 1999, an article titled "Centralization and the Designated Hitter" could have been written as a follow-up to those that might have been penned during recent seasons—"Interleague Play and the Designated Hitter" (1996) and "Radical Realignment and the Designated Hitter" (1997). The designated hitter seemed to always be in the mix whenever change was discussed.

Selig revealed plans for centralizing the governing powers of Major League Baseball. Baseball matters would be decided in the commissioner's office as had been done for many years in the National Football League and in the National Basketball Association. Beginning in 2000, the offices of the presidents of the American and National Leagues would be abolished, and the existence of separate American and National League umpires would go the way of the presidents. Player discipline and scheduling, which had both been under the aegis of the league offices, would now come under control of the commissioner's office. On September 15, in Cooperstown, NY, the owners voted 30–0 to approve the changes.

In September, Selig used the issue of consolidation to again raise the question of major realignment, and he also said that the designated hitter would be eliminated sometime in the near future. A centralized baseball structure seemed to be consistent with having both leagues play by the same rules. The pair of realities affecting a change in the DH rule continued to be the strong belief that the National League would never opt to have it, and the MLBPA would never agree to get rid of it. Whether any change regarding the designated hitter was near was about as uncertain as it had been for a long time.

However, Selig's success at bringing change to baseball was something to consider even though not much was currently happening on the DH front. The approval of his plan for the centralization of power was another example of what he had accomplished during his time as interim commissioner and then as commissioner. As reported in the *Milwaukee Journal Sentinel*:

No one thought he had a chance to push through revenue sharing, inter-league play or the wild-card playoff system, yet he did.

Accordingly, it would be foolish to bet against him when it comes to realignment and elimination of the DH.[25]

The 1999 Outstanding Designated Hitter Award was presented to a first-time winner. The Rangers' Rafael Palmeiro, who had begun his major league career with the Chicago Cubs in 1986 and then came to the American League with Texas three years later before moving to the Orioles in 1994, had returned to the Rangers for the 1999 season. Palmeiro had played first base prior to his second stint with the Rangers, but a pair of arthroscopic surgeries on his right knee in February and March led him to filling the designated hitter role in 135 games and limited him to 28 games at first base. He went on to have his best season with the bat, hitting .324 with 47 home runs and 148 RBI. Palmeiro was the winner of another award, and it was a strange situation indeed. He received the American League Gold Glove for First Base, although he only played 28 games at that position!

John Jaha was in the DH role in 130 games and at first base in eight others with Oakland. He hit. 276 with 38 homers and 111 RBI. The White Sox' Thomas was at first base in 49 games and was the team's designated hitter in 83 others. His hit .305 for the season while banging out 15 home runs and driving in 77 runs.

Both leagues posted outstanding slugging percentages. The American League's was .440 and the Nationals had a .430 slugging percentage, which was their all-time best. The Junior Circuit's .275 batting average was six points higher the Senior Circuit's, and AL domination in that area continued.

A pair of designated hitters retired following the 1999 campaign. The New York Yankees gave Davis his unconditional release on December 1, and the 39-year-old veteran put his bat away after a 19-year career. He had spent his first seven major league seasons in the National League and the final 12 in the American League, where he became one of the game's premier designated hitters. He finished his career by hitting .269 with 19 homers and 78 RBI in 141 games as a DH with the Yankees. The Red Sox' Jefferson, also in his final season, batted .277 in 58 games as the club's DH and two games at first base.

The attendance figures for 1999 mirrored the numbers for the previous season when the National League's 16 clubs outdrew the American League's 14 teams by 6.5 million fans. The Senior Circuit had five teams surpass the three-million mark in attendance — Arizona, Atlanta, Colorado, Los Angeles, and St. Louis — while only Baltimore, Cleveland, and New York reached three million admissions in the Junior Circuit.

The World Series pitted the Braves against the Yankees. New York, without benefit of a designated hitter, took the first two games in Atlanta by the scores of 4–1 and 7–2. When the series moved to Yankee Stadium in the Bronx, the Braves had to decide what they would do with the DH spot in their lineup. Manager Bobby Cox selected infielder José Hernandez for the third game and utility man Keith Lockhart for game four. The Yankees had Davis and Darryl Strawberry available to fill the role. When Hernandez learned that he would be the DH in the third game, he searched out Don Baylor, one of the Braves' coaches and a two-time ODH Award winner during the latter part of his playing career, to get some advice. The soon-to-be DH said, "I'll probably sit down with Don and get some tips. I don't want to get hit by a pitch the way Don did (when he played) but I'd like to try anything to get on base."[26]

The Yankees swept the series with 6–5 and 4–1 victories in the final two games. In that Fall Classic, none of the designated hitters in the pair of games in New York made significant impacts on the outcome of the games. The Yankees' designated hitters went a combined 1–for–7, and the pair of Braves DHs were 2–for–8.

Ten

In the New Millennium

The new millennium did not bring a new age of baseball when the designated hitter either disappeared in the American League or became a welcome addition to the National League game. A new Basic Agreement was approved in 2002, another debilitating strike was averted, and that was welcome news! The agreement included revenue sharing, a luxury tax, and prevented any contraction of major league teams through the 2006 season. The contraction of two teams, probably Minnesota and Montreal, had been another item on commissioner Bud Selig's "to do" list. The new Basic Agreement also provided for drug testing, and it increased the minimum salary to $300,000 in the first two years with a cost-of-living increase for the final three years of the pact. The agreement did not include any decision about the designated hitter or radical realignment.

A series of articles appearing in newspapers on April 16, 2000, showed the varied sides of designated hitting. One article described the feats of Kansas City Royals' rookie designated hitter Mark Quinn. He was batting a lofty .350 at the time and, as a right-handed batter, he was hitting .382 against right-handed pitchers. However, there was some question about how long Quinn would remain in the role, since he was not putting up the power numbers that the Royals were expecting to get out of the DH spot in the batting order. At the time of the article, Quinn had not hit a home run and had only driven in two runs. In another paper on the same day, there was a report that Seattle DH Edgar Martinez had hit a grand slam homer in the Mariners' 17–6 win over the Toronto Blue Jays. The long-time outstanding designated hitter had also flexed his muscles the previous night when he hit a three-run homer and drove in five runs. In the past, Martinez had put up both power numbers and a high batting average, and he appeared to be on target to do it again. The final article on April 16th was about Boston's Carl Everett, who also had a good day at the plate as a DH, going 3–for–4 with two doubles and four RBI. The difference between Martinez and Everett was that the former had made a career out of being a designated hitter, and the latter, a former National Leaguer, was not a fan of the role. Everett said:

> It's tougher, if you ask me. You're not warm. You always have to stay loose. You've got to do more exercising DHing than you're ever going to do just to stay loose. I think it's a tougher job than playing [in the field] and then trying to hit.[1]

Cal Ripken, Jr., had played 2,817 games over 19 years and not once had he been a designated hitter. During his record-setting 2632-consecutive-game streak, he never resorted to the "bat only" spot in the lineup as a way of keeping his streak alive. If there had been a time in his career when being a DH might have made sense, it would have been during the 1999 season when he had suffered with a bad back which limited him to playing only 86 games and ultimately led to surgery.

On May 9, in a concession to advancing age and declining healthy, the 39-year-old Ripken was in the lineup for the first time as a designated hitter. He went 1–for–4 with two RBI against the Toronto Blue Jays. Ripken explained:

> It's a new situation I'm dealing with, having come off back surgery.... We're going to do the things that allow me to play the most and get at-bats.... I'd like to play more than 86 games [this season], even if it means taking a day off here and there, and trying to DH, if that helps.[2]

Martinez was off to one of the best starts of his career. There were questions raised about whether or not this 37-year-old would be Hall of Fame material when he finally hung up his magic bat. The fact that he had been a designated hitter for most of his career was expected to work against him. That was coupled with the late start to his major league playing career. He had been an understudy third baseman for three seasons before becoming a Mariner regular at the position in 1990, at age 27. Injuries limited Martinez to a combined 131 games in 1993 and 1994. The following season he became Seattle's primary designated hitter for the first time.

Jayson Stark, a longtime baseball writer for the *Philadelphia Inquirer*, said:

> It's more difficult for a predominant DH to get into the Hall of Fame, but it's impossible to look at Edgar's career and not say he's one of the premier hitters of his time.
>
> If he continues to produce the way he has, and his career numbers creep up — say he gets a third batting title and moves past 2000 hits with a high lifetime average — you'd have to give him strong consideration.[3]

Bill James, the statistics guru and author of *Whatever Happened to the Hall of Fame? Baseball, Cooperstown and the Politics of Glory*, also expressed some enthusiasm about the prospect of Martinez eventually having a plaque in Cooperstown. He commented:

> It's hard to justify a Hall-of-Fame argument for a one-way player.
>   To do so requires a player who is exceptionally good as a hitter — and Edgar is quite a hitter. He's enormously valuable and has been for quite a long time. I wouldn't dismiss it [his chance] out of hand.[4]

The Mariners had not fared well in interleague games, and the team had a 21–29 record since Selig's plan was initiated in 1997. Their record ranked them 12th among the 14 American League clubs. Seattle manager Lou Piniella had a major problem when the games moved to the Senior Circuit's venues. He faced an annual dilemma about what to do with Martinez. Martinez was leading the majors with 57 RBI and was among the leaders with a .376 batting average and 15 home runs as "the 2000 interleague season" was set to begin.

Martinez had played seven games in the field in the three previous seasons of interleague play, all at first base. He had hit safely in all seven, going 9-for-26 for a .346 average, with four home runs and five RBI. He handled 64 chances in the field without committing an error.

The Seattle designated hitter's bat continued to sizzle during the first six games of the first round of the interleague matchups. Those games were played at Seattle's Safeco Field. In the six games against the San Diego Padres and the Colorado Rockies, Martinez was 10-for-24, with six RBI.

The following three-game series took the Mariners to San Francisco, where the teams played by National League rules. Martinez was at first base in game one as John Olerud took a seat on the bench. Martinez went 1-for-3 with an RBI in the opener. He was on the bench in the second game and then made a hitless pinch-hitting appearance in the series finale.

National Leaguer Tony Gwynn, who had gained membership in "the 3000-Hit Club" the previous season without benefit of being a designated hitter, found the American League's special rule to his benefit during the first round of interleague play. Suffering from an injured left knee, he was the Padres' DH when they were playing in an American League park. In the role that had been taboo for him up until that time, he went 9-for-24 in six games and was robbed of four other hits by outstanding defensive plays. In between at-bats he was able to ice his knee rather than going to the outfield for defensive duty. Gwynn said:

> Under the circumstances, being the DH was a good thing.... I was doing it because it was the only way I could be in there every day.

I knew I could do it. Do I want to do it? The answer is still no. That's not National League baseball. It's not the same…. If you're on base, it's OK. But if you make an out, you sit and wait and analyze.[5]

Not all American Leaguers were comfortable with the role either. Jorge Posada, the New York Yankees' regular catcher, was given some time off by manager Joe Torre, but the designated hitter role didn't agree with him. Posada recognized the need for rest from his duties behind the plate, but "rest" for him meant complete rest. He said, "I'd rather have a complete day off…. I'm not used to being a DH…. It's like pinch-hitting four times…. It's tough, especially if you're used to playing every day…. I told Joe Torre, 'I'm a terrible DH.'"[6]

Posada's stats as a DH supported his anti-designated hitter stance. He was 1–for–7 with five strikeouts in his two starts as a DH, compared with a .324 batting average with 12 home runs and 33 RBI in games when he was catching.

Torre was considering another player for the DH role, but for a very different reason. Second baseman Chuck Knoblauch had come from the Minnesota Twins to the Yankees in 1998. He had been a steady fielder with the Twins and the Yankees, and he was the league's leader in 1996 at the position with a .988 fielding average. Unexplainably, Knoblauch began to have trouble making throws from second to first. They would often bounce in the dirt in front of the first baseman or sail over his head into the stands. Knoblauch's difficulties were similar to the erratic fielding that Los Angeles Dodger second baseman Steve Sax had experienced in the early 1980s. The Dodgers' second baseman battled the erratic throws and eventually conquered "Sax Disease," as it was called. He went on to lead the American League with a .987 fielding average as a member of the Yankees in 1989.

Knoblauch was beginning to see more time as the team's designated hitter as a way to keep him from hurting the Yanks defensively. At first, he greeted the move positively, and he said, "I'm still playing, I still bat…. Plus it will give me a mental break to not think about defense."[7]

However, as the 2000 season progressed, Knoblauch saw less playing time. He finished the season playing at second in 82 games and batting as a designated hitter in 20 others, hitting .283.

During the postseason, he didn't see any playing time at second base. In the American League Division Series between the Yankees and the Oakland Athletics, which went to the Yanks, 3 games to 2, he was in the leadoff spot as the DH in games one and five, and had a pinch-hitting appearance in game three. He did not play in the other two games. He went 2–for–9 for the series.

Knoblauch was unhappy about his lack of playing time in the ALDS and asked, "Why don't they replace me on the roster? They don't have anything for me to do. I'm not sticking around if they do, I'll tell you that."[8]

He was in every game as a DH in the American League Championship Series against the Seattle Mariners, which New York took, 4 games to 2. He hit 6–for–23 in the six games leading off for the Yankees. He was then introduced to the DH's World Series dilemma. The Yankees defeated the New York Mets in the Fall Classic, 4 games to 1. The first two games were played in Yankee Stadium, and Knoblauch went a combined 0–for–8 as the club's leadoff hitter. The last three games were in Shea Stadium, and, with the DH not allowed, Knoblauch's only action was a pinch-hitting appearance in game five. He was 0–for–9 in the World Series.

If Knoblauch's erratic throwing continued in 2001, the Yankees' plan was to move him to left field, where he would have to make a different kind of throw. That was what happened, with rookie Alfonso Soriano taking over at second base.

Seattle's Martinez picked up another Outstanding Designated Hitter Award in 2000, becoming the first player to be chosen the season's best DH four times. He and Hal McRae had previously held the record with three awards. The 37-year-old Martinez hit .323 as a designated hitter (he hit .324 overall), and he drove in 145 runs, topping the DH RBI record of 133 that had been set by McRae in 1982.

In 2001, injuries played a huge role with regard to who was in the lineups as designated hitters. McRae was named manager of the Tampa Bay Devil Rays in April after Larry Rothschild was fired. One of McRae's first jobs was to find a DH for the club, and his choice was outfielder Greg Vaughn, who was nursing a sore right shoulder. Vaughn had bristled when the "D" word was used in spring training.

Vaughn took a different stance after McRae spoke to him.

> He called me in there and explained the situation to me…. I liked the openness, and taking the time to explain why he thought me playing DH would be better. I want to play, and he said this would help the team better.
>
> It was him coming to me and speaking to me about it. Plus, he's a former DH, and maybe he can give me some tips.[9]

However, it wasn't long before Vaughn was critical of his role as the club's primary DH, and he said that he wanted to return to being a full-time left fielder. In 40 at-bats while he was playing left field, Vaughn had hit .400 with five home runs. He was hitting a lowly .198 with six home runs in 116 at-bats as a DH. McRae addressed the subject, saying, "He can't play left field every day, so that's not even a question. We don't plan to play him any more than two or three consecutive days in the outfield. And I'll try to play him when there's going to be a day off the next day."[10] Vaughn ended up being in 136 games in 2001, hitting .233 with 24 home runs and 82 RBI.

McRae was always on the lookout for designated hitters. As the season went on, he thought he had found another candidate on the Tampa Bay roster who was well-suited for the role. Ben Grieve, the son of Tom, the Texas Rangers' general manager, had come from Oakland in January. He was in his fifth major league season. Grieve displayed the type of statistics that McRae liked to see when he was conducting "a DH talent search." Grieve was the Devil Rays' DH in 32 games, hitting .353 and averaging one home run every 23.8 at-bats. He also played 122 games in the field, but he batted only .238 and averaged a home run every 70.5 at-bats when he was doing defensive duty as well.

The Boston Red Sox had difficulty settling on their DH because of a March 12 hamstring injury to Manny Ramirez, who was ticketed to be the club's regular left fielder. Dante Bichette, who had spent the majority of spring training prepping for the DH role, was bitterly angry when he was told by manager Jimy Williams that he had lost his job to Scott Hatteberg. Bichette had played with Cincinnati for the most of the 2000 season and then had joined the Red Sox late in the campaign, appearing in 30 games, all of them as a designated hitter. Bichette said, "It totally blindsided me.... If I had any idea I was in competition for a job, it might have been a different camp. If somebody had respected me enough to have told me that, it would have been fine. This is a position I cannot accept at this point."[11]

Hatteberg never found his way into the early-season lineups. Because of his injury, Ramirez was the Red Sox' designated hitter. He put up good numbers in the DH slot, and it was early June before he made his first appearance in left field. Later in the campaign, Ramirez had a second stint as the DH because of injury. During the season, he had 327 at-bats as the club's designated hitter. He hit .333 and homered every 14.2 times at bat. Bichette would see action in 110 games, batting .286 with 12 homers and 49 RBI.

The Chicago White Sox' DH Frank Thomas went down with a torn triceps muscle in his right arm in early May and was lost to the club for the remainder of the season. Harold Baines was also with the White Sox, and he took over as the DH for the injured Thomas. However, the 42-year-old Baines soon went on the disabled list with a strained left hip flexor. His role the rest of the season was severely diminished. The long-time DH appeared in only 32 games and had a .131 batting average.

On June 21, the White Sox signed José Canseco to be their third DH of the campaign. Canseco had been released by the Anaheim Angels in spring training, and he had been playing with the Newark (NJ) Bears of the independent Atlantic League. Canseco played in 76 games with Chicago, hitting .256 with 16 home runs and 49 RBI.

Canseco retired after the 2001 season without reaching his goal of hitting 500 home runs. The former outfielder, who had been primarily in the designated hitter role since the 1994 season with the Rangers, finished 38 home runs short of 500.

Baines joined Canseco in retirement after the 2001 season, ending a 22-year major league career. Injuries had caused Baines to move into the DH slot full-time during the 1986 season with the White Sox. He finished his lengthy career 134 hits short of the coveted 3000-hit mark, and he fell 16 home runs shy of 400.

The Twins had DH troubles of their own. David Ortiz, their left-handed-hitting designated hitter, suffered a broken wrist on May 4 while sliding home, and he had surgery May 17. He had appeared in 130 games the previous season and hit .282 with 10 home runs and 63 RBI. Ortiz made it back to play a total of 89 games in 2001, but his batting averaged dropped to .234.

David Justice found himself in the DH role for the Yankees early in the campaign, and it wasn't working well for him or for the club. On May 11, he was hitting only .224. Torre thought he needed a dose of playing in the field, and Justice agreed, saying, "I'm doing what I've always done. The fact is, I'm an outfielder who's been asked to do a different role here, one that I've never done full-time. It's a learning process."[12]

Justice was in the outfield in two games against the Baltimore Orioles, but it wasn't a permanent change. He was moved between designated hitter and outfield duty for the remainder of the season. He was in a total of 111 games for the Yankees, and he hit .234 for the campaign.

The Athletics lost their designated hitter on June 30 when John Jaha announced his retirement. He had played parts of 10 seasons for Milwaukee and Oakland. A series of injuries had limited Jaha to 12 games in 2001.

The Seattle Times sponsored a contest to name the all-time All-Star team in advance of the Mid-Summer Classic that was scheduled for July 10 in Safeco Field. The players selected as the best-ever by position included Rogers Hornsby, Babe Ruth, Ty Cobb, Lou Gehrig, Ted Williams, and other greats of the game. Martinez was also there in the DH spot. He was the runaway winner at the position, garnering 1,476 of the 1,640 votes cast by the newspaper's readers.[13]

Martinez was in the starting lineup in the All-Star Game. He went

0–for–2 with a strikeout as the American Leaguers topped the National Leaguers, 4–1.

Seattle's primary designated hitter didn't escape the injury bug that had played havoc with DHs that season. He went on the 15-day disabled list on July 16 with a strained left quadriceps muscle. When he resumed playing, he continued his outstanding season. He picked up his fifth ODH Award in 2001, hitting .309 in 127 games.

Martinez had come to define the DH role, and he said that not being able to make up for a bad at-bat by doing something to help as a fielder "is a constant mental drain."[14] He also spoke about conditioning and added, "It's similar to what happens when you go from a manual-labor job to an office job.... You can get soft. It's easy to get out of condition taking four at-bats and sitting down. You're not as active. You swing and come back and sit. So I had to work extra hard on my conditioning."[15]

The Arizona Diamondbacks defeated the Yankees in the World Series, 4 games to 3. Games three, four, and five were played at the Stadium in the Bronx. The Yankees took all three matchups by a single run, 2–1, 4–3, and 3–2. Arizona's designated hitters contributed more to the offense than the Yanks' DHs, but that was not a surprise during a Fall Classic. Erubiel Durazo went 4–for–10 for Arizona in the three games in which designated hitters were in the lineups. New York countered with Knoblauch and Justice, who were a combined 2–for–12.

In 2001, there wasn't any reason for the Major League Baseball Players Association to soften its stance on keeping designated hitters in American League lineups. The average income that season for a full-time DH was $5,650,019, and that put them at the top of the league's salary list by position. First basemen were in second place with a $4,622,617 average salary. The salary figures for designated hitters were a bit misleading since only six players appeared in 80 or more games as a DH, and only five of them were signed to be full-time designated hitters. The sixth, Ramirez, had been expected to play the outfield for the Red Sox, but his nagging hamstring injury limited him to 55 games in left field in 2001. As had been the case for some time, most teams used a number of players as their designated hitters, and the DH role provided opportunities for flexibility in the lineup rather than have it as the sole responsibility of one or two players on the club's roster.

In 2002, the American League was playing its 30th season with the designated hitter. Throughout the history of the DH, there were players who detested the role, there were those who appreciated it, and there were those who excelled in it. All of that was represented in the new campaign.

The Blue Jays had a designated hitter controversy in the late 1980s when outfielder George Bell balked at the club's plan to have him be a DH. In 2002, Shannon Stewart had the same complaint. Coming off a .316 season, Stewart said that manager Buck Martinez had promised him the left-field job at a meeting in February. Martinez believed that the Blue Jays would be better defensively with Raul Mondesi, rookie Vernon Wells, and José Cruz patrolling the outfield. Jeffrey Moorad, Stewart's agent, weighed in, saying his client was "far too young and too athletic" to be a DH.[16]

The reluctant Stewart was a hitting machine early in the season, and he finished April with a .399 average and a .455 on-base-percentage. However, he suffered a hamstring injury and then struggled through a prolonged batting slump. He was a dejected DH by the end of May, and his batting average had fallen to .268, which was his lowest since April 10, 2000. He said, "I don't know, it's just one of those things where everything right now is just weighing on me and I'm trying to fight through it.... I don't know if I feel like I'm into the game, or if I'm trying too hard, or pressing."[17]

Stewart recovered his hitting stroke and was given more playing time in the outfield after Mondesi was traded to the Yankees in early July. He finished the season batting .303 in 141 games. Josh Phelps took over as the Blue Jays' primary DH on July 1, and he became one of the club's best hitters the rest of the way, finishing with a .309 average in 74 games.

In Cleveland, another player was ready to welcome the DH role if it came his way. Brady Anderson, who had been with the Red Sox and the Orioles since the late 1980s and had a 50-homer season with the O's in 1996, had been released by Baltimore at the end of the 2001 campaign after hitting .202. Indians' manager Charley Manuel had a number of jobs in mind for Anderson, including filling in as a designated hitter on occasion. Anderson's response to Manuel's plan was, "Whatever it is, I'm going to embrace it."[18]

The Indians already had a DH who was handling the job in fine fashion, but he would come down with some injuries later in the season. Early in April, Ellis Burks was third in the league with a .444 average and tops in the league with five multi-hit games. The former-outfielder-turned-DH commented about his successful start:

> As a player, you don't get caught up in stats or what's going on in this situation.... It's interesting when you're breaking down how we're winning or why we're winning, but I just try to do my thing. You know when you're swinging good, when your on-base percentage is good, because you're on base all the time.[19]

While Burks was streaking, Martinez was hobbling. The Seattle designated hitter ruptured a tendon behind his right knee on April 11 and had surgery the following day. In his return on June 27, he crushed a home run and delivered a two-run single later in the game to help the Mariners defeat the Athletics, 7–4. The crowd of 42,159 gave him a standing ovation before his first at-bat. Martinez, who plays the game with passion but with an impassive demeanor, commented about the crowd's response following the game, saying, "I was trying (to stay composed). I was kind of faking it. That was fun. That made me feel very good. I can't express what I felt in that at-bat.[20]

Carlos Baerga, a Red Sox DH who had only a few appearances as a designated hitter on his résumé, discovered a special form of assistance in the role. After two ineffective at-bats against the Mariners' James Baldwin, Baerga dashed to the video room to look at tape in an attempt to discover what he was doing wrong. That was not an opportunity that had been presented to him while he was playing two-way baseball. He recounted:

> I felt bad after I struck out with two men on base so I came here to watch the video. I saw I was jumping and I was far away from the plate when I had the chance to get two RBI. Maybe I'm the lucky one today. Being the DH I got the chance to look at the video while the other guys were on the field in the rain.[21]

Armed with fresh information, Baerga came to the plate in the fifth inning against Baldwin, and he hit a 1–1 pitch for a single that scored a crucial run.

On June 14, for the first time since 1972, a full slate of games was played in the major leagues without a designated hitter coming to the plate. All 14 of the interleague games were played in National League parks, and the two extra Senior Circuit teams faced each other. The strange situation that was caused by a quirk in scheduling continued until June 24, giving traditionalists 10 straight days of watching "nine-man baseball."

With a new round of interleague games, the Rockies were hoping to find the magic touch that had eluded them since play between the leagues began in 1997. While some designated hitters on National League teams had outperformed their American League counterparts in the games played in the American League parks, that was certainly not the case for the Rockies. There was ineptness displayed in whatever way one looked at the stats of Colorado's designated hitters. The combined batting average of all of their DHs during interleague play over the years was .193. Greg Colbrunn had gone 3–for–6 in his appearances in 1998, but a .250 average was the best any other Rockies' player had recorded.

In 2002, the Rockies' DHs were sparked by Larry Walker, who was in the role in seven of the nine games played in American League parks. Walker went 8–for–22 for a .364 average that was highlighted by a 4–for–5 outing against the Mariners on June 30. The Rockies' designated hitters' batting average for the nine games was .333, topping their previous high of .258 in 1997.

San Francisco Giants' outfielder Barry Bonds was upset with manager Dusty Baker after Baker inserted rookie Damon Minor in the designated hitter slot for the first interleague game of the campaign in which DHs were used. Bonds, who was looking at the positive side of the role for the game played in Yankee Stadium, said:

> That's embarrassing to me.... At my age, DH-ing is a vitally important role. For a lot of us veteran players, you want that opportunity because we're the horses of the game. If you want to keep your horse strong you need to manage his body the best you can.... You do what the manager says. But it's unfortunate if you've got a rookie DH-ing over a veteran player.[22]

Baker's response was "I just thought we had a better team with him playing left field. Also, the fans would probably run us both out of town if he was DHing. People come to see him play."[23]

Bonds brought an anemic .143 batting average as a designated hitter into the 2002 season. He was the designated hitter in three of the six games that were played in American League parks during the first round of the interleague season. He batted 2–for–8 with one home run in the three games, including the four bases on balls that he received in the final game in New York.

While all eyes were focused on the designated hitters when the Senior Circuit's teams were playing in the Junior Circuit's ballparks, Padres general manager Kevin Towers offered a novel suggestion. He proposed an interleague rule change in which DHs would be used in the National League's parks and not in the American League's parks. He felt that would be a way for fans to see how the other half lives, which he thought would be a useful educational experience for those on both sides of the DH debate.

Selig used the All-Star Game setting in Milwaukee to hold a town hall meeting with a live audience and an online hookup. Selig took questions about a number of situations facing the game. The topic of designated hitters in the city that had known both sides of the rule was not a major issue. When Selig addressed a question about it, he put it in its place, stating, "Would I like to have a standardized rule (between leagues)? I would, under the circumstances. But with all the problems we have facing base-ball, this is not something I spend a lot of time worrying about."[24]

In 2002, a new name appeared on the list of ODH Award winners. Burks, who had broken in as an outfielder with the Red Sox in 1987, was with them until 1993 when he became a member of the White Sox for a season. He went on to play in the National League with Colorado and San Francisco through the 2000 season. He joined the Indians in 2001. Burks, Cleveland's primary DH hit .303 and led all designated hitters with 32 home runs, 89 RBI, 90 runs scored, 150 hits, and 271 total bases. Ramirez finished second in the balloting after batting .356 with 11 homers and 51 RBI in 51 games as a designated hitter for the Red Sox.

Because of injury, Martinez had a sub-par season. For one of the few seasons in the recent past he was not in the running for the ODH Award. He played 97 games and hit .277 with 15 home runs and 59 RBI. Toward the end of the campaign, there was a sense that the soon-to-be 40-year-old might be playing his final major league season. On November 6, the Mariners decided not to pick up his $10 million option. However, before the ink was dry on that action, the club signed him to a one-year, $7.5 mil-lion contract for the 2003 season.

The Angels captured the 2002 World Series by beating the Giants in seven games. The Giants used four players, Tsuyoshi Shinjo, Shawon Dun-ston, Tom Goodwin, and Pedro Feliz, as their designated hitters in the first two and final two games of the series. The quartet was 3–for–16 for the Fall Classic. The Angels countered with Brad Fullmer, who had come from the Blue Jays after the 2001 season. Fullmer hit .289 during the reg-ular season, primarily as a designated hitter. He went 4–for–14 in the role in the World Series.

Martinez's 2003 season was also marred at times by nagging injuries. Early in April, he strained the tendon in his hamstring that had caused him trouble the previous season. Martinez was aware that something was going to be different for him when he was in the lineup. Bob Melvin, the Mariners' new manager who had replaced Lou Piniella, was going to pro-tect Martinez from possible injury, and he was going to pinch-run for him when someone else on the base paths might contribute more to the offense. Such was the price of being an aging ballplayer!

Baseball's best-ever primary designated hitter was disappointed, but he understood Melvin's reasoning:

> I understand it, but at the same time it's frustrating. I don't get frustrated because the manager takes me out. I'm frustrated that that's the situation and I have to accept it.
> I can tell when there's a really good possibility that I might come

Ellis Burks was given the outstanding Designated Hitter Award in 2002 (Cleveland Indians).

out. From the seventh inning on in any close game, there's a good chance I can come out.[25]

Martinez reached a personal goal in 2003. His line-drive single off White Sox reliever Gary Glover on May 2 went into the record books as the 2000th hit of his major league career. Perhaps he had nailed down one of those achievements that would help propel him into the Hall of Fame.

Throughout the season, there were new murmurs that 2003 was going to be Martinez's final season. The 40-year-old Seattle DH said that he was waiting to make his decision until after the campaign. Dick Stockton, who was announcing the Fox Television Game of the Week on Saturday, August 13, 2003, raised the question again as to whether or not Martinez might be elected to the Hall of Fame after he had been retired from baseball for five or more years. That honor would be a first for a player who spent over half of his career as a designated hitter. Stockton's opinion was that Martinez would be deserving of the honor, since he had excelled in a position that had been part of the game for over 30 years. He went on to say, "Martinez is the quintessential designated hitter. He hits the ball well to the opposite field, and he has the prettiest swing by a right-handed batter that you would ever want to see."[26]

Martinez faded a bit during the second half of the season, and ended with a .294 batting average with 24 home runs and 98 RBI. He played with a broken toe throughout September. On November 4, Martinez signed a one-year contract with a base salary of $3 million. With incentives, he could approach the $7.5 million that he made in 2002. He would be with Seattle for at least one more season, which would be his eighteenth.

The race for the season's outstanding designated hitter came down to a number of players who had excellent years as "10th men." The winner was announced at Baseball's Winter Meetings in New Orleans on Saturday, December 13, and it was Ortiz. He received 43 of the 80 votes cast. Martinez finished second in the balloting, and Thomas was third.

Ortiz had been a big addition to Boston's lineup. After being released by the Twins following the 2002 campaign, he was signed by the Red Sox on January 22 for a base salary of $1.25 million. The left-hander had posted career highs of 20 homers and 75 RBI while batting .272 in 412 at-bats for the Twins in 2002. However, he hit only .203 and struck out 30 times in 118 at-bats against left-handed pitchers.

Ortiz was a possible first baseman, a possible DH, or a bit of both. As the season unfolded, he became the club's primary DH, one of its most vocal cheerleaders, and a welcome addition to the clubhouse. The Red Sox, who had added a number of players as a result of general manager Theo

The Red Sox' David Ortiz was given the 2003 Outstanding Designated Hitter Award at Baseball's Winter Meetings in New Orleans on Saturday, December 13, 2003 (Boston Red Sox).

Epstein's deals, were getting "career years" from a number of the new-comers. Kevin Millar, Todd Walker, Ortiz, and Bill Mueller were contributing to the club's success in a number of areas. They made important offensive additions to a lineup that also included Nomar Garciaparra, Ramirez, Johnny Damon, Jason Varitek, Trot Nixon, and others.

Beantown was excited that 2003 might be the year when a new World Series championship flag would fly in Fenway Park, right next to the last one that had been put up there. It was dated "1918." The Red Sox made it to the postseason as a wild-card team, but lost to the Yankees in the ALCS.

Ortiz was right in the middle of the excitement, and some were promoting him for the league's Most Valuable Player Award. His contributions were described in this manner:

> Some guys might have better numbers, but how many big hits were in there? Some guys might hit for a higher average, but how much production is in there?[27]

Ortiz finished the campaign with an overall .288 batting average with 31 home runs and 101 RBI. He hit .310 with 27 homers and 73 RBI as a designated hitter. His .700 slugging percentage led all DHs with 100 or more at-bats. Ortiz led the team with 16 game-winning RBI.

Thomas was in the mix again. Thomas the DH and Thomas the first baseman had been different players throughout much of his career. That would not change early in the season. In 47 games as a designated hitter, he was batting .248, and in the 10 games he played in the field he had a .472 average with five doubles, four homers and 12 RBI. As the season progressed, Thomas became "instant offense" wherever he was in the lineup. He finished with a .267 batting average, and he led all DHs with 42 homers and 307 total bases. He also added 105 RBI to the White Sox' offense.

Rafael Palmeiro, the 1999 winner of the ODH Award, had another excellent season in the role. Playing for the last place Rangers in the American League West, he added some excitement for the fans when he hit his 500th career home run to join the special hitters' club. He rejected a trade to the National League Cubs in August, preferring to remain in Texas and be a part of the club's rejuvenation. He hit .260 with 38 home runs and 112 RBI, and his home-run and RBI totals placed him in a group of only three players in history to hit at least 35 homers and have at least 100 RBI in nine consecutive seasons. He joined Jimmie Foxx and Sammy Sosa in that club. His 38 home runs made him the only player in history to hit at least that many homers in eight consecutive seasons.

Dmitri Young was "Mr. Everything" for the terrible Tigers, who won only 43 games and finished in the basement of the American League Central. They went down to the final weekend of the season with the possibility of tying or surpassing the 1962 Mets' record of 120 losses, but narrowly averted the dishonor. The versatile Young played 75 games at DH, one at first base, 16 at third base, and 61 in left field. He hit .297 with 29 homers, 85 RBI, and 78 runs scored. He led all DHs with 167 hits.

Durazo was new to the DH role, having come to the Athletics from the Diamondbacks after the 2002 season. It was expected that he would add more power to the A's lineup than he did. He was tied for the lead among designated hitters in runs scored with 92 and in walks with 100, but he hit only 21 home runs and had 77 RBI with a .259 batting average in 154 games.

Injuries limited the performances of a number of players who were in the DH slot. Tampa Bay's Grieve was lost to the club in July when he had surgery for a blood clot in his right armpit. Anaheim's Fullmer was hitting .306 with nine homers and 35 RBI on June 26 when he tore a tendon in his knee that ended his season. The Angels released him after the season. Burks, who had won the ODH Award the previous season, had season-ending and, perhaps, career-ending elbow surgery in June. The Indians did not pick up the option on Burks' contract for 2004.

As has happened throughout the 30 years of the designated hitters' history, when one group of DHs moves on, there are others coming along. At least three players in 2003 showed that they might be among the outstanding designated hitters of the future.

Toronto's Phelps didn't have as strong a season in 2003 as he had during the second half of the previous campaign. He was in 119 games in 2003 and had a .268 batting average to go with 20 home runs and 66 RBI. He also struck out 115 times. Minnesota's Matthew LeCroy was in 107 games with 345 at-bats. He hit .287 with 17 homers and 64 RBI, but he had 82 strikeouts. Baltimore's Jack Cust showed some promise after a call-up late in the season, but he also had trouble with strikeouts, going down with a "K" in 25 of his 73 at-bats.

Another player began to express some interest in possibly applying for the DH role. In July, Bonds mentioned leaving the National League for a job in the DH league. He said:

> Couple of more years in the National League and maybe go DH in the American League. I'm not going to play in the field all the time after a certain point. I can hit, though...,
>
> In the American League, I can go DH and play two games a week [defensively] to keep myself going. In the National League, I can't do that.[28]

Two executives who had been supporters of the DH in the past expressed a change of heart in 2003. Former American League president Gene Budig, believing that the designated hitter had run its course, said, "Enough is enough. It's time to strike down the DH rule. Batters are bigger and stronger. There is no power outage in either league."[29]

Clark Griffith, who had been a Twins vice president when the rule was adopted, added that the DH "upset the balance of offense and defense in the game."[30]

The designated hitter debate continues, but it doesn't seem to be quite as loud as it once was. It appears to be safe as it is—"Yes" in the American League and "No" in the National League — at least until the next round of collective bargaining. The current agreement expires after the 2006 season.

ELEVEN

Awards and Accomplishments

David Ortiz, who won the Outstanding Designated Hitter Award in 2003, joined a list of 17 other players who had received the award since it was instituted in 1973. Eight of the award winners have received the honor more than once. The following are the Outstanding Designated Hitter Award winners from 1973 to 2003:

1973	Orlando Cepeda	Boston
1974	Tommy Davis	Baltimore
1975	Willie Horton	Detroit
1976	Hal McRae	Kansas City
1977	Jim Rice	Boston
1978	Rusty Staub	Detroit
1979	Willie Horton	Seattle
1980	Hal McRae ·	Kansas City
1981	Greg Luzinski	Chicago
1982	Hal McRae	Kansas City
1983	Greg Luzinski	Chicago
1984	Dave Kingman	Oakland
1985	Don Baylor	New York
1986	Don Baylor	Boston
1987	Harold Baines	Chicago
1988	Harold Baines	Chicago
1989	Dave Parker	Oakland
1990	Dave Parker	Milwaukee
1991	Chili Davis	Minnesota
1992	Dave Winfield	Toronto
1993	Paul Molitor	Toronto
1994	no selection because of strike	

1995	Edgar Martinez	Seattle
1996	Paul Molitor	Minnesota
1997	Edgar Martinez	Seattle
1998	Edgar Martinez	Seattle
1999	Rafael Palmeiro	Texas
2000	Edgar Martinez	Seattle
2001	Edgar Martinez	Seattle
2002	Ellis Burks	Cleveland
2003	David Ortiz	Boston

Entering 2003, two players who had spent considerable time as designated hitters were the career leaders in seven categories:

Outstanding Designated Hitter Awards	Edgar Martinez	5
Games Played	Harold Baines	1,652
At-Bats	Harold Baines	5,806
Hits	Harold Baines	1,688
Batting Average	Edgar Martinez	.323
Home Runs	Harold Baines	235
RBI	Harold Baines	978[1]

A list of the team-by-team top-hitting DHs through the years was produced by the Elias Sports Bureau:

Team	Player	Games	Average	HR	RBI
Anaheim	Chili Davis	587	.286	108	411
Baltimore	Harold Baines	602	.301	107	366
Boston	Jim Rice	530	.285	98	350
Chicago	Frank Thomas	798	.282	148	518
Cleveland	Andre Thornton	738	.254	125	459
Detroit	Rusty Staub	420	.271	57	287
Kansas City	Hal McRae	1,428	.294	145	823
Milwaukee	Paul Molitor	418	.310	37	187
Minnesota	Paul Molitor	380	.310	20	247
New York	Don Baylor	403	.266	69	259
Oakland	Dave Kingman	428	.236	98	290
Seattle	Edgar Martinez	1,214	.322	226	905
Tampa Bay	Jose Canseco	166	.266	41	121
Texas	Juan Gonzalez	293	.290	90	265
Toronto	Paul Molitor	376	.305	45	220[2]

Over the years, the DH role has helped deliver on Joe Cronin's, Lee MacPhail's, and the other early proponents' hopes for increased American League offenses. With very few exceptions, the American League had regularly trailed the National League in the combined batting averages of its players in the years prior to the inauguration of the designated hitter in 1973. The predominant argument made for having designated hitters in the Junior Circuit's lineups was to remedy that situation. That situation has been remedied!

From 1973 through 2003, with the exception of 1975 when the two leagues were tied with composite .258 averages, the American League has finished **every** season, with a higher combined batting average than the National League. In 1975, both leagues posted a .258 batting average. The average advantage from 1973 through 2000 was 6.9 points for American League hitters. The largest margins were 15 points in 1989, when the Junior Circuit's batters hit .261 to the National League's .246, and in 1996 when they hit .277 compared with the other league's .262.

From 1973 through 1997, the DH league topped the non–DH league in the number of home runs slugged by its players. With two more teams in its league (14 to 12) in 1987, the American Leaguers out-homered the National Leaguers by nearly 1000 home runs. Although the other seasons were not as overwhelming as 1987, there were still some impressive advantages produced by the league with nine "real bats" in its lineups.

From 1998 through 2000 (which are the last seasons for which I have figures), when the National League held a 16–14 team advantage, the Senior Circuit produced more home runs, with the largest advantage being 317 homers in 2000. However, because the National League had two more teams than the DH league, the average-homers-per team figure is important to consider. In each of those seasons, the American League continued to hold the advantage.

Besides batting average, there are two other sets of statistics that can be used to compare the offensive production of the leagues. The following statistics examine three offensive categories during the DH era. It is important to note that the National League regularly led in these offensive statistics prior to 1973. The three areas are: league batting average, league slugging percentage, and league on-base percentage.

Batting average (B.A.) is the number of hits divided by the number of official at-bats. A base on balls, a sacrifice, a hit-by-pitch, and a sacrifice fly do not count as an official at-bat.

Slugging percentage (S.P.) is the numbers of singles, doubles, triples, and home runs divided by the number of official at-bats. (The number of singles times one, plus the number of doubles times two, plus the number of triples times three, plus the number of home runs times four gives you the total you divide by the number of official at-bats.)

On-base percentage (O.B.P.) is the number of hits, walks, and hit by pitcher divided by the number of plate appearances.

I have included statistics for the three years prior to the institution of the designated hitter as well as those from 1973 to 2000.

	B.A.		S.P.		O.B.P.	
	A.L.	N.L.	A.L.	N.L.	A.L.	N.L.
1970	.250	.259	.379	.392	.325	.332
1971	.247	.252	.365	.367	.320	.319
1972	.240	.249	.344	.365	.308	.318
1973	.260	.255	.382	.376	.331	.325
1974	.259	.256	.372	.367	.326	.329
1975	.258	.258	.380	.370	.331	.330
1976	.256	.255	.361	.362	.323	.323
1977	.267	.262	.406	.397	.333	.331
1978	.262	.255	.385	.372	.329	.323
1979	.270	.261	.409	.385	.338	.328
1980	.270	.260	.400	.375	.335	.323
1981	.257	.256	.373	.364	.324	.322
1982	.265	.258	.403	.373	.331	.322
1983	.266	.256	.401	.376	.331	.325
1984	.264	.256	.398	.370	.329	.322
1985	.262	.253	.406	.374	.330	.321
1986	.262	.254	.408	.380	.333	.324
1987	.265	.261	.426	.404	.336	.331
1988	.260	.249	.391	.363	.327	.313
1989	.261	.247	.384	.366	.329	.315
1990	.260	.257	.388	.383	.331	.324
1991	.261	.251	.395	.373	.332	.320
1992	.260	.252	.386	.369	.332	.318
1993	.267	.264	.408	.399	.341	.330
1994	.273	.267	.435	.415	.348	.336
1995	.271	.264	.428	.408	.347	.334
1996	.278	.263	.445	.409	.354	.333
1997	.271	.263	.429	.411	.344	.336
1998	.272	.262	.432	.411	.343	.334
1999	.275	.269	.440	.430	.350	.345
2000	.276	.266	.444	.432	.352	.345[3]

The experiences of starting pitchers in the American League have changed dramatically over the years that the designated hitter has been a part of their game. During the first decade with the DH, starters, who were protected from having to leave games when they came to bat in crucial offensive situations, remained on the mound for as long as they were effective. Sometimes, this led to a route-going performance.

The number of complete games turned in by American League pitchers was higher than in the National League, where managers made greater use of pinch-hitters for the pitchers and then called on relievers.

Gradually, the regular use of relief pitchers found its way into the game plans of American League skippers as well. Now there is little difference between the two leagues in terms of the number of complete games pitched by starters. Route-going performances are now few and far between in both major leagues.

The following statistics show the number of complete games pitched in both leagues during the three seasons before the arrival of the designated hitter in the American League and for the years 1973–2000. I have not included statistics for the seasons when there was a strike, since the number of games played during those years varied in numbers. I have also identified the number of clubs in each league throughout this period, since it would have an effect on the total number of games played.

Complete Games

	A.L.	N.L.

There were 12 teams in both leagues from 1970 through 1976

	A.L.	N.L.
1970	382	470
1971	537	546
1972	(Strike)	

The first season of the designated hitter in the American League

	A.L.	N.L.
1973	614	447
1974	650	439
1975	625	427
1976	590	449

There were 14 teams in the American League and 12 teams in the National League from 1977 through 1992

	A.L.	N.L.
1977	586	321
1978	645	389
1979	551	362
1980	549	307

1981	(Strike)	
1982	445	289
1983	469	276
1984	398	234
1985	360	267
1986	355	224
1987	372	189
1988	352	270
1989	265	218
1990	229	200
1991	216	150
1992	242	177

There were 14 teams in each league from 1993 through 1997

1993	209	162
1994	(Strike)	
1995	(Strike)	
1996	163	127
1997	123	143

There were 16 teams in the National League and 14 teams in the American League from 1998 through 2000

1998	141	161
1999	109	128
2000	107	127[4]

With the increase in offensive production, there was also a rise in the American League pitchers' earned run averages. The following is a list of American League and National League ERAs during the DH era. I have included comparative figures for the three seasons prior to the institution of the designated hitter and for the seasons from 1973 to 2000.

Earned Run Average

	A.L.	N.L.
1970	3.72	4.05
1971	3.47	3.47
1972	3.07	3.46
1973	3.82	3.67
1974	3.62	3.62
1975	3.78	3.63
1976	3.52	3.51
1977	4.06	3.91

	A.L.	N.L.
1978	3.77	3.58
1979	4.22	3.74
1980	4.04	3.61
1981	3.66	3.50
1982	4.08	3.61
1983	4.07	3.63
1984	4.00	3.59
1985	4.15	3.60
1986	4.18	3.72
1987	4.46	4.08
1988	3.97	3.45
1989	3.89	3.50
1990	3.91	3.80
1991	4.10	3.69
1992	3.94	3.51
1993	4.33	4.04
1994	4.80	4.22
1995	4.72	4.19
1996	5.00	4.22
1997	4.57	4.21
1998	4.65	4.23
1999	4.86	4.57
2000	4.92	4.63[5]

The hope that improved offenses would ratchet up the attendance in American League parks was not as clear-cut a success as were the league's offensive figures. The Junior Circuit came into the DH era in 1973 after trailing the Senior Circuit in annual attendance since 1961. That season, the American League's 1.5-million attendance advantage was mostly the result of expansion, which had the AL fielding 10 teams for the first time while the National League remained with eight. A torrid attack by the New York Yankees' Roger Maris and Mickey Mantle on Babe Ruth's hallowed 60-home-run mark was also credited with bringing additional fans to Yankee Stadium and to ballparks throughout the league.

From 1962 through 1968, both leagues had 10 teams. The National League's lead was as small as 467,971 fans in 1968 and as large as 4.7 million in 1965 and 4.8 million in 1966.

In 1969, expansion brought two new teams to each league and the 12-team circuits welcomed 27.2 million to their ballparks, with the National League clubs drawing 15 million of the admissions. In 1972, only three

National League teams—Atlanta, San Diego, and San Francisco—*did not draw* more than a million fans, whereas only three clubs in the American League—Boston, Chicago, and Detroit—*drew* that many.

With the designated hitter in American league lineups beginning in 1973, the National League maintained its advantage through 1976, although the DH league was gradually closing the gap. In 1977, the American League surpassed the National League in attendance by 569,000 fans, but accomplished it primarily through the addition of two new clubs, Seattle and Toronto, each of which drew over 1.3 million customers.

Although the Junior Circuit took the lead in total attendance in 1977 and watched it grow almost annually through 1992, when it had 7.6 million more admissions than the Senior Circuit, the AL did it with two more clubs than the Nationals. The best test of admission figures when there were an unequal numbers of teams in the leagues was the average number of fans who came to each league's ballparks on an annual basis. The American League only held the edge in average-team attendance from 1989 through 1992.

The National League added two clubs in 1993—Colorado and Florida—and regained the lead in total attendance. From 1993 through 1997, when there were 14 teams in each league, the Americans had more admissions only in 1995. In 1998, the Senior Circuit became a 16-team league with the addition of Arizona and the move of Milwaukee from the American to the National League as part of realignment. The National League maintained the attendance advantage over the 14-team American League. For 2000 through 2002, the National League held per-team attendance advantages over the American League of 140,900, 135,450, and 101,400 paying customers.

Attendance in the DH league did post regular increases after the arrival of the designated hitter. However, it is not clear how much of those increases can be attributed to the extra bat in the lineups and the extra runs on the scoreboards. There were also extra teams in the league during most of the period. It's difficult to prove that the designated hitter spurred attendance in the way that the early proponents of the rule had hoped that it would do.

In conclusion, for most clubs, the place of the designated hitter has evolved into a role that is shared by a number of players on a club's roster. The DH role in not usually the sole property of one player who, because of age, or infirmity, is limited to playing only the offensive part of the game. The extra bat in American League lineups has been part of the increased offensive production that has given the American League a decided edge over the National League in most offensive categories.

The brand of baseball played in each league has drawn fans to their ballparks. Perhaps, the DH has helped the American League play catch-up with the National League in total attendance. However, it has not annually catapulted the DH league to the front of the attendance race.

What will the future hold? Probably, more of the same.

TWELVE

Strategies in the "Nine-Man" and "Ten-Man" Leagues

Discussions about the designated hitter often lead to discussions about baseball strategy. A number of the individuals who have shared their thoughts about the DH for inclusion in this book have commented about the different strategies that exist in the two leagues. This topic was also mentioned in a number of articles that I have included from media sources.

I will conclude the book by presenting scenarios that illustrate some of the differences between the leagues. American League fans will recognize its style of play, and those devoted to the National League will feel at home with theirs.

An American League manager often has fewer decisions to make about his offensive approach to a game when he has a designated hitter in the lineup. American League clubs rely on the nine hitters in the lineup who, by swinging their bats, provide the offensive output needed to win ballgames The National League plays "small ball" or "little ball" in which the strategic use of a bunt, a run and hit, a stolen base, a squeeze, and other offensive maneuvers are used to help manufacture runs.

"Small ball" has not been the exclusive property of the National League. There is some sentiment that the most effective offensive scenario is not the approach where the manager counts heavily on a power game that is provided by the presence of a DH and the other hitters in the lineup, but rather an offense that includes elements of "small ball" to go along with the "nine real bats" in the lineup. American League clubs such as the New York Yankees under manager Joe Torre and the Anaheim Angels under Mike Scioscia have used strategies that include the "small ball" offensive approach. Both Torre and Scioscia had been National League players, and they brought their experiences with "manufacturing runs" to their managerial positions in the American League. Torre had an 18-year career in the Senior Circuit and Scioscia played in the league for 13 seasons.

There are other Junior Circuit skippers who also use elements of "small ball" along with counting on the offensive contributions from the nine players in their lineups. In 2003, Kansas City Royals' manager Tony Peña, who played the first 10 years of an 18-year major league career in the National League, often had his club playing "small ball" as they battled for the American League Central title. Although they fell short of taking the title, Peña received the American League's Manager of the Year Award for 2003.

What follows are some examples of the different offensive approaches that a manager might use depending on which league he is in — the DH league or the non–DH league. The lineups in scenario # 1 are from actual games that were played in 1973. The lineups in the other scenarios are taken from the identified season, but the events did not actually happen as they are portrayed here.

1. **Strategic differences are seen in a pair of game lineups from 1973, the first season of the designated hitter. Each was used in a 6–4, nine-inning game. In one, National League manager Red Schoendienst uses pinch-hitters for the pitchers, pinch-runners, and a double switch. In the other, American League manager Eddie Kasko stays with his nine starting hitters.**

The St. Louis Cardinals defeated the Chicago Cubs, 6–4, on May 17. St. Louis manager Red Schoendienst's lineup and batting order:

Brock	lf	Anderson	pr
Melendez	rf	Folkers	p
Torre	1b	Tyson	ss, 2b
McCarver	1b	Bibby	p
Simmons	c	Granger	p
J. Cruz	cf	Stein	ph
Sizemore	2b	Segui	p
Kelleher	ss	Crosby	ph, 3b
Reitz	3b		

The Boston Red Sox defeated the Kansas City Royals, 6–4, on August 17.

Boston manager Eddie Kasko's lineup and batting order:

Harper	lf	Miller	cf
Aparicio	ss	Griffin	2b
Yastrzemski	1b	Evans	rf
Cepeda	dh	Moret	p
Cater	3b	Pattin	p
Fisk	c		

2. **A National League strategy at the bottom of the lineup in a game in 1981. A Philadelphia pitcher is replaced as part of an offensive move.**

The visiting Pittsburgh Pirates lead the Philadelphia Phillies, 3–1, in the bottom of the sixth inning. Larry Bowa, the Phils' number-seven hitter, doubles to lead off the inning. Bob Boone follows with a pop out to second base. *Dick Ruthven, the Philadelphia pitcher, is due to bat with one out. He has given up three runs, with two of them unearned as a result of Phillies' errors, and four hits. He has walked two Pirates and has struck out three. Manager Dallas Green sends pinch-hitter Del Unser to the plate to hit for Ruthven, and Unser grounds out to second with Bowa going to third base.* Lonnie Smith, the Phillies' lead-off man, flies to center field for the third out. The score remains 3–1 in favor of Pittsburgh. *Ruthven's work for the day is finished, and reliever Ron Reed comes into the game in the top of the seventh to face the middle of the Pirates' order.*

An American League strategy at the bottom of the lineup in a game in 1981. Cleveland's number-nine batter comes to the plate.

The visiting Detroit Tigers are leading the Cleveland Indians, 3–1, in the bottom of the sixth inning. Von Hayes, the Indians' number-seven hitter, doubles to lead off the inning. Duane Kuiper follows with a pop out to second base. *Mike Fischlin, Cleveland's number-nine hitter, comes to the plate, and he grounds out to second with Hayes going to third base.* Rick Manning, the Cleveland lead-off man, flies to center field for the third out. The score remains 3–1 in favor of Detroit. *Bert Blyleven, the Cleveland pitcher, has given up three runs, with two of them unearned as a result of Indians' errors, and four hits. He has walked two Tigers and has struck out three. In the top of the seventh he goes to the mound to face the middle of the Tigers' order.*

3. **A National League manager plays "small ball" early in a game in 1987. A sacrifice bunt is in order for San Francisco.**

The Los Angeles Dodgers hold a 4–2 lead over the visiting San Francisco Giants in the top of the third inning. Chris Speier, the Giants' number-eight batter, singles to left to start the inning. *Atlee Hammaker, the San Francisco pitcher, comes to the plate, and manager Roger Craig gives him the signal to lay down a bunt. Hammaker bunts the second pitch to the Dodgers' third baseman Mickey Hatcher who throws Hammaker out at first base.* Speier advances to second, and lead-off hitter Mike Aldrete comes to the plate. *Hammaker has done his job.*

An American League offensive approach early in a game in 1987. Oakland attempts to advance the baserunner without sacrificing an out.

The Kansas City Royals hold a 4–2 lead over the visiting Oakland Athletics in the top of the third inning. Tony Phillips, the Athletics' number-eight batter, singles to left to start the inning. *Alfredo Griffin, batting ninth in the order, comes to the plate, and manager Tony LaRussa gives him the signal to hit away. He hits the second pitch for a single to right field, and Phillips races to third base. Griffin has done his job.* Lead-off hitter Mike Davis comes to the plate.

4. A National League offensive strategy in a game in 1983. With no one out, Cincinnati wants to move the runners into scoring position.

The Cincinnati Reds lead the visiting St. Louis Cardinals, 4–3, in the bottom of the fifth inning. Mario Soto, the Reds' pitcher, leads off the inning. He tops the ball toward third base and beats it out for an infield single. Gary Redus, Cincinnati's lead-off hitter, draws a walk to put runners at first and second. *Eddie Milner, the Reds' second hitter, drops a sacrifice bunt down the third-base line drawing in the third baseman, and he is thrown out at first. Soto goes to third and Redus to second.* With one out, Dave Concepcion comes to the plate.

An American League offensive strategy in a game in 1983. New York's number-two batter steps to the plate with a hit in mind.

The New York Yankees lead the visiting California Angels, 4–3, in the bottom of the fifth inning. Rick Cerone, the Yankees number-nine hitter, leads off the inning. He tops the ball towards third base and beats it out for an infield single. Willie Randolph, New York's lead-off hitter, draws a walk to put runners at first and second. *Ken Griffey, Sr., the Yankees' second hitter, singles to left field, and Cerone scores and Randolph ends up at second base.* With no outs, the score is tied, 4–4, and the Yankees have runners at first and second. Dave Winfield comes to the plate.

5. A National League manager moves the runner in a game in 1993. The Chicago running game sets up a run-scoring opportunity.

The visiting Chicago Cubs lead the Atlanta Braves, 5–3, in the top of the eighth inning. With one out, Sammy Sosa, the Cubs' fifth hitter, lines a single to center field. *With Rick Wilkins, the number-six hitter, at bat, Sosa steals second base on the second pitch.* With a 3–1 count, Wilkins singles to right field and Sosa scores.

An American League batter advances the runner in a game in 1993. A Minnesota hit moves a runner into scoring position.

The visiting Minnesota Twins lead the Toronto Blue Jays, 5–3, in the top of the eighth inning,. With one out, designated hitter Dave Winfield, the Twins' fifth hitter, lines a single to center field. *Brian Harper, the sixth hitter, singles to right field on a 3–1 count, and Winfield goes to third base.*

6. A National League manager plays "run-and-hit" in a game in 1977. A Houston batter takes advantage of an open area in the infield, and the base runner takes an extra base.

The Houston Astros lead the visiting New York Mets, 4–2, in the bottom of the seventh inning. The first batter, Astros' pitcher Joaquin Andujar, strikes out. Houston lead-off hitter Cesar Cedeño draws a walk. *Enos Cabell comes to the plate with one out. On a 2–1 pitch, Cedeño takes off for second and, with the Mets' second baseman moving toward second base to take a throw from the catcher, Cabell grounds the ball between first and second and into short right field. Cedeño races to third base.*

An American League manager decides to hit away in a game in 1977. A California batter's single moves the baserunner into scoring position.

The California Angels lead the visiting Seattle Mariners, 4–2, in the bottom of the seventh inning. The first batter, Andy Etchebarren, the Angels' number-nine hitter, strikes out. California's lead-off hitter Gil Flores draws a walk. *Jerry Remy comes to the plate with one out. On a 2–1 pitch, Remy singles to short right field and Flores goes to second base.*

7. A National League manager uses the "double switch" in a game in 1988. Los Angeles maneuvers to move a pitcher out of the number-nine spot in the batting order.

The Los Angeles Dodgers trail the visiting Chicago Cubs, 7–4, in the top of the seventh. Dodger reliever Jesse Orosco is due to lead off in the bottom of the seventh inning. Orosco walks the first two batters in the top of the seventh. *Los Angeles manager Tom Lasorda goes to the mound to bring in Brian Holton to replace Orosco. Lasorda also sends Franklin Stubbs to*

right field to replace Danny Heep. Lasorda tells home plate umpire Steve Rip-
pley that Stubbs will bat number-nine in the lineup (where Orosco was in
the order) and Holton will be in the number-seven slot in the order (where
Heep was).

8. An American League manager plays for the "three-run homer" in a game in 1974. Baltimore sets the stage for a big inning.

The Baltimore Orioles trail the visiting Minnesota Twins, 5–3, in the bottom of the seventh inning. Orioles' manager Earl Weaver has Mark Belanger batting ninth in the order. Belanger leads off the bottom of the seventh with a double down the left-field line. Al Bumbry follows with a base on balls, putting base runners at first and second with no one out. Number-two hitter Rich Coggins sends a short fly to right field for the first out of the inning. Bobby Grich, batting in the third spot in the order, grounds to first base and a force out is made on Grich at second base with Belanger going to third. *Tommy Davis, the Orioles' designated hitter, comes to the plate. Tom Burgmeier, the Twins' pitcher, makes two throws to first base in an effort to keep Grich from extending his lead. The count goes to 2–2 on Davis. He swings at the next pitch and drives the ball into the left-field stands for a three-run homer.* The Orioles take the lead, 6–5. Weaver's favorite strategy pays off. His philosophy is that you don't give outs away by employing a sacrifice bunt or an attempted steal in the wrong situation. He did not want to take away the opportunity for the power hitters in the lineup to do their jobs.

9. A National League manager uses the running game in 1985. Philadelphia protects its pitcher and adds to the club's lead.

The Philadelphia Phillies lead the visiting New York Mets, 3–2, in the bottom of the eighth inning. The Phils' number-five hitter, Tim Corcoran, flies deep to center field for the first out of the inning. Ozzie Virgil, the sixth hitter in the order, singles to left field. Glenn Wilson comes to the plate and singles to right. Virgil goes to third base. Luis Aguayo, the Phils' number-eight hitter, is the next batter. Relief pitcher pitcher Larry Andersen, who entered the game with two outs in the top of the eighth inning, is scheduled to follow Aguayo. Manager John Felske wants to have Andersen in the game in the ninth inning, but he would also like to have a larger lead. *On a 2–1 pitch, Wilson takes off for second base. On the throw to second in an attempt to get Wilson out, Virgil races to home plate and slides safely under the return throw to the catcher.* The Phils' lead is 4–2. Aguayo and Andersen strike out to end the inning. Andersen returns to the mound in the top of the ninth with a two-run lead and attempts to hold the Mets.

An American League manager lets the bats do it in a game in 1985. A timely Boston single adds to the club's lead.

The Boston Red Sox lead the visiting Detroit Tigers, 3–2, in the bottom of the eighth inning. Number-five hitter Mike Easler, Boston's designated hitter, flies deep to center field for the first out of the inning. Dwight Evans, the sixth hitter in the order, singles to left field. Rich Gedman comes to the plate and singles to right. Evans goes to third base. Mike Barrett, the Red Sox number-eight hitter, strikes out for the second out of the inning. *Glenn Hoffman, batting number-nine in the order, singles to center and Evans scores.* Boston's lead is 4–2. Lead-off hitter Steve Lyons grounds out to shortstop to end the inning. Relief pitcher Bob Stanley, who had entered the game with two outs in the top of the eighth inning, returns to the mound in the top of the ninth with a two-run lead and attempts to hold the Tigers.

10. A National League manager forces the other team's skipper to make a decision in a game in 1996. A Cincinnati pitcher comes to the plate in a crucial situation.

The Cincinnati Reds are trailing the visiting San Diego Padres, 5–2, going into the bottom of the eighth inning. The Reds' Eric Davis leads off with a triple. Number-five hitter Eddie Taubensee follows with a single, scoring Davis to make the score 5–3. San Diego reliever Todd Worrell walks Bret Boone, putting a runner at second and the tying run at first. Willie Greene grounds out to first base, with Taubensee and Boone advancing to third and second with two outs. *Number-eight hitter Chad Mottola, who is two-for-two in the game, including a home run, comes to the plate. San Diego manager Bruce Bochy tells Worrell to intentionally walk him, putting the go-ahead run on base. The move brings up the Reds' pitcher Jeff Brantley, who came out of the Reds' depleted bullpen and pitched an easy 1-2-3 inning in the top of the eighth inning, to the plate. Cincinnati manager Ray Knight ponders whether or not to send up a pinch-hitter.*

An American League manager contemplates his next move in a game in 1996. What does the Milwaukee manager say to his pitcher?

The Texas Rangers are trailing the visiting Milwaukee Brewers, 5–2, going into the bottom of the eighth inning. The Rangers' Juan Gonzalez leads off with a triple. Number-five hitter Dean Palmer follows with a single, scoring Gonzalez to make the score 5–3. Milwaukee reliever Graeme Lloyd walks designated hitter Mickey Tettleton, putting a runner at second and the tying run at first. Rusty Greer grounds out to first base, with

Palmer and Tettleton advancing to third and second with two outs. *Number-eight-hitter Mark McLemore, who is two-for-two in the game, including a home run, comes to the plate. Milwaukee manager Phil Garner considers his next move. He goes to the mound to talk with Lloyd.*

11. A National League team squeezes in a run in a game in 1986. Good base running and a well-paced bunt produce a go-ahead run.

Atlanta and St. Louis are tied, 2–2, going into the bottom of the eighth inning. Cards' pitcher Bob Forsch walks number-eight hitter Glenn Hubbard to start the inning. Braves' pitcher David Palmer comes to the plate. He attempts to bunt on the first pitch but fouls it off. He lays the second delivery down between third and the pitcher's mound, and third baseman Terry Pendleton makes an excellent play to get Palmer at first with Hubbard going to second. Lead-off batter Bill Sample hits a slow roller toward second base and beats it out as Hubbard goes to third. *Rafael Ramirez comes to the plate for Atlanta with one out, and count goes to 2–0. On the next pitch, Hubbard breaks for home and Ramirez lays down a bunt toward first base. He is thrown out at first, and the go-ahead run scores.* Dale Murphy flies out to end the inning. The Braves lead, 3–2.

An American League hitter delivers a sacrifice fly in a game in 1986. An Oakland fly ball produces a go-ahead run.

Kansas City and Oakland are tied, 2–2, going into the bottom of the eighth inning. Royals' pitcher Charlie Leibrandt walks number-eight hitter Mickey Tettleton to start the inning. Stan Javier, batting in the number-nine spot in the order, hits a slow grounder to third and he is thrown out at first base with Tettleton going to second. Lead-off batter Tony Phillips hits a slow roller toward second base and beats it out, and Tettleton goes to third. *Bruce Bochte comes to the plate for Oakland with one out, and the count goes to 2–0. On the next pitch, Bochte hits a fly ball to deep center, and Tettleton tags up and scores from third base for the go-ahead run.* Carney Lansford flies out to end the inning. The A's lead, 3–2.

12. A National League manager plays another version of "small ball" in a game in 1995. Off with the crack of the bat, a Chicago runner scores and a second runner advances to third base.

The Chicago Cubs lead the visiting Pittsburgh Pirates, 3–2, going into the bottom of the seventh inning. Ozzie Timmons, batting in the seventh slot in the order for the Cubs, leads off with an infield single. Rey Sanchez, the Cubs' number-eight batter, hits the ball to the right side and is out at first base. Timmons advances to second. Pinch-hitter Lance Johnson, batting for pitcher Steve Trachsel, singles to left field, and Timmons stops at third base. Matt Franco replaces Johnson at first base as a pinch-runner. On a 1–0 count, Franco breaks on the pitch and slides safely into second, beating catcher Don Slaught's throw. Timmons remains at third base. With runners at second and third and one out, manager Jim Riggleman signals for the "contact play." On a ground ball hit to anyone in the infield except the pitcher or directly at the third baseman, Timmons will break for home with the crack of the bat, and Franco will head to third. *With a ball and two strikes on Brian McRae, he hits a ground ball toward the second baseman. Timmons, having broken for home on contact, scores easily and Franco ends up on third base.* With two outs, the Cubs lead, 4–2.

An American League manager goes for a big inning in a game in 1995. A run scores for Detroit on a double play.

The Detroit Tigers lead the visiting New York Yankees, 3–2, going into the bottom of the seventh inning. Alan Trammell, batting in the seventh slot in the order for the Tigers, leads off with an infield single. John Flaherty, the Tigers' number-eight batter, grounds a single to short left field. Trammell advances to second. Danny Bautista, the number-nine hitter, singles to left field, and the bases are full with no outs. *Yankee manager Buck Showalter pulls his infield in for a play at the plate. Chad Curtis, the Tigers' lead-off hitter, hits a grounder to the left of the shortstop. He cannot make a play at home, and he starts a 6-4-3 double play. Trammell scores on the twin-killing.* With two outs, the Tigers lead, 4–2.

13. A National League club "works the count" in a game in 1996. The Atlanta hitters make the pitcher throw a lot of pitches, which might have an effect on his performance later in the game.

The Atlanta Braves and the Philadelphia Phillies are tied, 0–0, going into the top of the third inning. Marquis Grissom, Atlanta's lead-off hitter, comes to bat for the visiting Braves. On a 3–1 pitch he grounds a single into right field. Mark Lemke, the second hitter attempts to bunt the first pitch and fouls it off. He takes two balls on the next two pitches and then fouls off a second bunt attempt. He swings and fouls off the next two pitches before taking balls three and four for a base on balls. Phils' pitcher Terry Mulholland works carefully to Chipper Jones, the number-three hitter, and falls behind 2–0. The count goes to 2–2 and Jones hits a fly ball to short center field for the first out of the inning. Fred McGriff, the clean-up hitter, works the count to 2–2 and then singles to left field with Grissom scoring the first run of the game. Runners are now at first and second base. David Justice, the number five hitter, takes a called strike on the first pitch. Mulholland then delivers two balls before Justice swings and misses, making the count 2–2. Justice watches the next pitch come in low and outside and the count goes to 3–2. He fouls off two grounders to the right side. On the next pitch he lines a ball to the left fielder for the second out of the inning. Ryan Klesko, the sixth hitter in the order, pops out to the second baseman on a 2–0 pitch for the final out of the top of the third inning.

The Braves take a 1–0 lead. The six batters who came to the plate in the inning worked the count in their at-bats, and Mulholland made 34 pitches in the inning.

An American League club takes the lead in a game in 1996. Cleveland batters do not "work the pitcher" in a 13-pitch inning.

The Cleveland Indians and the Milwaukee Brewers are tied, 0–0, going into the top of the third inning. Kenny Lofton, Cleveland's lead-off hitter, comes to bat for the visiting Indians. He swings at the first pitch and grounds a single into right field. Julio Franco, the second hitter, walks on a 3–1 pitch from Ben McDonald. McDonald works carefully to Carlos Baerga, the number three hitter, and falls behind 2–0. On the next pitch, Baerga hits a fly ball to short center field for the first out of the inning. Albert Belle, the clean-up hitter, hits the first pitch from McDonald and singles to left field with Lofton scoring the first run of the game. Runners are now at first and second base. Eddie Murray, the designated hitter batting in the fifth spot in the lineup, takes a called strike on the first pitch. Murray lines the next pitch to the left fielder for the second out of the inning. Manny Ramirez, the sixth hitter in the order, pops out on the first pitch to the second baseman for the final out of the top of the third inning.

The Indians take a 1–0 lead. McDonald made 13 pitches to the six batters who came to bat in the inning.

14. A National League team legs out a lead in 1984. It is not a Dodgers' run-and-hit play, but the results are the same.

The San Francisco Giants and the visiting Los Angeles Dodgers are tied, 2–2, in the top of the 10th inning. Greg Brock, the Dodgers' fourth hitter in the batting order, opens the inning with a grounder to the shortstop for the first out. The next batter, Mike Marshall, walks on a 3–1 pitch. Ken Landreaux, the sixth hitter, works the count to 3–2. The Giants' pitcher, Greg Minton, makes two throws to first base to keep Marshall close to the bag. *On the next pitch from Minton, Marshall attempts to steal second base. Landreaux lines a single into medium left field. Because Marshall was running on the pitch, he makes it to third base.* With runners at first and third and one out, the next batter, Mike Scioscia, hits a fly ball to left field, and Marshall tags up after the catch and scores the go-ahead run. Bill Russell the Dodgers' number-eight hitter, grounds out to second base to end the inning.

An American League team hopes for a hit to take the lead in 1984. The Oakland baserunner isn't in scoring position when a fly ball is hit to left field.

The Texas Rangers and the visiting Oakland Athletics are tied, 2–2, in the top of the 10th inning. Carney Lansford, the A's' fourth hitter in the batting order, opens the inning with a grounder to the shortstop for the first out. The next batter, designated hitter Dave Kingman, walks on a 3–1 pitch. Davey Lopes is sent in to pinch-run for Kingman. Bruce Bochte, the sixth hitter, works the count to 3–2. *Texas pitcher Dave Schmidt throws twice to first base to keep Lopes close to the bag. On the next pitch from Schmidt, Bochte lines a single into medium left field. Because Lopes wasn't running on the pitch, he only makes it to second base. With runners at first and second, the next batter, Mike Davis, hits a fly ball to left field for the second out of the inning.* The baserunners remain at first and second base. Mike Heath, the Athletics' number-eight hitter, grounds out to second base to end the inning.

15. A National League club calls on timing to make up for a lack of speed in a game in 1999. A base runner gets into scoring position with two outs.

The visiting Arizona Diamondbacks lead the Montreal Expos, 3–2, in the bottom of the sixth inning. Rondell White, the Expos' number-three hitter, lines out to center field for the first out of the inning. Clean-up hitter Vladimir Guerrero grounds out to third base for the second out. Number-five hitter Michael Barrett singles to left field. Barrett does not have great speed and is not a threat to steal second. The next hitter, Chris Widger, works the counts to 2–1. *The next pitch is a strike, and as the pitch crosses the plate, Barrett takes off for second base on a delayed steal. The shortstop and second baseman are playing back, and the second baseman is late getting to the bag to take the catcher's throw. Barrett is safe at second base.* With the count 2–2, Widger hits a line drive into the right-field corner. Barrett scores from second to tie the score, 3–3, and Widger slides into second base. Wilton Guerrero come to bat with two out.

An American League club advances a runner to third base on a two-out double in a game in 1999. Another hit will be needed to tie the game.

The visiting Toronto Blue Jays lead the Tampa Bay Devil Rays, 3–2, in the bottom of the sixth inning. Designated hitter José Canseco, the Devil Rays' number-three hitter, lines out to center field for the first out of the inning. Clean-up hitter Fred McGriff grounds out to first base for the second out. Number-five hitter John Flaherty singles to left field. Flaherty does not have great speed and is not a threat the steal second. The next hitter, Wade Boggs, with a 2–2 count, hits a line drive into the right-field corner. Barrett goes to third base and Boggs slides into second base. Quinton McCracken comes to bat with two out.

Chapter Notes

One

1. William Leggett, "Now Half the Nines Are Tens," *Sports Illustrated*, 22 January 1973, 27.
2. Ford C. Frick, *Games, Asterisks, and People* (New York: Crown Publishers, 1973), 155, 156.
3. John Thorn, "Our Game," *Total Baseball*, Eds. John Thorn, et al. (New York: Total Sports, 1999), 9.
4. Geoffrey. C. Ward and Ken Burns, *Baseball An Illustrated History* (New York: Alfred A. Knopf, 1994), 377.
5. Bowie Kuhn, *Hardball* (New York: Times Books, 1987), 55.
6. "A Matter of Designation," Sports of the Times, *New York Times*, 4 February 1973, Sec. 5, 2.

Two

1. "Pinch-Hit Method Stays Unchanged," New York Times, 2 December 1972, Sec. 1, 47.
2. Lee MacPhail, Letter to author, 2003.
3. Bowie Kuhn, Hardball (New York: Times Books, 1987), 55.
4. Wells Twombly, "Now the 10th man," New York Times Magazine, 1 April 1973, 21, 23.
5. The Sporting News Official Baseball Guide for 1974, 283.
6. "Mailbox: Comparative Speaking," New York Times, 11 February 1973, Sec. 5, 2.
7. "Now the 10th man," New York Times Magazine, 1 April 1973, 17.
8. William Leggett, "The 10th Man Cometh," Sports Illustrated, 5 February 1973, 15.
9. "Kasko, Denied DH in Own Park, Lashes Out at Inter-League Rule," New York Times, 13 March 1973, Sec. 1, 46.

10. Joseph Durso, "The 10th Man Theme: American League's Overture to Lost Fans," New York Times, 4 February 1973, Sec. 5, 2.
11. "The 10th Man Cometh, 13.
12. "Now the 10th man," New York Times Magazine, 1 April 1973, 17.
13. "The 10th Man Cometh," 15.
14. "The 10th Man Cometh," 15.

Three

1. Murray Chass, "Fisk's 2 Homers Set Boston Pace," New York Times, 7 April 1973, Sec. 1, 24.
2. Mel Antonen, "DH at 30: Hit, Miss," USA Today, 14 July 2003, Sec. 3, 2.
3. Bill Dawson, "DH at 30; Rule still enrages purists, but many hitters relish role," The San Diego Union-Tribune, 12 May 2003, Sec. 3, 2.
4. Wells Twombly, "Now the 10th Man," New York Times Magazine, 1 April 1973, 21.
5. Mike Bass, "Burgess Was A Hitter Ahead Of His Time," St. Louis Post-Dispatch, 19 September 1991, Sec. 4, 1.
6. "Now the 10th Man," 23.
7. "Now the 10th Man," 23.
8. "Now the 10th Man," 26.
9. Dawson, "DH at 30; Rule still enrages," Sec. 3, 2.
10. "DH: More Excitement in the Games, But Scoring Shows Little Increase," New York Times, 20 May 1973, Sec. 5, 3.
11. "DH: More Excitement in the Games...," Sec. 5, 3.
12. "DH: More Excitement in the Games...," Sec. 5, 3.
13. "Now the 10th Man," 19.
14. Bob Fowler "Designated-Hitter Rule Helps Twins," The Sporting News Official Baseball Guide for 1974, 25.

15. Frank Quilici, Letter to author, 2003.

16. Frank Quilici, Letter to author, October 5, 2003.

17. Eddie Kasko, Telephone conversation with author, February, 26, 2003.

18. "Some Players and Mangers Frown on DH Rule," The Sporting News Official Baseball Guide for 1974, 282.

19. "Some Players and Managers...," The Sporting News Official Baseball Guide for 1974, 282.

20. "Feeney Still Spurns DH," New York Times, 6 September 1973, Sec. 1, 47.

21. "Sanderson Looks for a Trade," New York Times, 15 March 1974, Sec. 1, 30.

22. "Tom Van Arsdale Is Traded to Hawks," New York Times, 9 November 1974, Sec.1, 36.

23. Daryl Van Schouwen, "Interleague Play Could Eliminate AL's '10th Man'; Endangered Species: DH," Chicago Sun-Times, 18 January 1996, Sports, 94.

24. Red Smith, "And Next, the Designated Manager," New York Times, 30 August 1974, Sec. 1, 25.

25. Frank Lucchesi, Telephone conversation with author, March 11, 2003.

26. Bruce DalCanton, Letter to author, 2003.

27. Sonny Siebert, Letter to author, 2003.

28. Siebert, Letter to author, 2003.

29. Leonard Koppett, "Designated-Hitter Rule Restores Homer Parity," New York Times, 12 October 1975, Sec. 5, 3.

30. "Designated Hitter Must Go, Says Fan," New York Times, 6 July 1975, Sec. 5, 2.

Four

1. Joseph Durso, "The Designated Gimmick," New York Times, 17 August 1976, Sec. 1, 39.

2. "The Designated Gimmick," Sec. 1, 39.

3. Dave Garcia, "Reluctant Baylor Still DH Success," Denver Rocky Mountain News (Colorado), 21 May 2000, Sec. 3, 10.

4. "Reluctant Baylor Still DH Success," Sec. 3, 10.

5. Bill Lee, Letter to author, 2003

6. Willie Horton, E-mails to author, August 28, 2003 and September 3, 2003.

7. Bobby Winkles, Letter to author, 2003.

8. Thomas Boswell, "Time to End 9th-Bat Split," The Washington Post, 31 July 1980, Sec. 6, 1.

9. "Time to End 9th-Bat Split," Sec. 6, 1.

10. "Time to End 9th-Bat Split," Sec. 6, 1.

11. Bill Shannon, "It's Time To Designate The Designated Hitter For Oblivion," New York Times, 17 August 1980, Sec. 5, 2.

12. "National League Rejects DH," New York Times, 13 August 1980, Sec. 4, 20.

13. "National League Rejects DH," Sec. 4, 20.

14. Bill Giles, Telephone conversation with author, February 3, 2003.

Five

1. Phil Elderkin, "Royals' designated hitter 'adjusts' his way past the defense," The Christian Science Monitor, 21 October 1980, 10.

2. "Royals' designated hitter 'adjusts' his way past the defense," 10.

3. "Royals' designated hitter 'adjusts' his way past the defense," 10.

4. Dick Drago, Letter to author, 2003.

5. Ira Berkow, "Players," New York Times, 15 June 1982, Sec. 4, 25.

6. Total Baseball, Sixth Edition (New York: Total Sports, Warner Books, 1999), 2284, 2320.

7. John Mayberry, Conversation with author, July 27, 2003.

8. George Medich, Letter to author, 2003.

9. Medich, Letter to author, 2003.

10. Thomas Boswell, "Series Opens On a Speedy Note Today," The Washington Post, 11 October 1983, Sec. 4, 1.

11. "Series Opens On a Speedy Note Today," Sec. 4, 1.

12. Jim Kaat, Letter to author, 2003.

13. Kaat, Letter to author, 2003.

14. The Bill James Historical Baseball Abstract (New York: Villard Books, 1986), 263.

15. "Kingman Gets to Play," New York Times, 28 September 1984, Sec. 1, 26.

16. Paul Splittorff, Letter to author, 2003.

17. Dave Anderson, "Sports Of The Times; D.H. Confusion Requires Action," New York Times, 13 October 1984, Sec. 1, 49.

18. Bill Virdon, Letter to author, 2003.

19. Ralph Houk, Letter to author, 2003.

20. "Sports People; Designated Survey," New York Times, 8 November 1984, Sec. 2, 20.

21. "D.H. Rule Backed By Wide Margin," New York Times, 9 December 1984, Sec. 5, 8.

22. Thomas Boswell, "The DH Moves On Deck in NL," The Washington Post, 25 April 1985, Sec. 5, 1.

23. "The DH Moves On Deck in NL," Sec. 5, 1.

24. "The DH Moves On Deck in NL," Sec. 5, 1.

25. "The DH Moves On Deck in NL," Sec. 5, 1.

26. "D.H. Defeated In Fans' Poll," New York Times, 21 April 1985, Sec. 5, 2.

27. Joseph Durso, "Designated Hitter Will Remain As Is," New York Times, 12 December 1985, Sec. 2, 28.

Six

1. Dave Anderson, "Chub Feeney Is a Fan Again," New York Times, 10 December 1986, Sec. 4, 28.

2. Katie Feeney, Letter to author, 22 November 2002.

3. Katie Feeney, Letter to author, 2003.

4. Ira Berkow, "From Dante to Darling," New York Times, 11 June 1986, Sec. 4, 27.

5. Thomas Boswell, "The Great DH Debate," The Washington Post, 3 August 1986, Sec. 3, 1.

6. George Bamberger, Telephone conversation with author, February 20, 2003.

7. Neil MacCarl, "Cecil Fielder is more confident Jays' designated hitter; feels no pressure with Cliff Johnson gone," The Toronto Star, 1 March 1987, Sec. 7, 2.

8. Pat Gillick, Letter to author, 2003.

9. Ira Berkow, "Rasmussen Makes Comeback, Of Sorts," New York Times, 28 July 1987, Sec. 1, 17

10. Major League Rule Book.

11. "Rasmussen Makes Comeback, Of Sorts," Sec. 1, 17.

12. Dave Perkins, "Bell quiet after meeting with manager. Team will monitor his work habits," The Toronto Star, 3 March 1988, Sec. 2, 1.

13. "Designated hitter role prolongs Bell's career, Jays say," The Toronto Star, 23 February 1988, Sec. 1, 1.

14. John Romano, "Bell says he won't play as Blue Jays DH," St. Petersburg Times, 19 March 1988, Sec. 3, 1.

15. Bruce Lowitt, "Giamatti speaks his piece," St. Petersburg Times, 11 March 1987, Sec. 3, 1.

16. "Giamatti speaks his piece," Sec. 3, 1.

17. Neil MacCarl, "Bell happy to DH if the money is right," The Toronto Star, 10 April 1988, Sec. 7, 1.

18. "Pitcher Rhoden makes history as Yankee DH," St. Petersburg Times, 12 June 1988, Sec. 3, 4.

19. "Designated hitter is bane of baseball," USA Today, 4 April 1989, Sec. 3, 6.

20. Bruce Lowitt, "A Fan of Tradition," St. Petersburg Times, 21 March 1989, Sec. 3, 1.

21. "A Fan of Tradition," Sec. 3, 1.

22. Dan Shaughnessy, "The new commissioner is on deck," The Boston Globe, 18 October 1988, 33.

23. Dave Anderson, "Memo to Giamatti: Make It One Game, Not Two," New York Times, 2 April 1989, Sec. 8, 13.

24. "Memo to Giamatti: Make It One Game, Not Two," Sec. 8, 13.

25. Eugene J. McCarthy, "Another Good Season for Baseball," The Christian Science Monitor, 26 April 1989, 19.

26. "Lasorda opposes all-star DH but Cardinals' Guerrero likes it," The Toronto Star, 11 July 1989, Sec. 2, 3.

27. "Bell accepts DH role under Gaston's rule," USA Today, 11 August 1989, Sec. 3, 6.

28. "Another Good Season for Baseball," 19.

29. Hal Bodley, "Series: 'Modest Little Sports Event,'" USA Today, 19 October 1989, Sec. 3, 3.

Seven

1. Vahe Gregorian, "Commissioner Not In Favor Of Change," St. Louis Post-Dispatch, 8 April 1990, Sec. 3, 24.

2. "Vincent Will Follow Giamatti's Agenda," St. Louis Post-Dispatch, 14 September 1989, Sec. 4, 1.

3. Art Rosenbaum, "Hubbell's All-Star Feat Explained," The San Francisco Chronicle, 4 September 1990, Sec. 4, 4.

4. "Is D.H. Out of Order? The designated hitter may be an endangered species," New York Times, 20 October 1990, Sec. 1, 44.

5. Allan Ryan, "Questions about Bell bedevil Blue Jays," The Toronto Star, 15 November 1990, Sec. 4, 6.

6. "Parker becomes an Angel," The Toronto Star, 15 March 1991, Sec. 3, 4.

7. David Bush, "Less Talk, More Hits: That's Harold Baines," The San Francisco Chronicle, 25 June 1991, Sec. 2, 1.

8. Total Baseball, Sixth Edition (New York: Total Sports, Warner Books, 1999), 655.

9. Dennis Brackin, "Kelly says pitchers cannot really be expected to hit," Star Tribune (Minneapolis, MN), 17 October 1991, Sec. 3, 8.

10. Joe Strauss, World Series '91; Twins Notebook; Vincent: Game 3 ultimate argument against DH," The Atlanta Journal and Constitution, 24 October 1991, Sec. 4, 10.

11. World Series '91; Twins Notebook....," Sec. 4, 10.

12. Larry Dierker, "Compromise possible on designated hitter," The Houston Chronicle, 18 May 1992, Sec. 1, 5.

13. Larry Dierker, "Tomahawk belongs in Hall, but DH doesn't," The Houston Chronicle, 29 October 1991, Sec. 1, 6.

14. "Tomahawk belongs in Hall,...." Sec. 1, 6.

15. Steve Aschburner, "Not a crossover hit; After two decades, DH still a matter of debate," Star Tribune (Minneapolis, MN), 23 August 1992, Sec 3. 16.

16. Lowell Cohn, "N.L. Plays Correct Version of Baseball," The San Francisco Chronicle, 27 August 1992, Sec. 5, 3.

17. "N.L. Plays Correct Version of Baseball," Sec. 5, 3.

18. Mel Antonen, "White Sox get Bell from Cubs; Patterson, Sosa move across town," USA Today, 31 March 1992, Sec. 3, 1.

19. John Lindsay, "Dave Winfield Is Playing Like A Young Lion At 40," Saint Louis Post-Dispatch, 27 September 1992, Sec. 6, 3.

20. Archie McDonald, "Mum's word for Gaston; Jays' manager keeping plans under wraps," The Ottawa Citizen, 16 October 1993, Sec. 6, 1.

Eight

1. G. Richard McKelvey, For It's One, Two, Three, Four Strikes You're Out at the Owners' Ball Game (Jefferson, NC: McFarland & Company, Inc., Publishers, 2001), 170.

2. Larry Dierker, Letter to author, 2003.

3. Hal Bodley, New AL chief wants brawls curtailed, USA Today, 9 June 1994, Sec. 3, 3.

4. "Kansas Chancellor Budig Is Elected AL President," Chicago Sun-Times, 8 June 1994, Sec. 1, 6.

5. Bill Arnold, Mark Camps, "Beyond the Boxscore," The San Francisco Chronicle, 30 August 1994, Sec. 4, 4.

6. Alan Truex, "Interleague play close to becoming a reality; If union Oks it, DH phase-out likely," The Houston Chronicle, 18 January 1996, Sports, 1.

7. "Interleague play close to becoming a reality...," Sports, 1.

8. Hal Bodley, "Designated hitter problem could stall interleague play," USA Today, 7 June 1996, Sec. 3, 5.

9. Murray Chass, "When Pitchers Grab The Bats, the Sound Often Heard Is 'Whiff'," New York Times, 4 February 1996, Sec. 8, 6.

10. "When Pitchers Grab The Bats...," Sec. 8, 6.

11. Shirley Povich, "Baseball No Longer Speaks Same Language," The Washington Post, 20 March 1996, Sec. 6, 3.

12. "Baseball No Longer Speaks...," Sec. 6, 3.

13. Murray Chass, "An Old Tale of Two Leagues Focuses on the D.H.," New York Times, 9 July 1996, Sec. 2, 12.

14. "An Old Tale of Two Leagues...," Sec. 2, 12.

15. Murray Chass, "The D.H. Is 25 Years Old, but Now the Question Is Whether It Will Get to 30," New York Times, 5 April 1998, Sec. 8, 2.

16. Tim Brown, "DH rule still stirs controversy; Interleague play likely to bring issue to the front burner again," Denver Rocky Mountain News, 7 April 1996, Sec. 3, 17.

17. "DH rule still stirs controversy...," Sec. 3, 16.

18. Patrick Reusse, "Gaetti likes the NL brand of ball," Star Tribune (Minneapolis, MN), 11 October 1996, Sec. 3, 6.

Nine

1. Hal Bodley, "Survey on rules says dump DH," USA Today, 8 July 1997, Sec. 3, 5.

2. I.J. Rosenberg, "Radical, and red hot," The Atlanta Journal and Constitution, 7 August 1997, Sec. 6, 1.

3. Jerry Crasnick, "Kinder, gentler, less radical realignment in the works," The Denver Post, 30 August 1997, Sec. 3, 5.

4. Murray Chass, "In Chicago, a Catch to Interleague Play," New York Times, 8 April 1997, Sec. 2, 16.

5. G. Richard McKelvey, The MacPhails: Baseball's First Family of the Front Office (Jefferson, NC: McFarland & Company, Inc., Publishers, 2000), 300.

6. McKelvey, 300.

7. "Owners come up with plan to eliminate designated hitter," The Houston Chronicle, 30 August 1997, Sports, 7.

8. "Owners come up with plan to eliminate designated hitter," Sports, 7.

9. Bob Costas, "Costas on the designated hitter," The Sporting News, 25 September 1997.

10. Lou Gorman, Letter to author, 2003.

11. Joe Goddard, "When it comes to Sox memories, Baines reigns," Chicago Sun-Times, 1 August 2000, Sports, 93.

12. Daryl Van Schouwen, "The Quiet Man; Baines lets bat — and character — do the talking," Chicago Sun-Times, 27 July 1997, Sports, 13.

13. "The Quiet Man...," Sports, 13.

14. Paul Hoynes, "Hart Says Series Makes

DH Case," Plain Dealer (Cleveland, Ohio), 5 October 1997, Sec. 3, 12.

15. Bruce Jenkins, "Fehr, Orza Keeping the DH Afloat," The San Francisco Chronicle, 23 May 1998, Sec. 5, 2.

16 Tom Haudricourt, "Union bristles at DH banter," Milwaukee Journal Sentinel, 12 April 1999, Sports, 5.

17. "All-Stars Designate Desire For DH," The Denver Rocky Mountain News, 8 July 1998, Sec. 6, 22 R.

18. Paul Molitor, Letter to author, 2003.

19. Jack McKeon, Letter to author, 2003.

20. Marc Topkin, "Bochy: No DH is no edge to me," St. Petersburg Times, 20 October 1998, Sec. 3, 3.

21. Ron Kroichick, "Healthy Debate," The San Francisco Chronicle, 2 June 1999, Sec. 5, 1.

22. Mike Sullivan, "Baines Remains," Columbus (Ohio) Dispatch, 7 September 1999, Sec. 2, 5.

23. Thomas Stinson, "Gwynn last of a kind; No other in NL in reach of 3000 hits," The Atlanta Journal and Constitution, 23 May 1999, Sec. 7, 12.

24. "Gwynn last of a kind...." Sec. 7, 12.

25. Tom Haudricourt, "Next for Selig? Realignment. He plans to eliminate designated hitter, too," Milwaukee Journal Sentinel, 19 September 1999, Sports, 15.

26. Geoff Baker, "Now Atlanta Faces The DH, Too," The Toronto Star, 26 October 1999, Sports.

Ten

1. Steve Conroy, "Everett a big hit in the DH role," The Boston Herald, 16 April 2000, Sec. 2, 17.

2. Dave Sheinin, "Orioles Notebook; At 39, Ripken Plays a New Role," The Washington Post, 10 May 2000, Sec. 4, 6.

3. Larry Stone, "Late start stymies Edgar's Hall pass," The Seattle Times, 28 May 2000, Sec. 3, 8.

4. "Late start stymies....," Sec. 3, 8.

5. Bill Center, "Gwynn finding a comfort level at DH after all," The San Diego Union-Tribune, 10 June 2000, Sec.4, 8.

6. Thomas Hill, "Jorge Signals He's No Hit In DH Role," New York Daily News, 18 June 2000, Sports, 49.

7. Roger Rubin, "Knoblauch Seconds DH Move," New York Daily News, 22 June 2000, Sports, 77.

8. Buster Olney, 2000 Playoffs; Knoblauch

Starts and Sounds Off," New York Times, 9 October 2000, Sec. 4, 4.

9. Carter Gaddis, "Players feel need to play better," Tampa Tribune, 19 April 2001, Sports, 8.

10. John Romano, "Two HR-game can't sell Vaughn on DH," St. Petersburg Times, 22 May 2001, Sec. 3, 3.

11. Bob Hohler, "Lineup Moves Infuriate Two," Boston Globe, 1 April 2001, Sec. 6, 1.

12. Peter Botte, "Justice Move Has Joe Fielding Queries," New York Daily News, 12 May 2001, Sports, 48.

13. Bob Sherwin, "The Ultimate All-Stars; M's Martinez swings along with Babe and Ty on the readers' dream team," The Seattle Times, 1 July 2001, Sec. 3, 1

14. Mel Antonen, "DH at 30: Hit, Miss," USA Today, 14 July 2003, Sec. 3, 2.

15. "DH at 30: Hit, Miss," Sec. 3, 2.

16. Bob Elliott, "The Buck Starts Here; Jays Have Changed Under Martinez And Today's Opener Is Their First Test," The Toronto Sun, 1 April 2002, Sports, 3.

17. Geoff Baker, "Stewart in designated funk," The Toronto Star, 24 May 2002, Sec. 3, 11.

18. Paul Hoynes, "Anderson makes most of his starts in outfield," Plain Dealer (Cleveland), 7 April 2002, Sec. 4, 6.

19. Scott Priestle, "Burks Say Don't Read Too Much Into His Hot Start," Columbus Dispatch (Ohio), 10 April 2002, Sec. 5,

20. Bob Sherwin, Martinez flips M's power switch," The Seattle Times, 28 June 2002, Sec. 4, 1.

21. Rich Thompson, "Roll that tape; Baerga gets helpful hint," The Boston Herald, 19 May 2002, Sec. 2, 6.

22. Henry Schulman, "To DH or not to DH? That's the rub," The San Francisco Chronicle, 8 June 2002, Sec. 3, 4.

23. "To DH or not to DH?.." Sec. 3, 4.

24. Thomas Stinson, "All-Star Report; Selig sizes up the game," The Atlanta Journal and Constitution, 10 July 2002, Sec. 4, 4.

25. Bob Sherwin, "Martinez well aware of growing shortfalls," The Seattle Times, 24 April 2003, Sec. 4, 9.

26. Dick Stockton, Fox Television Game of the Week, 16 August 2003.

27. Garry Brown, "Mates pushing Ortiz for MVP," The Republican (Springfield, MA), 25 September 2003, Sec. 3, 2.

28. Peter Barzilai, "Bonds considering switch to DH at end of career," USA Today, 8 July 2003, Sec. 3, 6.

29. "DH at 30: Hit, Miss," Sec. 3, 2.
30. "DH at 30: Hit, Miss," Sec. 3, 2.

Eleven

1. "DH Turns 30," Rocky Mountain News (Denver, CO), 4 April 2003, Sec. 3, 1.

2. Elias Sports Bureau as reported in USA Today, 14 July 2003, Sec. 3, 2.

3. John Thorn, Pete Palmer and Michael Gershman, "The Annual Record," Total Baseball, Seventh Edition, (Kingston, NY: Total Sports Publishing, 2001).

4. "The Annual Record."

5. "The Annual Record."

Index

Index

Index

Index